APPLIED WORD/ INFORMATION PROCESSING

AN INTRODUCTION

CAROLYN CRAWFORD DOLECHECK

Associate Professor
Department of Computer and Office Information Systems
Northeast Louisiana University
Monroe, Louisiana

DANNY W. MURPHY

Administrator, Office Systems
City of Phoenix
Phoenix, Arizona

WS44CB
PUBLISHED BY
SOUTH-WESTERN PUBLISHING CO.
CINCINNATI, OH DALLAS, TX LIVERMORE, CA

ISBN: 0-538-70460-8

Library of Congress Catalog Card Number: 90-64428

1 2 3 4 5 6 7 8 9 H 9 8 7 6 5 4 3 2 1

Printed in the United States of America

Acquisitions Editor: Ben Willard
Developmental Editor: Jane Phelan
Production Editor/In-House: Alan Biondi
Production Editor/Out-of-House: Cinda Johnston
Art Director: Patty Veerkamp
Designer: Jim DeSollar

CONTENTS

PREFACE

One of the most dramatic changes in the information systems world has been how we use word processing. Although secretaries and word processing operators continue to use word processing extensively, executives, professionals, and students at all levels use word processing on a regular basis. Word processing has become a universal skill used by individuals in both their personal and professional lives.

The third edition of APPLIED WORD/INFORMATION PROCESSING: AN INTRODUCTION reflects the current trends in word/information processing. All concept chapters and function descriptions have been updated to reflect current word processing software and equipment. To alleviate unnecessary keying, templates are available for numerous exercises and documents.

OVERVIEW OF CONTENT

The third edition of APPLIED WORD/INFORMATION PROCESSING: AN INTRODUCTION is organized into two parts. Part 1 includes five chapters of word/information processing concepts, and Part 2 includes seven sections of hands-on word processing applications.

Word Processing Concepts

Becoming familiar with basic word/information processing concepts gives students a broader understanding of these technologies. Students will not only appreciate the importance of learning word processing but also realize the need for expanding their knowledge into other technologies. Skills and technologies do not work in isolation. One is dependent on the other, and all are necessary to maximize productivity and efficiency in the workplace. All of the concept chapters have been completely revised, and Chapters 3, 4, and 5 are new.

These features are incorporated into each chapter to help students understand the concepts:

- Objectives, to establish a guide for study.
- Meaningful photographs of equipment and software, to add realism.
- Key terms highlighted in the text, defined in the margin and glossary, and listed at the end of the chapter, for ease in reviewing.
- End-of-chapter activities, to provide an organized review of the chapter.

Chapter 1, *Information Processing in the 90s,* discusses the significance of word/information processing and identifies the skills necessary to utilize word processing. Students learn about the different types of word processing equipment and the purpose and features of the main applications software.

Chapter 2, *Document Processing Systems*, discusses the phases of the document production cycle, including the methods and equipment for originating, processing, reproducing, and distributing documents. Students learn about storing documents for retrieval, making backup copies, and maintaining file security.

Chapter 3, *Know Your Computer*, identifies the hardware and software components of a computer. Students are introduced to a variety of input devices, monitors, storage devices, and printers. They will learn about the processing unit and the differences between an operating system and applications software. Students will become familiar with the advantages of a graphical user interface (GUI) and a character-based operating system. Section 1 of Part 2 applies the concepts presented in this chapter.

Chapter 4, *Managing Your Files*, explains the procedures involved in maintaining an effective file management system. Students will learn to name files; format and label disks; display directories; copy, delete, and rename files; and create and organize directories. They will also develop an understanding for converting files from one software to another or into ASCII format. These activities are applied throughout Part 2.

Chapter 5, *Ergonomics in the Automated Office*, discusses the features of an ergonomically designed office and their effect on worker performance. Helpful guidelines and exercises for relieving stress caused by VDTs are included.

Document Processing Applications

Part 2 of APPLIED WORD/INFORMATION PROCESSING: AN INTRODUCTION is organized into seven logical sections progressing from simple to more complex applications: (1) entering and saving text; (2) editing files; (3) enhancing text and adjusting document format; (4) setting specialized tabs and formatting tables; (5) formatting and editing multipage documents; (6) preparing form documents; and (7) using specialized features.

Thirty-six word processing functions and operations are introduced and applied in short exercises and documents. Directions for each function are written in generic style consistent with the popular software packages. Space is provided for students to list the steps for performing each function using their software.

Students will learn to use the new functions through two types of activities: exercises and documents. The exercises, new in this edition, are short and enable students to immediately apply the new functions before confronting them in a longer document.

■ TEMPLATE DISK

Document files for numerous exercises and some of the documents are stored on a template disk prepared for selected word processing software. The activities can be prepared without the template disk; however, the template disk enables students to concentrate on learning the new function rather than on keying.

Exercises and documents recorded on the template are identified throughout the text with a diskette icon. The file names, listed with the activities, are generally the same as the exercise/document name.

■ INSTRUCTOR'S MANUAL

A comprehensive instructor's manual accompanies the text and includes

- Suggestions for using the text.
- Strategies for using the template disk.
- Two objective tests covering Part 1.
- Four production tests covering the functions and documents in Part 2.
- Guidelines for administering and grading production tests.
- Answers to the end-of-chapter exercises.
- Solutions to all documents.

Carolyn Crawford Dolecheck
Danny Wilson Murphy

PART I

WORD/INFORMATION PROCESSING CONCEPTS

Information processing is the fundamental activity of all offices. To be able to process information in an automated office, workers must possess skills in basic computer operations, be aware of the various software and hardware used to process this information, understand and complete the various steps in the document production cycle, and understand and adjust the factors in their work environment that affect their performance and well-being.

To provide this basic information, Part 1 presents five chapters of word/information processing concepts and terminology. Almost all office workers are involved in some way with originating, processing, printing and reproducing, distributing, and storing documents; therefore, the material in Part 1 is focused on the relationship between word processing and other software applications, the document production cycle, the various parts of the computer and peripheral devices to produce documents, the importance of and techniques for managing computer files, and ergonomic issues facing VDT workers.

CHAPTER 1

WORD/INFORMATION PROCESSING IN THE 90s

CHAPTER OBJECTIVES

After completing your study of Chapter 1, you should be able to:

1. Discuss the significance of information processing in the coming years.
2. Identify the skills necessary for workers in the word/information processing area.
3. Discuss the importance of word processing as it relates to the rest of information processing.
4. Identify the different types of word processing equipment.
5. Describe the purpose and features of various application software.

INTRODUCTION TO INFORMATION PROCESSING

Welcome to office automation! You have made a wise decision to prepare yourself for working with computers. During the 80s, most business offices in America computerized to some extent. In the 90s, only a few offices will not contain a computer.

Yes, the 90s will see not only the end of the century but also the end of the "Pre-Information Age." Over the last few decades, we have shifted from an agricultural and industrial economy to an information and service economy. Information and the ability to manage information have significant value.

How can information be valuable? A business mailing list is a good example of how information is valuable. To a company that sells products, knowing the names and addresses of potential customers is very important. Mailing lists can be purchased, sometimes for large sums of money. Collecting and maintaining these lists can be very profitable.

In both business and personal affairs, computers are becoming an increasingly important part of our lives. Consider, for example, the way banks transfer funds. Funds are transferred electronically from one computer to another; physical money is never moved.

Significance of Information Processing

Computer technology has been the catalyst for many of the changes we have experienced over the past few decades. The computer's ability to process different kinds of information has made the shift to the Information Age possible.

Computers, however, are just machines. They are not capable (so far) of independent thought. It is people who make the Information Age work. People must understand how to operate computers and process information.

Information processing Technologies involved with creating, processing, and distributing information.

The fastest growing careers are in the fields of information processing and office automation. As technology changes, new jobs are created—jobs that are interesting, challenging, and rewarding. The secretarial role, for example, is changing considerably. Employers frequently expect the support personnel they hire to have many skills that they themselves do not possess. Career paths with "administrative titles" are available for persons who are computer literate and knowledgeable about various software applications. Support personnel have access to more information than ever before, and their ability to manage information can alter the way companies do business.

Thus, computers and the information age have not, as some suggest, dehumanized people. Rather, computers have provided an excellent opportunity for people to change their lives. People, however, must be willing to learn about and participate in the Information Age. The time you spend learning about information processing will pay you dividends now and for years to come.

Forms of Information

Information comes in many different forms: text, numbers, graphics, images, and voice. Letters, memos, and reports consist mainly of text. Statistical reports consist primarily of numbers. Graphics include charts, graphs, and illustrations generated by a computer. Images include photographs or any art that is read by a scanner.

Software Programmed instructions for a computer.

Information processing refers to the technologies involved with creating, processing, and distributing information in its various forms. Information is processed by a computer by means of **software**, or programmed instructions. Software enables us to use the computer for a specific application. Because there are many different applications for a computer, there are many different kinds of **application software**. Later in this chapter you will gain an overview of the primary application software that make up information processing. The emphasis of this text, however, is on word processing. Part 2 of this text will help you to master many features of your word processing software.

Figure 1.1
Information Processing in the 90s

Source: *Courtesy of International Business Machines Corporation*

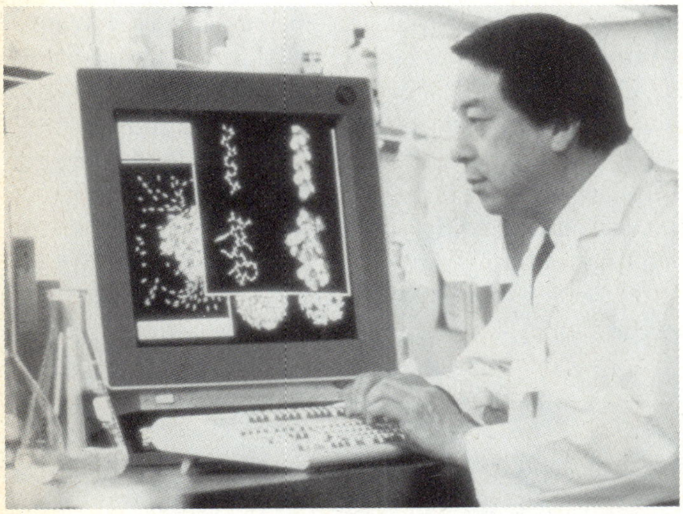

Source: *Courtesy of International Business Machines Corporation*

Source: *Courtesy of NeXT Computer, Inc.*

Source: *Courtesy of International Business Machines Corporation*

INFORMATION PROCESSING SKILLS

Application software has made many tasks easier, and it has changed the way these tasks are accomplished. Creating documents with graphics, for example, used to be very difficult, and thus graphics were generally only incorporated into sophisticated reports. Now some word processing programs include a graphics feature that enables the user to mix product diagrams, logos, charts, or pictures within text documents. Likewise, information that used to be found in paper files or research books can now be located quickly by accessing a remote database file using a telephone and special communication software. Tasks, such as creating graphics or searching databases, that were performed by specialized people are becoming routine. As tasks become computerized, workers must develop new skills and accept new responsibilities.

If you are preparing to become a secretary, support person, or information manager, you will want to become familiar with a variety of software programs and become proficient at word processing. A 1990 survey of classified ads revealed word processing to be the most requested skill for secretaries (54 percent). Following word processing in the survey were organizational skills, communication skills, and telephone skills.[1] Communication skills included the following:

- **Language arts skills.** Grammar, punctuation, word usage, and spelling. Thorough study and successful completion of grammar and writing courses are most desirable.
- **Careful proofreading and editing ability.** The ability to detect mistakes in keying, formatting, and language arts is most important. Some originators do not spend much time on these aspects of a document; they expect support personnel to have these skills.

Figure 1.2
Word Processing Skills Are Central to Many Application Software

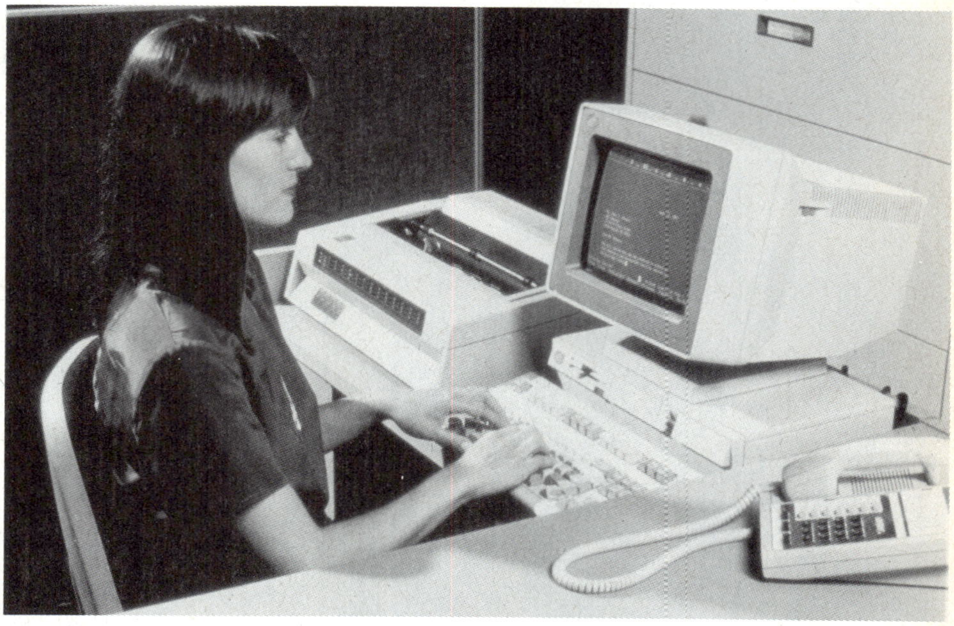

Source: *Courtesy of International Business Machines Corporation*

[1]Dartnell Institue of Business Research Corporation, *Secretarial Want Ad Survey, 1990.*

- **Ability and willingness to use references.** The dictionary, reference books, equipment and software documentation (directions for operating a system), and any other manuals written for word processing users and operators.

IMPORTANCE OF WORD PROCESSING

Word processing has become a universal skill that many people use in both their personal and professional lives. Originators (including U.S. Supreme Court judges, attorneys, executives, office workers at all levels, authors, and students) who possess good keying skills are realizing that they can easily create documents using word processing software. No longer is word processing confined to a few specialized office workers. Obviously, however, the skill of users and the sophistication of the software they use vary depending upon their needs.

Word processing is also an underlying tool of other application software. For documents to be transmitted via electronic mail, the user must key and edit the message. Before documents are typeset using desktop publishing software, they are keyed and edited with word processing software. Spreadsheets and database applications require that numbers and text be entered. Without a basic knowledge of word processing software, using these other programs is more difficult.

Compund document Document that combines information from two or more application software.

Word processing is also becoming increasingly important as a new kind of document emerges, called a compound document. A **compound document** consists of files within various applications linked together. The final document may consist of text from a word processing file, data from a spreadsheet, and a chart from a graphics file. If the spreadsheet file is changed, the numbers in the graphic file are updated automatically. A compound document is not a static entity, but a series of links that can be updated. Some of the new word processing programs such as WordPerfect and Microsoft Word can link spreadsheet files, database files, and graphics into a single document.

Figure 1.3
Compound Document

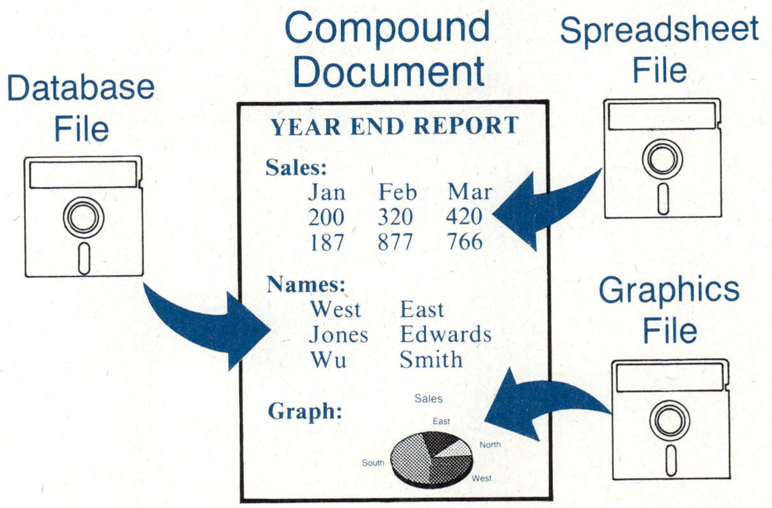

INFORMATION PROCESSING EQUIPMENT

A wide variety of word processing equipment and software is used in offices today, depending upon the user's need. Dedicated word processors may be appropriate for offices with heavy word processing needs, while electronic typewriters may be better for other offices. Frequently, however, you will find a combination of computers and electronic typewriters. To evaluate the kinds of equipment necessary for an office, you must understand their features.

Electronic Typewriters

Electronic typewriters (ETs) are used by those who need to be able to key a wide variety of short documents and switch from one job to the next quickly and easily. ETs are ideal for handling short documents such as letters and memos as well as labels, forms, and envelopes. ETs include automatic features such as centering, underscoring, bold, decimal alignment, word wrap, and error correction. Other models include the additional features of document assembly, merge, search and replace, and block move/copy/delete/print. (You will learn the purpose of these features later.)

ETs are very durable because they operate with microchips rather than mechanical parts. Additionally, ETs offer the benefits of being (1) easier to use than computers, (2) able to handle forms easily (unlike computers), and (3) able to perform many of the same word processing functions as computers.

ETs are available in a number of configurations. They can be enhanced (at a cost) by adding three important features: display, upgradability, and compatibility with personal computers (PCs).

- *Display screens*: Displays enable the user to edit and view the text on the display before printing. Displays are usually a half page and are capable of displaying bold and underlining, centering, and various size pitches. Some ETs include split screens and popup windows.
- *Upgradability*: Upgrading consists of adding such options as additional internal memory, external storage devices, and other features. Upgradabiilty is important because it enables the ET to continue to be used as the tasks to be performed become more complex.
- *PC compatibility*: Some ETs, primarily those from IBM, have the abiity to use application software designed for a computer. Compatibility allows the ETs to be used for many tasks.

Dedicated Word Processors

In terms of evolution, ETs and dedicated word processors came before computer-based word processing. A **dedicated word processor** is much like a computer, but with a single purpose—it is designed to perform a few specialized tasks, whereas a computer can perform many different tasks. A dedicated word processor usually consists of a monitor, a keyboard, and a way to store information on a disk or tape. A dedicated word processor has the word processing application program built in. Other application software cannot be used on a dedicated word processor.

Figure 1.4
Electronic Typewriters Are Available in a Number of Configurations

Source: *Courtesy of International Business Machines Corporation*

Source: *Olivetti USA, Inc.*

Dedicated word processors are designed for high production of text documents. A benefit of dedicated word processors is the keyboard, which is designed exclusively for word processing. Special keys handle common functions such as tab set, copy, and move. The disadvantages of dedicated word processors are that they are more expensive than a computer and they are limited to word processing.

Wang and Displaywriter used to be the two most popular dedicated word processing systems. Now there are versions of the dedicated word processor software available for the computer. For example, MultiMate software for the computer has replaced the Wang dedicated word processor just as DisplayWrite software has replaced the Displaywriter dedicated word processor.

Computers

Because of their versatility, computers have become one of the most commonly used tools for word processing. In Chapter 3 you will learn about the components of a computer.

■ APPLICATION SOFTWARE FOR INFORMATION PROCESSING

Application software Computer program designed to do a certain kind of task, such as word processing.

Application software makes it possible for computers to process information in its various forms. The most popular of these applications are described on the following pages.

Figure 1.5 Application Software

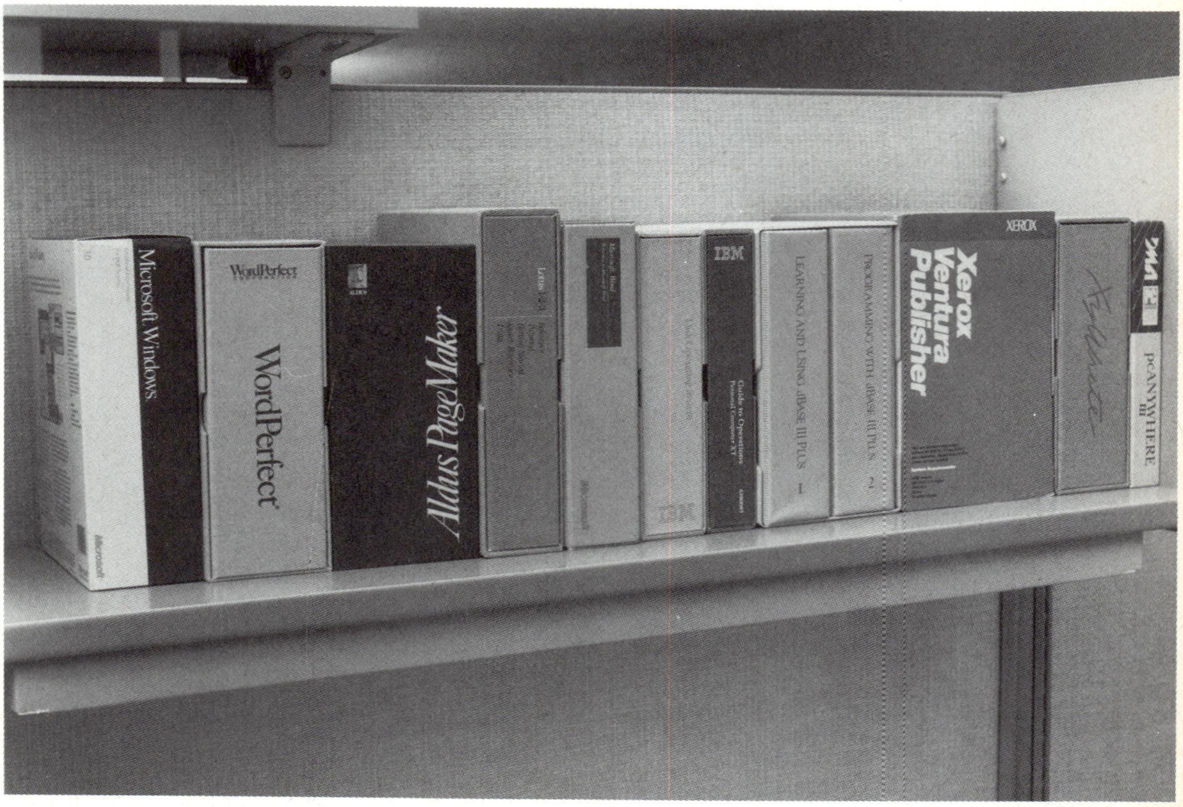

Word Processing

Word processing, the most popular application software, allows users to produce attractive text documents in the most efficient manner. Word processing software enables the user to perform these basic steps:

Enter text:	Key a document.
Edit text:	Insert, delete, move, and search and replace text.
Format text:	Change left, right, top, and bottom margins. Change text to bold, underline, or italic. Change the size and typeface of characters. Indent text and use headers and footers.
Save text:	Store text on a disk.
Print text:	Control the printer so that the hard copy contains bold, italic, and other print features.

In addition to basic text entry and editing, most word processing programs have the ability to check spelling and combine documents with lists of information. New word processing programs have even more features. Some programs have extremely sophisticated formatting features, approaching the level of desktop publishing software. Some programs allow graphics or other files to be incorporated into the document.

As word processing programs evolve, additional features are added or existing features are refined, making the software easier to use. Upgrades to software are indicated by the version number. Each new version of the software has a higher number. WordPerfect and MicroSoft Word have evolved from version 2.0 to 5.1. WordStar has gone from version 2.0 to 6.0. Generally, a small increase in the version number (5.0 to 5.1) means that minor changes have been made. Most software companies allow registered owners of their product to purchase new versions at a minimal cost. Popular word processing programs include DisplayWrite, MicroSoft Word, MultiMate, and WordPerfect.

Figure 1.6
Word Processing Software with Graphics Integrated

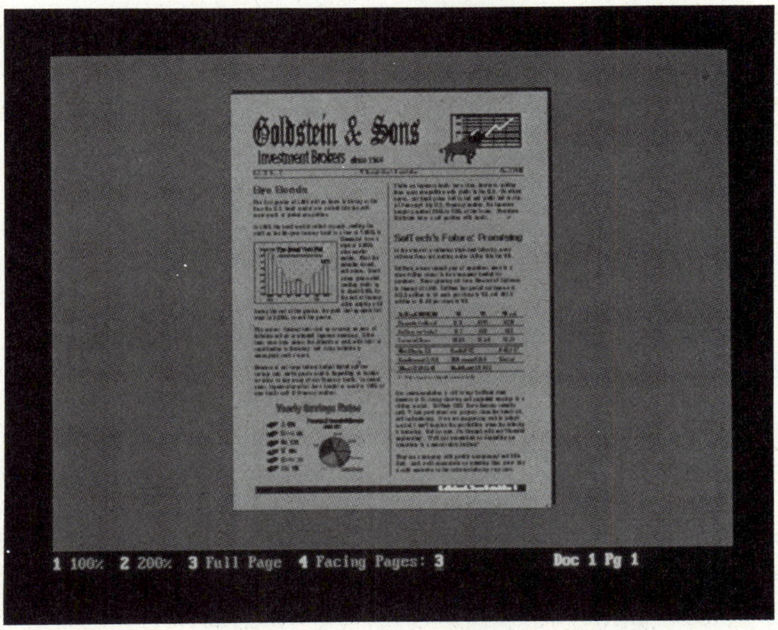

The design of word processing applications is basically either menu driven or command driven. A menu-driven application presents menus for the operator to choose from; each menu includes a series of options or submenus. With a command-driven application, the user presses specific keys to perform various tasks.

A menu-driven application is easier to use because you can refer to the menus for the appropriate option. As you become familiar with the application, however, you can be slowed by having to select from the menus. For example, to bold text using a menu-driven software, you would first strike the keys to bring up a menu and then select the bold menu. In a command driven application, bold could be done with far fewer keystrokes. Many new programs such as WordPerfect 5.1 and Display-Write 5 (Figure 1.7) combine the merits of both designs of software by providing menus for beginners and a complete set of commands.

Figure 1.7
DisplayWrite 5 Combines Menus and Commands

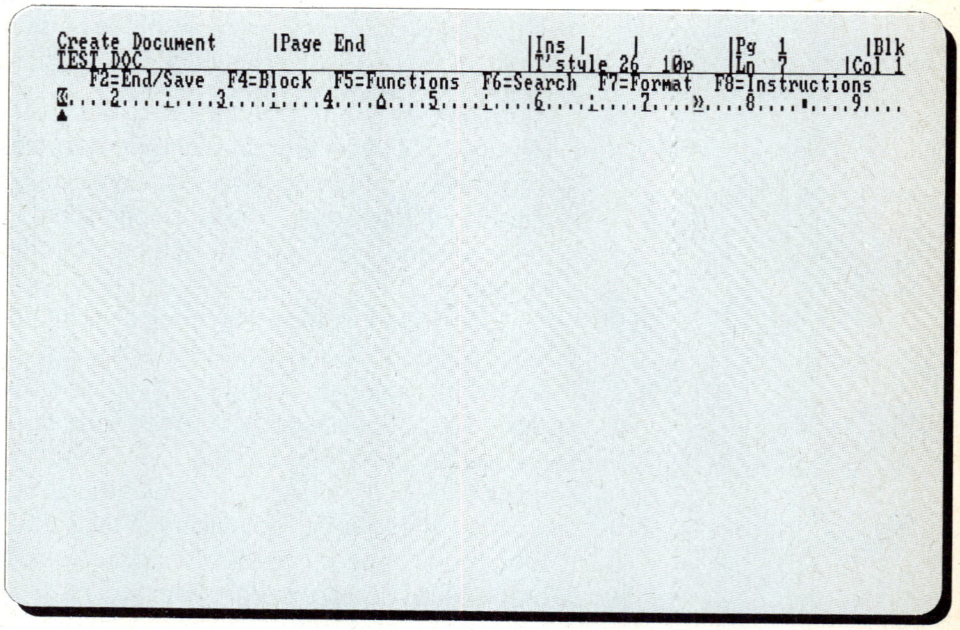

Desktop Publishing Applications

Desktop publishing Microcomputer-based publishing system.

Desktop publishing is related to word processing in that both applications are used to produce documents. They differ in that desktop publishing software has more formatting capabilities than word processing software and can print graphics with text. Desktop publishing software is sometimes called page layout software because it is used primarily to arrange text and graphics on a page. It uses a WYSIWYG (What You See Is What You Get) display—the document is displayed as it will look when printed. This feature is necessary because when combining text and graphics, you must be able to see how the page will look when printed.

Most desktop publishing programs require that the text portion of the document be created with word processing software. Desktop publishing programs have very limited editing capabilities. Two of the most popular desktop publishing programs are Aldus Pagemaker and Ventura Publisher. These, and many other desktop publishing programs, are able to create high-quality documents that at one time would have required the services of a professional printer.

Figure 1.8
Desktop Publishing

Source: Micro Display

Database Applications

Database application Software that stores and retrieves related data.

A **database** is an organized collection of facts (data) about a related topic. Its purpose is to manage different kinds of information. Database applications enable the user to perform these functions:

- Create a new database and enter information.
- Search and find information by using simple commands.
- Create useful lists based on a search.

To create a database you must first determine its structure by planning the kind of information that will go into the file. If you were creating a database to be used as a mailing list, for example, you would include the first name, last name, address, city, state, and ZIP code. Each of these elements is a field. A set of fields is called a record—in this case a record would be the information for one individual. Once a database has been structured, data can be entered and records can be added, deleted, or revised.

The object of creating a database is to be able to locate specific information quickly and easily. Sorting, or the ability to locate random records in any order, is one of the most important features of a database. If you had a database of names and addresses, you could sort the database and find people who live in California. The database application would search through the files and list the names where the state matched *California.* Some database applications also provide a means for creating and printing reports.

Popular database applications include Dbase III, Dbase IV, Oracle, Paradox, and R:base.

Spreadsheet Applications

Spreadsheet application Software that keeps financial records.

A **spreadsheet** manages numbers and keeps track of financial information. Businesspeople use a spreadsheet application to calculate costs and profits, plan schedules, create finanacial plans, determine sales forecasts, or analyze expenses. Before computers became affordable, spreadsheets consisted of large paper ledgers with the entry of numbers and calculations completed manually.

Electronic spreadsheets organize data much like a paper spreadsheet, except the software uses the computer's screen and memory to keep track of the numbers. Numbers and text are entered into the spreadsheet and various calculations are performed. Calculations can be entered as formulas in the spreadsheet so that they can be updated. Spreadsheets enable users to perform the following functions, although programs may not have all of these features.

- Enter numbers, text, and formulas.
- Create graphs from the numbers and calculations.
- Print reports based on the numbers in the spreadsheet.

Numbers and text are entered in rows and columns. The point at which a row and column intersect is called a cell. Each cell may contain a number, text (label), or a formula that causes cells to be added, subtracted, divided, etc. Notice from Figure 1.9 that rows are labeled along the left side of the screen starting at *1*. Columns are labeled along the top of the screen starting with the letter *A*. Each number occupies a single cell.

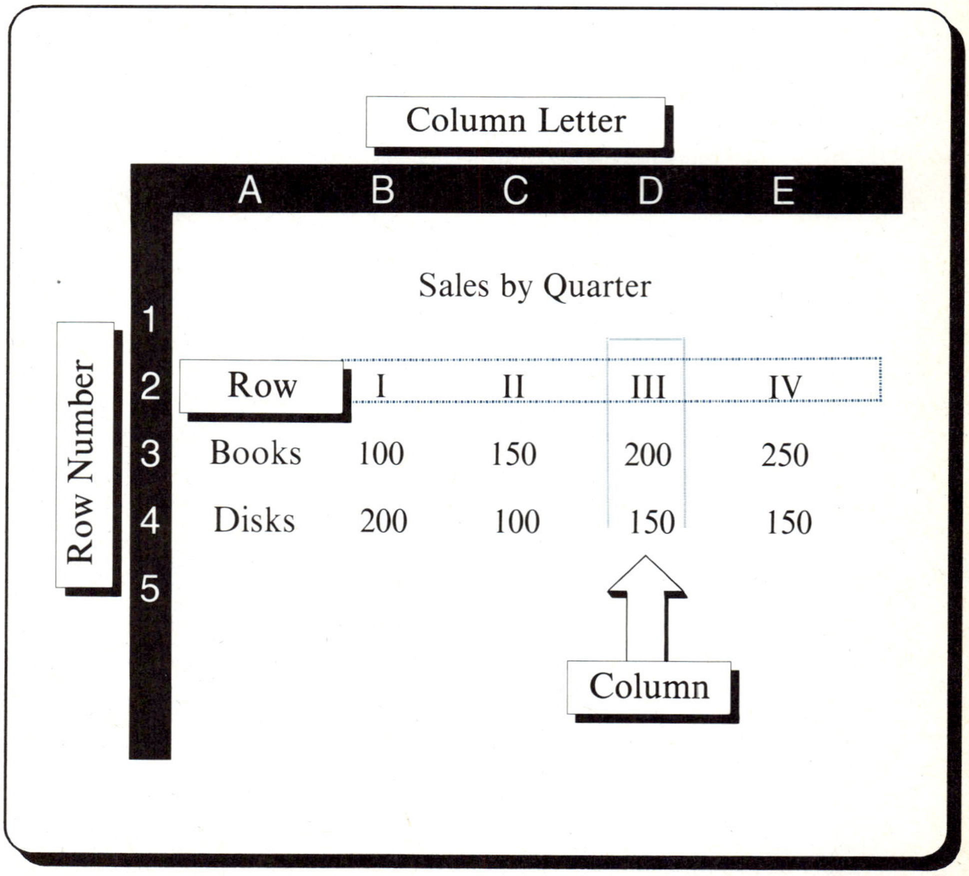

Figure 1.9
Spreadsheet Software

In addition to managing numbers, spreadsheet programs usually provide a means for graphing numbers. Different spreadsheet programs are capable of generating different kinds of graphics. Figure 1.10 is a sample graph from the spreadsheet program Quattro.

Most spreadsheet programs have the ability to create and print reports. Some spreadsheets have the ability to format the reports much like a word processing program. The text and numbers can be formatted as bold or italic and the text size can be changed.

The most popular spreadsheet application is Lotus 1-2-3. Other spreadsheet programs are Quattro Professional, Excel, and Supercalc 5.

Figure 1.10
Graph Created from a Spreadsheet

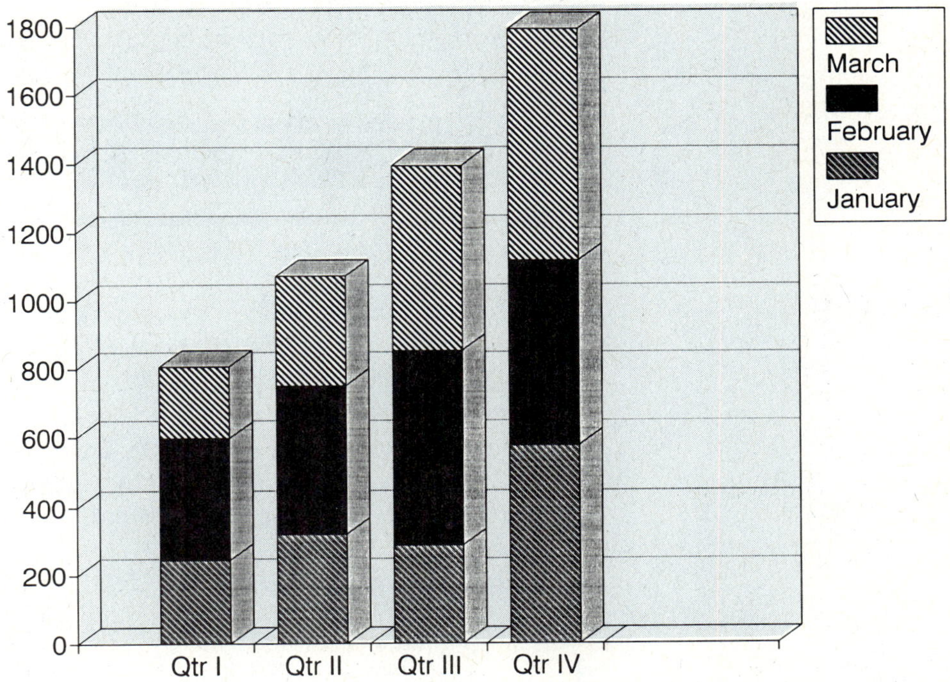

Graphics Applications

Graphics Charts, graphs, logos, and designs created by a computer graphic software.

Graphics software has become very popular as computer systems have become better able to display and print graphics. The two main types of graphics software include drawing and painting programs and presentation programs. These programs overlap somewhat, as many drawing programs can produce presentation quality graphics and many presentation packages have powerful drawing capabilities.

Drawing and painting programs are mainly used by graphic artists and drafting engineeers to produce designs and art. Manufacturing companies use these programs to design products such as automobiles or boats. An aircraft company might use a drawing program to design the parts of an engine or even the entire aircraft. Such advanced applications are called Computer-Aided Design (CAD). Figure 1.11 shows the screen from the drawing program DrawPerfect. Painting programs are good for blending and shading a drawing. Painting programs are used to produce more artistic designs.

Figure 1.11
Work Screen of a Drawing Program

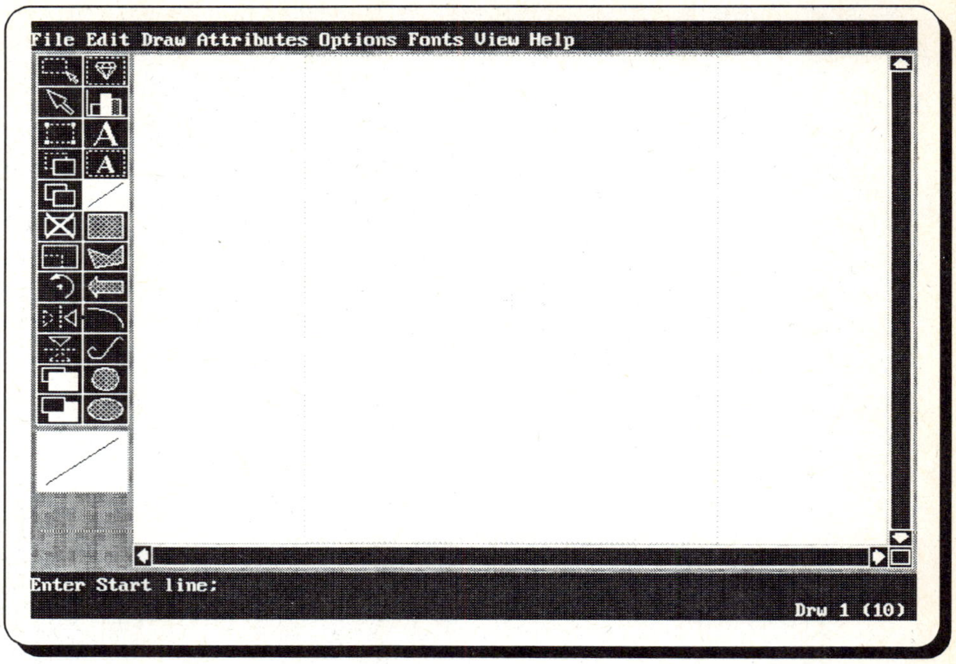

Presentation programs are used to produce all of the elements associated with a formal presentation: graphs, charts, diagrams, and speaker's notes and handouts. Some programs are able to create a slide show. A special device projects the images on the computer's monitor through an overhead projector to the audience. Some programs can generate animated images. Examples of presentation software include Aldus Persuasion and Powerpoint for the Macintosh. An example of presentation software is shown in Figure 1.12.

Communications and Network Applications

One direction both computers and software are taking is toward connecting computers. In the office, people are finding that as information can be moved from one computer to another computer, productivity increases. Two kinds of application software are used to facilitate this communication between computers: (1) communication software and (2) network software.

Communication software uses a *modem*, a special device that connects a telephone to a computer. The modem enables the computer to send and receive data with another computer over the telephone.

Network Group of computers linked together for sharing information; also called a local area network.

A network consists of special software, special boards that plug into computers, and cables that connect the computers. A **network** (common term for local area network, which will be discussed in Chapter 2) enables users to send and receive files and share applications that are on other computers. Examples of network applications are Lotus Notes, IBM Office, and WordPerfect Office.

Groupware Software that runs on a network and supports group activities and management.

Some applications are especially suitable for a network. **Groupware** is software that runs on a network and supports group activities. Groupware provides for scheduling by automatically finding time slots when people and resources are available. *Electronic mail*, which enables individuals to send messages and files to each other using a computer, is a core application of groupware. *Project planning* coordinates group tasks, goals, completion dates, resources, and other information.

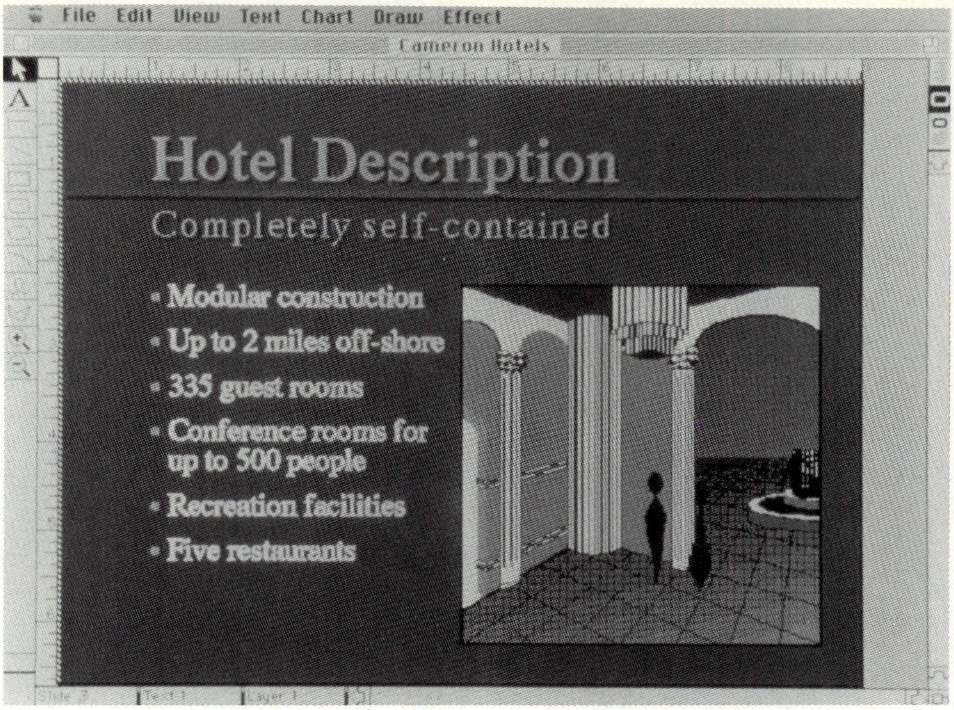

Figure 1.12
Presentation Software

■ SUMMARY

Information processing and office automation offer an almost unlimited future for individuals who have the necessary skills and are willing to become involved. The pace of change requires those working in this field to have a wide range of skills and to maintain those skills. Employees need to be computer literate, knowledgeable about software, and able to utilize good communication and organizational skills. Persons who are skilled in word processing are in the most demand, but knowledge of other applications such as spreadsheets, databases, desktop publishing, graphics, and communication is also important.

EXERCISES

KEY TERMS

Information processing
Software
Application software
Compound document
Electronic typewriter
Dedicated word processor
Groupware
Word processing
Desktop publishing
Database
Spreadsheet
Graphics software
Network

COMPLETION

1. Information has different forms including ____________________, ____________________, ____________________, ____________________, and ____________________.
2. Software is a series of ______________________________ for the computer.
3. Software that enables the user to incorporate text and graphics on the same page and use various type fonts is __________________.
4. Word processing software is designed to be either ________________ -driven or ______________-driven.
5. ________________ are produced by linking files from two or more application software.
6. ______________________ are best used in offices in which a variety of short documents are processed and the user must move from one application to another frequently.
7. The main word processing steps include ________________________, ___________________, _________________, ____________________, and _____________________ text.
8. A __________________ word processor produces text documents only.
9. To forecast sales, create financial statements, plan budgets, and manipulate numerical data, you would use ______________ software.
10. To create and retrieve files of related information, you would use ________________ software.

DISCUSSION QUESTIONS

1. List two ways in which information is valuable to businesses.
2. List three tasks that computers could perform in an office.
3. What are the five forms of information? Give an example of each in the office.
4. What skills are necessary for support personnel in today's office?
5. What type of jobs are best handled on electronic typewriters?
6. What are the advantages and disadvantages of using a dedicated word processor in an office.
7. What is the difference between menu-driven software and command-based software? Which is easier to use?
8. Define and explain the purposes of these application programs: desktop publishing, database, spreadsheets, graphics, network.

CHAPTER 2

DOCUMENT PROCESSING SYSTEMS

CHAPTER OBJECTIVES

After completing your study of Chapter 2, you should be able to:

1. Discuss the various methods and equipment used to originate information.
2. Explain the activities involved in processing a document.
3. Discuss how documents may be printed and reproduced.
4. Explain the several ways documents may be distributed to receivers and list the advantages of each.
5. Identify the forms in which documents may be stored.
6. Explain the need for making backups of storage media and protecting records from unauthorized access.

Every office produces information. The procedures, methods, and equipment used to produce information vary from manual to automated; however, the steps to produce documents such as letters, memos, and reports are quite similar in automated offices. Your study of document processing, however, will focus on how automated equipment can be used in each phase of the **document production cycle**.

Document production cycle Series of steps for producing a document.

Document production consists of five steps: origination, processing, printing and reproduction, distribution, and storage. As you study this material, you will see that some of these steps overlap and are sometimes repeated.

■ ORIGINATION

Information to be communicated must be captured in some way and input (entered) into the computer for processing into a finished document. The **originator** who creates the document may input information into the document cycle in various ways. The method of origination often depends on the skills of the originator and the equipment available.

Keying

With computers in 95 percent of all offices[1] and the increasing popularity of laptop portable computers, many originators today are finding that keying their thoughts as they are composed is extremely efficient.

Often the originator keys and prints the first draft and marks revisions on the printed copy using proofreaders' marks. Then an assistant retrieves the stored document, revises it making the changes marked on the rough draft, **formats** the document attractively on the page, and prints and reproduces the final copy.

Format Document design including side margins, top and bottom margins, tabs, line spacing and other features.

Handwriting

For those who have not developed keyboarding skills, handwriting is a popular method of origination. Because handwriting is slow and the material must eventually be keyed, handwriting is generally inefficient. Statistical data and documents with unusual formats, however, are often prepared more efficiently and accurately if they are handwritten.

Figure 2.1
Handwritten Document with Unusual Format

FINAL PRICE AFTER MARKDOWN

	Amount of Discount			
Original Price	Red Tag 10%	Blue Tag 20%	Yellow Tag 30%	Green Tag 40%
$799.95	$719.96	$639.96	$559.97	$479.97
749.95	674.96	599.96	524.97	449.97
699.95	629.96	559.96	489.97	419.97
649.95	584.96	519.96	454.97	389.97
599.95	539.96	479.96	419.97	359.97

[1]Patricia M. Fernberg, "Value-Added Supports Stimulate Growth," Modern Office Technology (January 1990), Vol. 35, No. 1, p. 108.

Machine Dictation

Machine dictation is an accepted and widely used tool of origination. Physicians who must quickly record patient information, executives who travel or work after hours, as well as those who are not comfortable keying their own documents find machine dictation most efficient. After a document is dictated, an administrative assistant or transcriptionist listens to the recorded dictation and keys the document. Several types of dictation/transcription equipment systems are popular.

- Small, portable, battery-operated dictation units are popular because they can fit into a pocket, purse, or briefcase and can be used anywhere. Portable dictation equipment uses a small microcassette tape, which can be easily mailed to the office for transcription.

Figure 2.2
Portable Dictation Unit

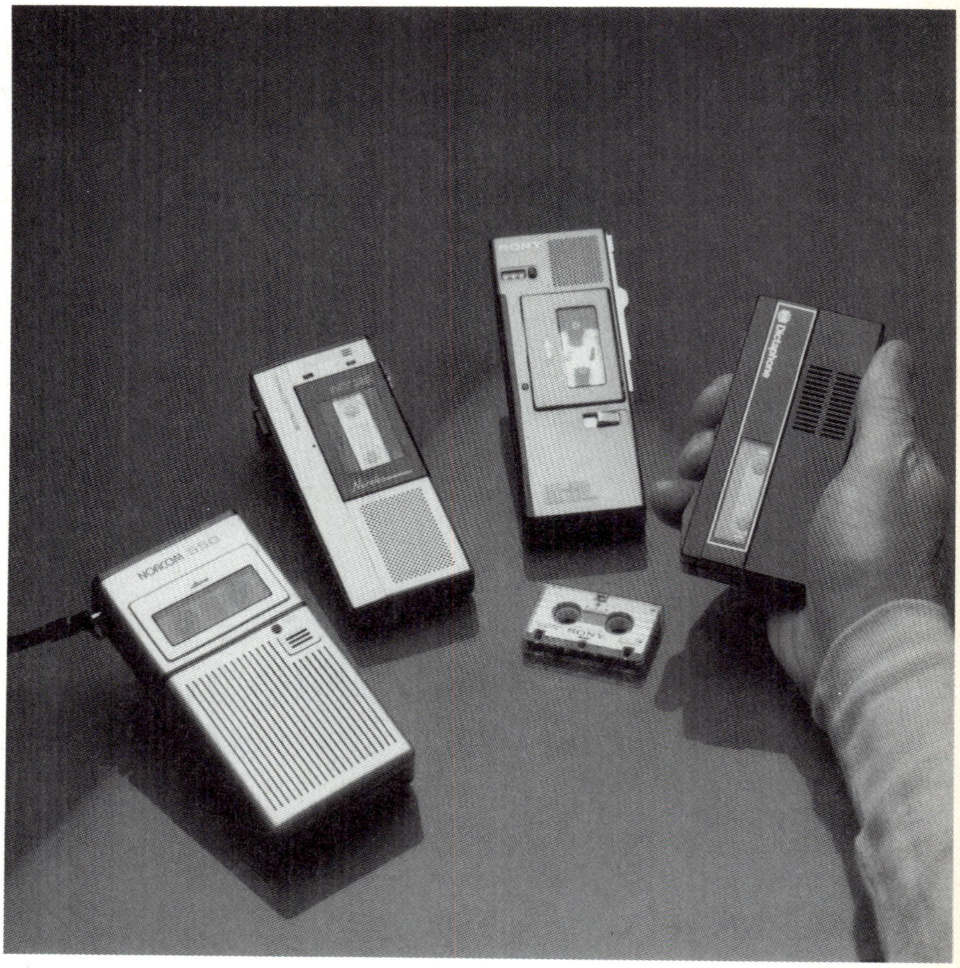

- Desktop machines are placed on desks of executives and managers who dictate frequently in their offices. Generally these machines store dictation on minicassette tapes.

- Central dictation systems are gaining in popularity and are used in organizations such as insurance companies that have many people who dictate their correspondence. Dictation is recorded on a central recording unit using the telephone or a microphone.

Figure 2.3
Centralized Dictation System

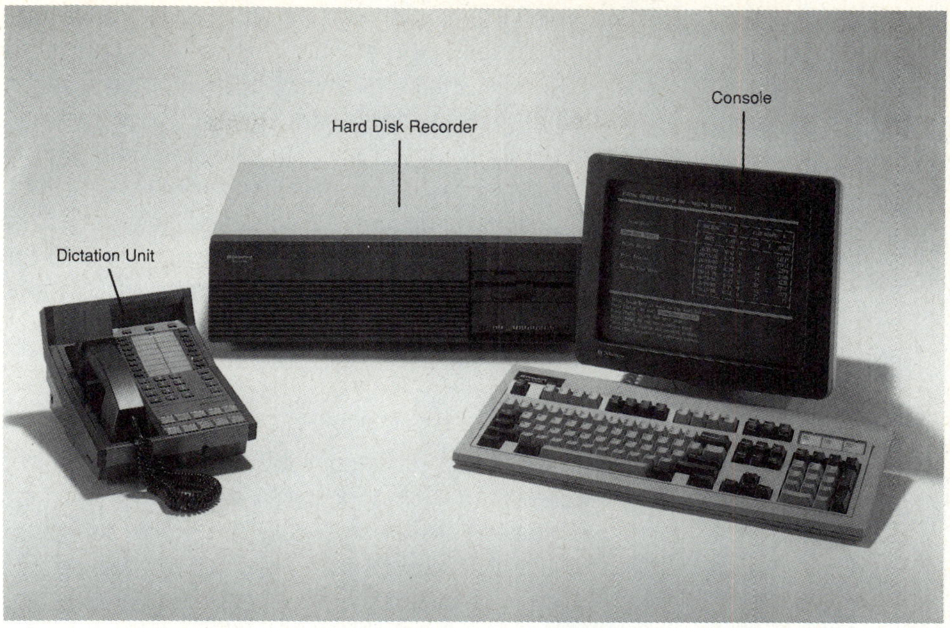

Source: *Dictaphone Corp., Stratford, CT*

Centralized dictation systems are often classified by the type of media used to record the dictation: endless loop, discrete, or hard disk digital units.

An endless loop system contains a continuous magnetic tape that holds the dictation until it is transcribed; the dictation is erased when new dictation is recorded over it.

Discrete systems utilize several cassette tapes. The system automatically switches from one tape to the next as tapes are filled or priorities change.

The newer hard disk dictation systems digitize the voice. Messages can be edited on disk just as information can be edited with a computer. Similar to a computer, a hard disk is a random access medium allowing users to locate dictation and make changes easily. Additionally, hard disk dictation systems allow multiple access by originators, random access for transcribers, and prioritization schemes. Centralized systems also allow users to dictate from locations away from the office. Unlike discrete systems, dictation on a hard disk system is never handled by the originator or the transcriber.

Scanners

Scanner Machine that reads printed copy and stores information on a computer disk.

Text in printed form can be entered into the computer using a **scanner** and then saved on disk. A scanner, originally known as an OCR (optical character recognition), can read a printed page of text or graphics and store the information on disk, thereby eliminating the need to rekey text. Text pages can be scanned in about 25 seconds, or about 20 times faster than the average typist can rekey a page.[2] A few scanner models recognize some handwritten characters, but most do not.

Some scanners interface so well with the most popular word processing software that the scanned text is formatted automatically during the scanning process. For example, if the user plans to revise and print the document using

[2] "Teach Your PC to Read," brochure from DEST Corporation, San Jose, California (January 1990), p. 1.

WordPerfect software, WordPerfect formatting commands such as centering, underlining, tabs, and bold are automatically entered.

Font Characters with the same typeface and size.

You should be aware, however, that scanners require special software if they are to scan a variety of **fonts** as well as graphics. Inexpensive scanners are limited in the fonts they accept; they do not scan graphics at all. Also, the text copy must be sharp and contain no stray marks.

After a document is scanned, you must always proofread for characters that may have been misread since scanners on the average fail to recognize ten or more characters per page. Some scanners insert a # or @ symbol (or any other symbol the user specifies) at each point where a character is unreadable. You should check for misread characters, such as an *O* substituted for a *C*, unexplained numbers at the top of the page, and missing portions of text.

In addition to capturing text material, scanners are used for many other applications: desktop publishing, databases, information storage, and facsimile. Scanners are heavily used for incorporating graphics and photos into desktop publishing documents such as reports, manuals, and newsletters. A scanner is essential for preparing image databases for organizations such as real estate agencies and police departments. Realtors often scan photographs of houses for sale, and police departments scan mug shots of criminals; these scanned images are added to databases for easy reference by many people. Scanners are also used for scanning documents for permanent storage on optical disks.

Scanner technology is improving at a rapid rate, and the scanner market is becoming stronger each year as scanners become more sophisticated and less expensive. Scanners are becoming a popular computer peripheral as more companies introduce scanners and users discover more uses for them.

Figure 2.4
Scanner Workstation

Source: *DEST*

Voice Recognition

Computer and software engineers have been working on voice recognition technology input for several years, and experts predict major commercial use by the end of this decade. Some systems already accept single words or phrases from a limited vocabulary; these are used primarily to control computer programs. Someday office workers will be able to dictate their documents directly into the computer without using a keyboard or other input devices.

Other tools such as a light pen, a mouse, and touch-sensitive screens are sometimes used as input devices, usually in conjunction with a keyboard.

PROCESSING

The processing stage of the document production cycle may involve several activities: formatting, keying and printing a draft, editing, incorporating other files, and proofreading. Depending on the complexity of the document, the word processing specialist may not complete all of these activities or may complete them in a different order.

Formatting

Default Preset software settings such as margins and line spacing.

Generally, the format of each document is selected before it is keyed. Most word processing programs offer **default** (predetermined) formats that are acceptable for routine correspondence. If the document is a draft that will be heavily edited, the final formatting may be completed after revisions are made.

Keying

Although some part of the document may have been keyed by the originator or scanned, keying is a significant part of the document production process. Of course, documents that are handwritten or dictated must be keyed.

As documents are keyed, errors are corrected during screen proofing. If the intent is to revise a document before final printing, a draft copy (sometimes formatted in double spacing) is usually printed. After the document is keyed, it should be saved on a disk before revision or printing.

Editing

Editing Revising a document.

The editing capabilities of word processing software make revising a document so easy that originators now expect to edit their documents at least once before final printing. Using standard proofreaders' marks, the originator can mark any desired changes on the printed copy. Text can be inserted easily, deleted, moved, and replaced. When copy is revised, only the revisions are keyed.

Figure 2.5
Edited Hard Copy

Current date

Mrs. Elizabeth Chittenden
3800 Beach Blvd. Apt. C
Pascagoula, MS 39567-2250

VISIT THE ~~BEAUTIFUL~~ *EXCITING* ORIENT

As a *valued* subscriber to DAILY LIVING, you have an opportunity to visit the beautiful Orient for 18 days and 17 nights for ~~as low as~~ *only* $2,350. Flights from San Francisco depart October 15, November 20, and December 5.

During your 18-day~~s~~ *visit* you will ~~visit~~ *tour* these exciting oriental cities:

Singapore -- *4 days*
Bangkok -- *3 days*
Hong Kong -- *4 days*
Taipei -- *3 days*
Tokyo -- *4 days*

Your oriental vacation includes: round-trip jet transportation via World Airlines; an escort *on* ~~accompanies~~ every departure; baggage handling (except through customs areas); travel information; American breakfast daily*, and accommodations at first-class hotels.*

For more details, read the enclosed four-page brochure which describes activities planned for each city. Call toll free 1-800-555-3321 *weekdays from 8:30 a.m. to 9:00 p.m. (EST)* for more information or to make *your* reservations.

Geok Ng
MARKETING MANAGER
doc code

Enclosure

Some originators may request that more than one version of a document be prepared. For example, different versions of a resume may be prepared—each one for a different job title. An attorney may wish to prepare several versions of an estate planning document for a client who wishes to study several options; the primary document remains the same, but selected sections are modified. All these versions are saved until the client and attorney agree on an appropriate version. All but the selected version may then be erased. To prepare different versions, copy the original into another file and make the revisions.

Incorporating Other Files

As you have already learned, as a part of your office work you will probably use other computer application software in addition to word processing. Sometimes files created with another computer program are incorporated into word processing documents. For example, a chart or bar graph created with a graphics program may be **imported** into a report.

Imported Retrieved from another file and incorporated into a document.

Figure 2.6
Report with Imported Graphics

Other studies indicate a definite awareness and sensitivity to economic conditions on the part of small business managers. For example, a survey of small businesses found 67% of the firms experienced sales decreases during recessions. Only 16% reported "no effect," while 17% stated sales actually increased during recessions. Small manufacturing firms producing products that improve efficiency or cut costs were among those firms reporting sales increases [21]. While most firms can expect downturns during recessions, the magnitude varies greatly with different industries, customers, competitors, locations and a host of other factors in these microeconomic admixtures.

In an attempt to sort through all these factors, this study addresses specific questions as they relate to small business development. How are entrepreneurial behaviors and objectives strengthened by the economy? What might previous empirical studies suggest as a model for future research? How could researchers use multivariate designs in field studies to control for economic constraints in the model? What data would allow researchers to identify microeconomic conditions promoting startup, expansion, maintenance or retrenchment in small businesses?

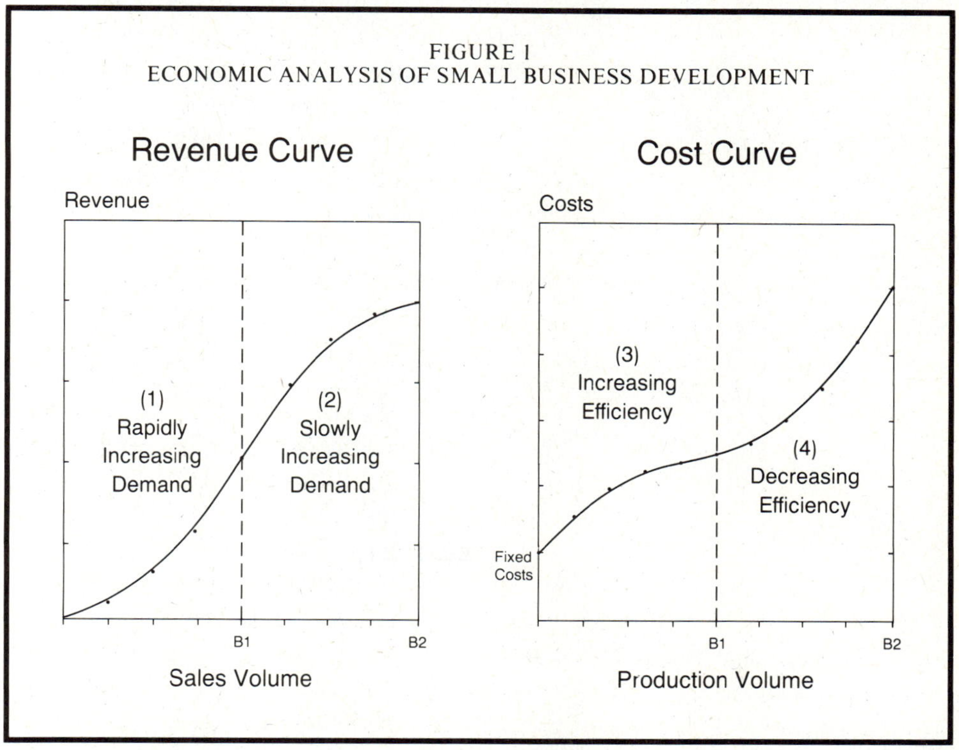

To determine if your word processing program supports graphs from other software, you will have to check your software manual. Also, business pictures known as Clip-Art, available from software vendors, may be incorporated into a word processing file (see Figure 2.7).

Figure 2.7
Vendor Prepared Graphics

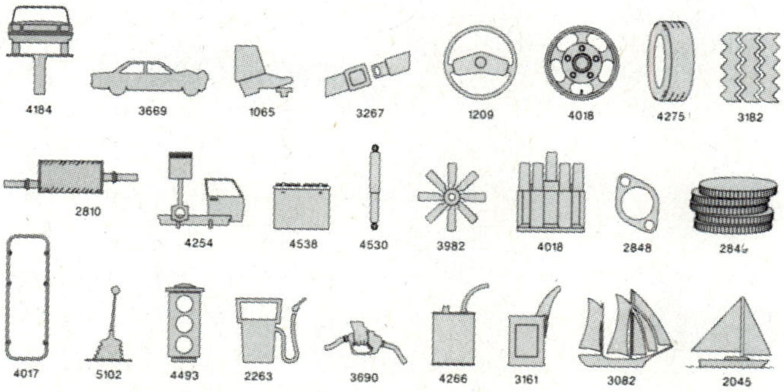

Data stored in spreadsheet and database files may also be imported into text documents. For example, names and addresses of clients saved in a database file may be used in conjunction with word processing to prepare form letters. Also, some spreadsheet files may be converted to a word processing file and processed as a part of the text document. Software programmers are constantly working to design application software programs that are compatible to help you produce documents more efficiently.

Proofreading

Proofreading Checking a document for accuracy.

One of the most important steps in the processing cycle is **proofreading,** checking the document for accuracy and format. A document should be proofed from the screen and again after it is printed. The document should be checked for several kinds of errors: keyboarding, omissions or additions of text, and formatting.

Spelling Checker. The first step in proofing a document is checking for possible keying errors. Word processing programs commonly provide a proofreading capability that checks for spelling errors, or they support a separate spelling checker package. A spelling checker locates keying errors by comparing each typed word to those in a glossary or dictionary in the program. You should be aware, however, that a spelling checker will not detect a miskeyed word if it is a correctly spelled word. For example, if you key *form* for *from* or omit the *s* from *sales*, a spelling checker will not catch the errors. Neither will a spelling checker find omitted words or miskeyed numbers. Some checkers, however, will detect double words such as *the the* or double capital letters as in *TExas*. Always use the spelling checker feature of your software, but do not depend on it to detect all errors.

Most spelling checkers will allow you to add words to the glossary. Proper nouns and specialized terminology, such as legal or medical, that occur often in your work should be added to the glossary. If you add them, the spelling program will not highlight them for you to check during the spell checking process.

Proofreading Techniques. Each document must be carefully proofread; however, proofreading is a skill that is developed through practice. You should find the following techniques helpful as you proofread your documents. Before printing the first draft, you should:

Scrolling Moving the cursor through a document.

- Proofread from the screen by **scrolling** line by line through the document.
- Use the spelling checker to locate misspelled words.

After printing, you should:

- Carefully read the hard copy at least twice:
  *Read for content—does it make sense? Some proofreaders state that reading the document aloud helps detect content and omission errors.
  *Read for keying errors that may not have been detected by the spelling checker. Check each word for errors. Check punctuation.
- Verify dates, amounts, names and addresses; check against an original document, if available. If numbers are totaled, verify by using the word processing math feature or a calculator.
- After checking for content and keying errors, check the format of the printed document—margins (top, bottom, side); right margin justification; line spacing (especially if it was changed within the document); page numbers and headers/footers on multiple-page documents.

Thesaurus Listing of synonyms and antonyms.

Other Document Checking Aids. Many word processing software packages provide a **thesaurus** to aid in selecting synonyms (words with the same or similar meanings) for selected words in a document. Also, antonyms (words with the opposite meaning) are usually listed in a thesaurus.

Figure 2.8
Thesaurus Screen

```
     Several grammar checking software packages which are
compatible with most word processing software are available

compatible=(a)
  1 A ·agreeable
    B ·congruous
    C ·harmonious

  2 D ·appropriate
    E ·fitting
    F ·suitable

compatible-(ant)
  3 G  clashing
    H ·inappropriate

1 Replace Word; 2 View Doc; 3 Look Up Word; 4 Clear Column: 0
```

Several grammar checking software packages that are compatible with most word processing software are available for checking a document for subject and verb agreement, parallel structure, sentence length, passive voice of verbs, pronoun antecedents, gender-biased terminology, reading level, and other troublesome writing areas. By following the suggestions for proofreading, using a thesaurus when you want to vary word choice and a grammar checker to detect possible grammar errors, you should produce accurate and well-received documents.

PRINTING AND REPRODUCTION

Depending upon the purpose, documents may be printed on different kinds of printers. The first draft is sometimes printed on a draft-quality printer; the final copy is printed on a letter-quality printer. Sometimes the draft-quality printer is connected to the computer while the letter-quality printer is shared with other users via a network. Typically only one copy is printed on a letter-quality printer for the following reasons:

Queue Order of jobs waiting for processing such as printing.

- To prevent a long print **queue** when the printer is shared with others.
- To reduce costs since copies printed on letter-quality printers, espcially laser printers, are more expensive than those produced by other means.

If more than one copy of a document is needed for filing or sending to secondary readers, photocopies are made. Photocopiers have been heavily used for many years, but until recently the quality of copies was not as good as the original copy. Now, however, photocopiers have been improved significantly. Photocopier models differ according to their capabilities, but the following list presents features that are now available on various models:

- The quality of photocopies can be as clear and sharp as the original.
- Photocopiers produce copies at rates from 10 to 100 copies per minute.

- Some photocopiers accept plain paper of varying sizes.
- Double-sided copies can be made from single- or double-sided originals.
- Some photocopiers reproduce copies in color.
- Some photocopiers reduce and enlarge copy.
- Some new models of photocopiers perform several operations in addition to copying—scanning, printing and electronically transmitting.

DISTRIBUTION

Once the document is processed, it must be distributed to the receiver(s). Distribution can be completed in several ways.

Traditional Mail

Traditional means of distribution (mail and courier services) often are used when (1) the document is lengthy, (2) it is not needed immediately, (3) the document must be a signed original, or (4) the sender or the receiver does not have electronic mail equipment. Special courier services usually require one day for delivery and are expensive. More and more offices are automating, however, and distribute many of their messages electronically.

Electronic Mail

Electronic mail (E-Mail) Written messages transmitted from one machine to another.

Offices purchasing various automated systems for instantly distributing written messages are using **electronic mail (E-mail)**. Electronic mail is becoming popular because written messages can be sent and received in minutes rather than in days, which traditional mailing systems require. Electronic mail is generally considered to include several technologies that transmit documents—facsimile, computer message systems, voice mail, and telex.

Facsimile Machine that transmits an exact copy to another facsimile machine.

Facsimile. Business experts predict that within the next few years all businesses, even small ones, will have **facsimile (fax) machines**. Fax machines scan documents and then transmit them over telephone lines to other fax machines that reproduce copies of the original. These devices can transmit and receive all kinds of images—graphics, photographs, handwriting, and text. Documents are distributed at the speed of a telephone call; reproduction at the receiving end is about 15 seconds per page.

Offices are now installed with PC-to-fax boards (which include a telephone jack and special communications software) in the computers so that users may communicate with a facsimile machine. From their PCs, users can send documents to a fax or receive documents from a fax device. With PC-to-fax transmission, those receiving documents can store them, if they wish, without printing a copy. Receivers may also modify the documents, and then transmit to the sender or to someone else.

Fax machines are appearing on individual desks, in automobiles, and in homes. Fax telephone numbers now appear on company stationery and personal business cards. A very common statement today is, "I'll fax it to you." Fax machines are especially popular in Far East countries (especially Japan), where languages contain thousands of characters that cannot be transmitted by computer.[3]

[3] Elizabeth A. Hanscom, "Electronic Mail: A Fivefold Message," Office Systems'89 (March 1989), p. 28.

Figure 2.9
Facsimile Machine

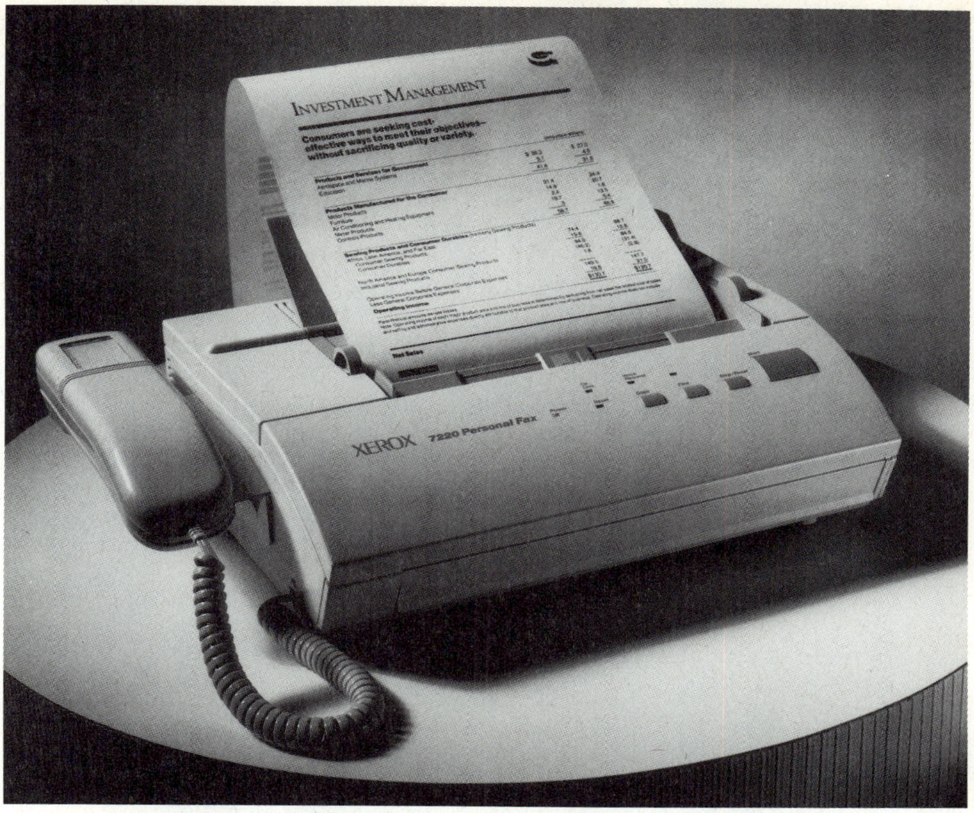

Source: Photo courtesy of Xerox Corporation

Electronic mail by facsimile offers these benefits to users:

- All kinds of images can be transmitted over telephone lines.
- Written messages travel as quickly as a telephone call.
- Fax machines are easy to operate, requiring little training for the user.
- Local fax distribution costs nothing—the same as a local call.
- Fax output is usually error free.
- Written messages are more easily understood than spoken ones—especially for those who speak a different language.
- Fax machines are inexpensive when compared to other means of quickly transmitting written documents.

Computer-Based Mail. Written messages created and transmitted by computers are also called electronic mail. E-Mail combines computer hardware and software that enable users to send messages and be signaled when messages are received. Messages are keyed at a computer and transmitted over telephone lines or a communications network to other computers. These messages can be read at the receiver's computer and printed. If the receiver is not available, the message is stored in the receiver's electronic mail box until it is read.

Computer-based mail requires that the sending and receiving computers have either communications software or network software. As you learned in Chapter 1, a network connects computers for sharing information. Networks installed within a small radius such as a building are called **local area networks** (LAN). Workers key the messages at their computers and transmit them over the LAN mail system. By using LAN mail, workers do not have to leave their offices or suffer from "telephone tag" (trying to reach someone who is not in the office and then waiting for a return call). If a response is necessary, the receiver can transmit it through the LAN mail system.

Figure 2.10
Sample LAN Mail Message Menu with Sample LAN Mail Message

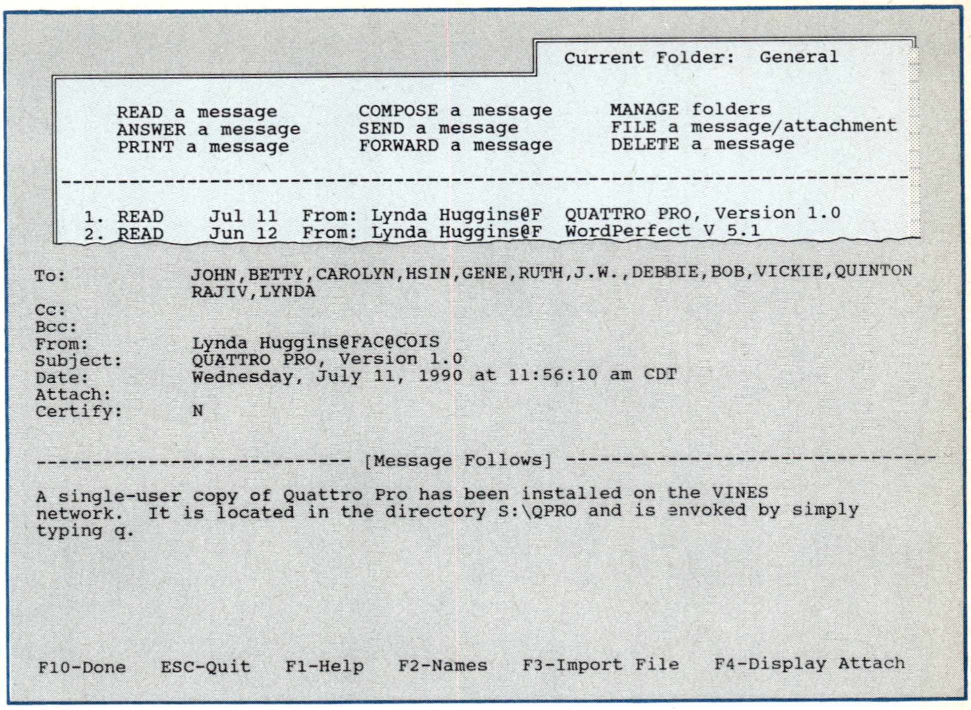

Wide area network Computers linked together over long distances for sharing information.

Wide area networks (WAN) allow users to send and receive messages through their computers over long distances, even to other countries. Messages may be transmitted over telephone lines or communication satellites.

A computer mail message may be sent to one person or several people on the same network. For example, if the sales manager needs important sales figures from several sales representatives, one computer mail message can be sent to all of them. If all representatives are at their computers, they can send the requested information immediately using the computer mail network.

You will learn about other capabilities of local area networks when you study storage, backup, and security of files later in this chapter.

Voice Mail. Voice mail systems (also categorized as electronic mail) process voice messages sent over telephone lines for storage and replay. They are different from telephone answering machines because of their computer-based flexibility. These systems answer unanswered phones and give callers a selection of choices, including leaving messages, talking to someone other than the intended recipient, and integrating voice and text messages. Commands during transmission are given through touch-tone telephones. Printed copies of the voice message cannot be made with today's technology.

Telex. Printed messages sent by telex machines traditionally have been transmitted over dedicated lines (lines used only for telex messages); however, telex over ordinary telephone lines is becoming available. Teleprinters that are used for sending and receiving are usually installed in large organizations. Although the technology is old and other electronic mail systems are more popular, telex systems are being improved by eliminating the need for dedicated lines and using personal computers for document creation. In most foreign countries, telex is the primary form of electronic mail; therefore, many firms in the United States communicate with firms in other countries via telex.

STORAGE, BACKUP, AND SECURITY

You now have a good idea of how documents may be originated, processed, printed and reproduced, and distributed in an automated office. The last step in the cycle involves storing documents for retrieval at a later time, duplicating storage media, and maintaining security of files.

Storage

Hard copy Paper containing printed or handwritten material.

The primary function of the office is to process information; usually that information must be saved for later use or be used to provide a permanent record. In the electronic office, files of information may be stored in different forms: as hard copy, on magnetic media such as disks or tapes, on optical disks, or on microforms. Often files are stored in more than one form.

Hard Copy Files. Although records in the electronic office are almost always filed on some form of electronic media, paper records are still kept. Many people still feel more comfortable when they have access to paper records. In fact, more paper records are produced than ever before because more information is being processed; and with automated equipment, hard copies are easily and quickly produced. Offices, therefore, still must have space and filing cabinets for these hard copy files and maintain an accurate filing system.

File server Hard disk computer to which a number of other computers are connected by a network.

Magnetic Media. Documents produced with word processing or other information systems may be stored on diskettes, hard disks within the computer, a LAN file server, magnetic tape, or an optical disk. Where they are stored will depend on the automated equipment available and electronic filing procedures established for the organization. Storage of documents on disk or tape is more cost effective than storing hard copies. For example, an optical disk with 256 megabytes of storage could contain all of a student's college work, as well as a complete dictionary, thesaurus and other resources vital to a particular field of study.[4]

Backup Duplicate copy.

Files are saved on diskettes when the computer does not have a hard disk or when diskettes are used for making **backups**, a duplicate copy of a file or diskette. (You will learn about making backups in the next section of this chapter.) The operator labels the diskettes and maintains a filing system for easy retrieval.

Documents keyed at a standalone computer with a hard disk are usually stored on the hard disk. Since about 85 percent of all PCs sold in the United States in the early 1990s contain hard disks,[5] you will likely store your documents on a computer with a hard disk. The filing system you establish for storing these documents for retrieval must provide for fast and accurate retrieval. (In Chapter 4, you will study how files are managed on a hard disk.)

You learned when you studied computer-based electronic mail that computers linked by a local area network can communicate with each other. Because of the ability to share information, LAN installations are growing in popularity. Predictions are that eventually networked PCs will outnumber standalone computers.

Not only can workers send mail messages to each other through the network, but they can access company data and various application software stored on the LAN file server. A LAN file server is a centralized computer housing a large

[4]"What the Future Has in Storage," brochure from NeXT, Inc., Palo ALto, California (1990), p. 6.

[5]Steve Davis, "The Hard Facts About Hard Disks," Today's Office (January 1990), Vol. 24, No. 8, p. 52.

capacity, high-speed hard disk that is used for storing files and software and managing the network. For example, persons using a LAN store files containing data needed by others on the LAN server; therefore, users needing certain information simply retrieve it from the network server through their computers. (You will learn in a later section about securing files to limit access to those who do not need the information.)

Magnetic Tape. Magnetic tape is a storage medium used for backing up files on a hard disk or LAN server. It is available in cassette, reel, or cartridge form. Documents are retrieved from magnetic tape only if the original storage disk becomes unreadable.

Optical disk Large capacity disk that scans and stores information using a laser beam.

Optical Disk. Optical disks, sometimes called **laser disks**, use laser beams to read and write data to and from specially treated, nonmagnetic disks. They are primarily used for storing databases, reference materials, and permanent files. Optical disks can store massive amounts of information in any form—text, data, image, or voice.

Figure 2.11
A Read\Write\Erasable Optical Disk

Source: Courtesy of 3M Optical Recording

Two of the most common optical technologies are Compact Disk-Read Only Memory (CD-ROM) and Write Once/Read Many (WORM). CD-ROM users typically access large databases such as tax laws or periodical references prepared by another organization and stored on the CD-ROM disk for reading only. WORM disks permit the user to write (save) data on it, but the disk cannot be erased or rewritten. WORM disks are primarily used for library materials and other databases that must be updated periodically. Erasable optical disks are available, but they are very expensive and therefore are not widely used. Optical disks can be used only in computers with special disk drives and are expensive when compared to costs of other storage media. As the technology is improved and prices are reduced, optical disks will likely become a popular storage medium.

Microforms. Not all records can be stored on computer disks. For example, business forms with signatures are stored on microforms. **Microforms,** which reduce storage space by 95 percent, are rolls or sheets of film containing exact duplicates of documents; these duplicates are so small that special equipment must be used to read them. Microforms may be enlarged and reproduced. The computerized filing and retrieval system designed for microforms makes documents readily available for use.

Microforms Film containing miniature duplicates of documents.

Figure 2.12
Microform Film

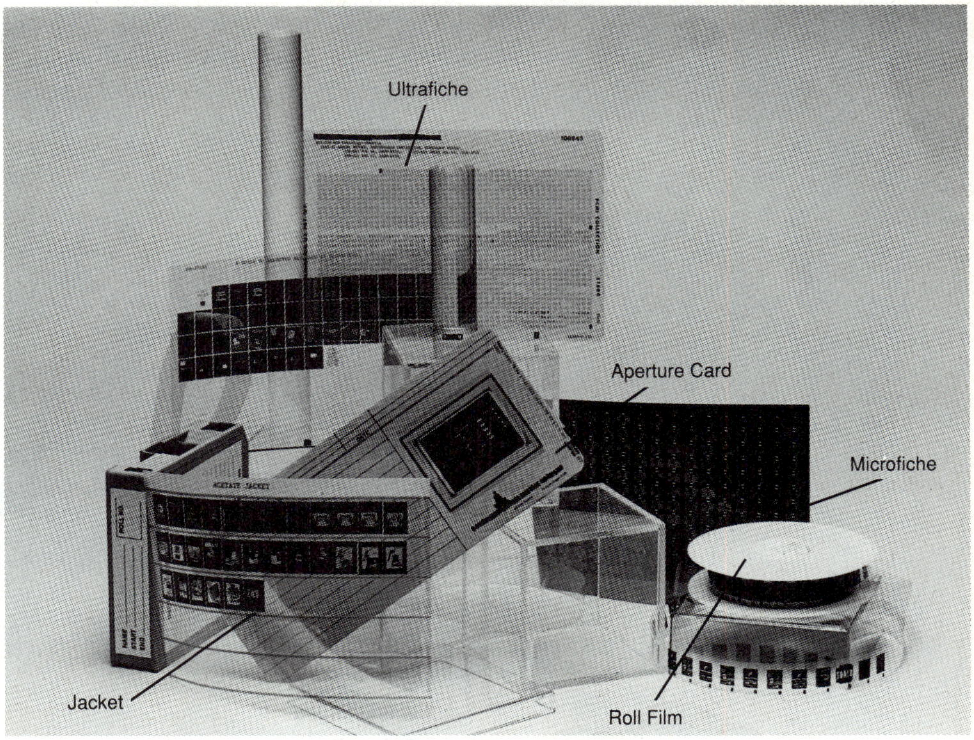

Backup and Security of Media and Records

Diskettes and hard disks are the primary media for storing documents created with word processing. Even with careful handling, these disks can become unreadable after extended use. Hard disks sometimes malfunction, which could destroy the stored information. Also, the user may accidentally delete a file or reformat a disk. For these reasons, backup copies (duplicates) of all storage media should be made on a regular basis, daily for many offices. Backup disks or tapes can then be used if the original disk is unreadable for any reason.

Disks may be backed up using a special copy command, which you will learn in Chapter 4. Those users who must make frequent backups of hard disks or network file servers would be wise to use special backup software; several software packages are available from software vendors.

Media failure is not the only security concern of users. Stored information must be protected from theft and unauthorized access. Companies are establishing many different security measures, such as using passwords and establishing access rights for users. A **password** is a confidential code that must be used to identify authorized users. A password must be keyed when a user logs into a network. Passwords also may be assigned to confidential documents stored on diskettes or hard disks with a special word processing command. Only those who know the password may access the document.

Password Confidential code.

Network users must also have **access rights** in order to read or revise certain files. For example, a user may have "read only" access rights, meaning that the user may read the file but cannot modify it. Others on that network, however, may have full access to the file, which means they can edit it. The network manager sets access rights and may establish passwords.

Access rights Computer setting that controls which users may read or modify a file.

Important documents may also be protected by using encryption software. **Encryption** is the process of coding a document or file so that it cannot be read. The encrypted file is scrambled with letters, numbers and symbols and cannot be read until it is decoded with the encryption software, which requires the user to key the set password for that file. Confidential documents are sometimes encrypted if they are distributed by E-Mail.

Encryption Process that makes a file unreadable until it is decoded.

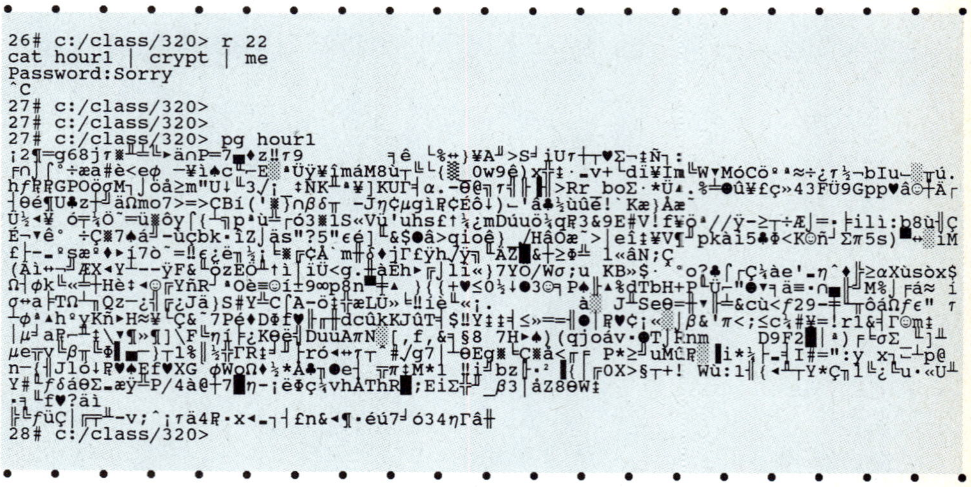

Figure 2.13
Encrypted Document

Another problem area concerning records security is the computer virus. **Computer viruses** are programs written by unethical people to infect software programs and operating systems. Viruses cause damage to hard disks and destruction or contamination of information. Viruses, which are invisible to users, are easily spread from disk to disk and computer to computer because they attach themselves to a program or file. Any disk used on an infected computer will likely become infected. If that disk is used at another computer, it will infect that computer system.

Since over one hundred computer viruses have been identified and spread so easily, causing serious problems in computer systems, organizations as well as individuals are establishing guidelines for detecting and preventing computer virus invasion of their systems. To reduce the risk of infecting your computer with a computer virus, follow these suggestions:

- Make backups often.
- Place write-protect tabs on boot and software diskettes.
- Do not borrow or lend program disks.
- Do not let others use their disks in your computer.
- Never use diskettes from educational laboratory computers in your home or work computer.
- Do not use pirated (unauthorized) copies of software.
- Be careful if you download software from bulletin boards.
- Using anti-virus software, periodically check your computer hard disk and diskettes for viruses.

SUMMARY

Office technology affects how documents are produced in each step of the document production cycle. This cycle of origination, processing, printing and reproduction, distribution, and storage, backup, and security may be completed by using a variety of automated hardware and software systems.

Documents may be originated by being keyed, handwritten, machine dictated, scanned, voice recorded directly into the computer, or input with other devices such as a light pen, mouse, or touch-sensitive screen. The processing step may include formatting, keying, editing, incorporating other files, and proofreading. A variety of printers may be used for producing a hard copy that may then be reproduced with a photocopier. Document distribution may be accomplished by traditional mailing services or one of several electronic mail devices: facsimile, computer-based mail including LAN or WAN, voice mail, or telex. Documents are traditionally stored in hard copy form, in addition to being saved on media including diskettes or hard disks, magnetic tape, optical disks, or microforms. In case of media failure, documents are duplicated onto backup media. To maintain confidentiality and provide additional safekeeping of documents, passwords, access rights, and encryption may also be applied. In addition, measures are taken to prevent invasion of computer viruses, which destroy data and disks.

The document production cycle may appear to be long and complex; in reality, however, today's technology speeds up each step of the process, produces a more attractive and accurate document, and provides more security of information.

EXERCISES

KEY TERMS

Originator
Format
Scanner
Defaults
Spelling checker
Scrolling
Electronic mail
Facsimile
LAN
WAN
Backup
File server
Optical disk
Microforms
Password
Access rights
Encryption
Computer virus

COMPLETION

1. One who composes a document to be produced with word processing may be called a/an ____________________.
2. Of the traditional methods employed to originate documents, ______________________ is the most inefficient.
3. A ______________________ can read printed text or graphics into a computer's memory for further processing and storage on disk.
4. Setting margins, line spacing, right margin justification, and other document specifications is called ______________________.
5. Checking the document for accuracy of content, spelling, punctuation, and format is called ______________________.
6. The word processing software feature that detects keyboarding errors and highlights them for the user to correct is ______________________.
7. A __________________ scans documents and transmits them over telephone lines to another machine where duplicate copies are reproduced.
8. Computers linked together within a small radius with cables and special software for sharing information form a ____________________________.
9. A duplicate copy of a file or disk is called a ____________________________.
10. __________________________ is the process of coding a document or file so that it cannot be read until it is decoded with special software.

DISCUSSION QUESTIONS

1. List the five origination methods or tools originators may use to capture information for processing into documents using word processing. Identify at least one advantage of each method.
2. Itemize several activities that may be completed during the processing stage of the document production cycle, and briefly summarize the importance of each activity.
3. List at least five techniques for proofreading a document.
4. Discuss reasons that one final copy of a document should be printed on a printer and additional copies reproduced on a copier.
5. Explain why facsimile is so popular for transmitting written messages.
6. Briefly outline the benefits of computer-based electronic mail.
7. List five forms in which documents may be stored for retrieval. Discuss at least one advantage and disadvantage of each form.
8. Review the reasons for making backups of magnetic media.
9. Identify three ways documents stored on disks and networks may be protected from unauthorized use.
10. What guidelines should one follow to protect computers from computer virus invasion?

CHAPTER 3

KNOW YOUR COMPUTER

Chapter Objectives

After completing your study of Chapter 3, you should be able to:

1. Identify the five hardware components of a computer.
2. Describe several input devices.
3. Describe the types of monitors available for microcomputers.
4. Identify the two parts of the processing unit.
5. Describe the main types of printers and the features used with a microcomputer.
6. Distinguish between an operating system and application software.
7. Explain the difference between graphical user interface and character-based operating systems.

Just as you don't need to know all the components of your automobile in order to drive it, you do not need to know everything about a computer to operate it. However, you do need to know some of the elements of a computer to effectively use one.

Hardware Parts of a computer that include the monitor, keyboard, and processing unit.

A computer consists of hardware and software. **Hardware** includes the keyboard, the monitor, disk drives, central processing unit (CPU), printer, and other physical parts. Software gives the computer life—it's the reason people use computers. This chapter will introduce you to the computer and discuss its main features.

Figure 3.1
Parts of a Computer

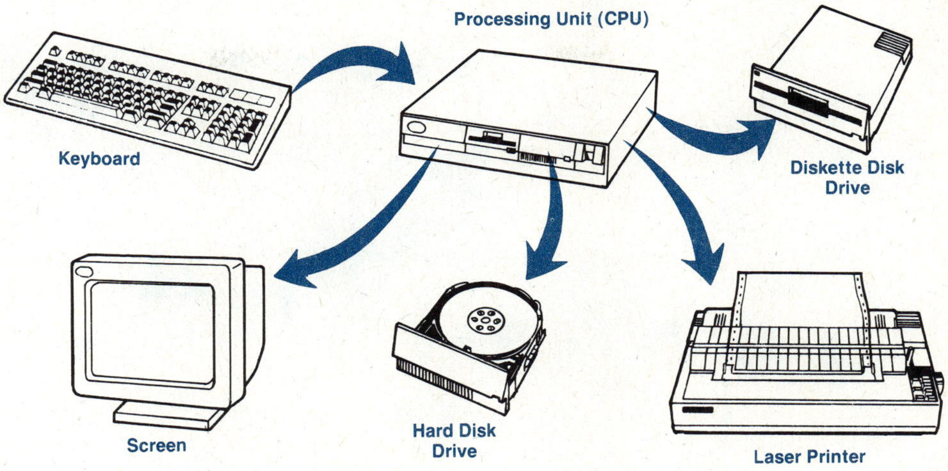

INPUT DEVICES

Information must be entered, or input, into the computer before it can be processed. Input devices are the means we use to communicate with a computer so that it can produce useful information. Although a variety of input devices exists, the keyboard is the most common.

The Keyboard

As you key, the computer reads each keystroke and displays it on the screen. The alphanumeric keys of a computer are located in the same position as those of a typewriter. Although the keyboard of a typewriter and computer keyboards are similar, many differences exist. The computer has additional keys not found on a typewriter. These keys are used to issue commands to the computer, control the cursor, and perform editing functions. As you read about the various parts of the keyboard, refer to Figure 3.2 to learn where these keys are located on the IBM enhanced keyboard.

Function Keys

Function keys Special keys on a computer that are programmed by the application software.

Function keys are programmed by the application software to perform specific tasks. Function keys, therefore, serve various purposes depending upon the application software being used. For example, the F1 function key may bring up a help screen in one word processing program but save a file in another program. Function keys are numbered and are found either at the top of the keyboard or at the left side of the keyboard. Most IBM keyboards contain 10 or 12 function keys,

Figure 3.2
IBM Enhanced Keyboard

labeled from F1 to F10 or F12. An IBM PC enhanced keyboard has 12 keys located across the top of the keyboard; a standard IBM PC keyboard has 10 function keys located on the left side.

Special Keys

The Alt (Alternate) and Ctrl (Control) keys expand the uses of the function keys in a similar way to the shift keys expanding the alphanumeric keys on a typewriter. Some word processing programs such as WordPerfect are programmed so that a function key can accomplish four different tasks when struck either by itself or along with either the Shift key, the Alt key, or the Ctrl key.

The purpose of the Esc key is also defined by the software; however, it is normally used to exit (or Escape) from a program, command, or screen. The Caps Lock key capitalizes the alphabetic characters but leaves the numeric keys in the unshifted mode. The Tab key works much the same as it does on a typewriter.

Toggle key On/off key.

The Insert key is used to add text between characters. Striking the Insert key turns the insert mode on. In the insert mode, characters are inserted to the right of the cursor. For some software, the text in front of the cursor is pushed forward; in other software, striking the Insert key sets Typeover or Replace mode, which deletes the existing text as new text is keyed. The Insert key is called a **toggle key** or an on/off key. Striking it once puts the computer into insert mode. Striking the key again will take the computer out of this state.

The Delete key is used to delete a single character. Text is deleted to the right of the cursor.

Cursor Movement Keys

Cursor Screen symbol that indicates where the next character will be displayed.

The **cursor** is a symbol on the screen, such as a block or underline that indicates where the next character entered will be displayed. Generally, cursors blink so they can be easily identified. As text is keyed or the space bar is struck, the cursor moves one space to the right.

Cursor movement keys Special keys that move the cursor to various points in a document.

To move through existing text without adding extra spaces, you would use the **cursor movement keys**. These keys, marked with arrows, move the cursor up, down, left, or right. To move the cursor quickly, some programs combine the Alt or Ctrl keys with the arrow keys. Other cursor movement keys include the Home, End, PgUp, or PgDn keys. These keys will move the cursor longer distances than a character or line. For example, they may move the cursor to the beginning or the end of the document or page.

Figure 3.3
Screen Showing Square, Underline, and Pointer Cursors

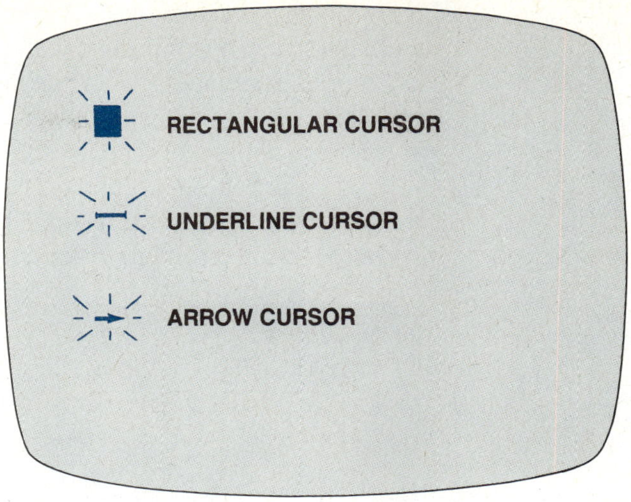

Numeric Keypad

The numeric keypad, located at the far right of the keyboard, is used to enter statistical data or move the cursor. To enter numbers, the NumLock key must be toggled on. When there are many numbers to key, it is more efficient to use the numeric keypad rather than the numbers located across the top of the keyboard. The keypad is usually arranged similar to a calculator; for some keypads, numbers are arranged to conform to the touch-tone telephone.

Other Input Devices

Although the keyboard is the most commonly used input device, there are other ways to communicate with a computer. Most of these devices, however, are generally not used with word processing applications.

Mouse Small input device for moving the cursor.

A **mouse** is a small hand-manipulated device that controls cursor movement on the screen. It can be used to select objects on the screen or perform operations. Certain kinds of programs, such as graphics programs or desktop publishing programs, require the use of a mouse. Some word processing programs now support a mouse.

Figure 3.4
Mouse

Source: BULL HN INFORMATION SYSTEMS, INC.

Touch screens consist of special monitors and software. Selections are made from the screen by touching it with a finger or some other object. Touch screens are often used in situations where keyboards are either unnecessary or awkward. For example, grocery stores use touch screens to display product information. Touch screens are not appropriate for entering large amounts of data.

A **light pen**, a variation of the touch screen, is a special pointing device with a light-detecting sensor at its tip. The pen is connected to the computer and used to point to the screen and to make selections.

Figure 3.5
Light pen

Source: *Courtesy of International Business Machines Corporation*

■ MONITOR

Just as we must communicate with the computer, so it must be able to communicate with us. A computer must have not only input capability but also output capability.

The most common output device is the monitor. A printer, also an output device, is discussed later in this chapter.

Monitors display characters as they are keyed and **prompts** or messages from the computer. Monitors, also called screens, displays, or VDTs (video display terminals), are connected to the computer with a cable. Like a television monitor, the computer monitor has controls for brightness, contrast, and vertical and horizontal hold. Text can be displayed on all computer monitors, but special monitors are necessary to display graphics. The monitor usually displays about a half page (25 lines). Full-page displays are common, however, for desktop publishing.

Figure 3.6
In addition to partial- and full-page monitors, the Macintosh line also includes a two-page monitor, shown here, center.

Source: Photo Courtesy of Apple Computer, Inc.

Monochrome and Color

Monochrome monitor One color display on a dark background.

The two general kinds of monitors are monochrome and color. **Monochrome screens** display a single color such as white, green, or amber on a dark background. Many have excellent resolution (display characters clearly). Resolution is determined by the number of dots, or pixels, that are displayed on the screen.

Color screens are becoming increasingly popular as the use of graphics and desktop publishing increases. Several standards for displays are available, including CGA (Color Graphics Adaptor), the EGA (Enhanced Graphics Adaptor), and the VGA (Video Graphics Array). These display systems differ in the clarity and sharpness of the display and the number of colors they can produce. Many software packages have been written to work with these display systems.

Some monitors are better suited to specific tasks. For example, the Monochrome Display Adaptor (MDA) will not display graphics. The Color Graphics

Adaptor (CGA) will not display text and graphics sharply enough for some applications. Desktop publishing requires monitors that have a very sharp display.

Flat Displays

Originally monitors were about the size of a television screen—large and heavy. With the advent of laptop computers, new lightweight, flat monitors were developed that enable the computer to indeed be portable. Although at one time the characters on a flat screen were difficult to read, technology has improved the resolution of flat screens.

Figure 3.7
Laptop with a Flat Screen Monitor

Source: Reprinted with permission of Compaq Computer Corporation. All Rights Reserved.

PROCESSING UNIT

The processing unit is the central part of a computer. The processing unit might be thought of as the "box" in which the disk drives are contained and to which the keyboard and monitor are attached. The processing unit may sit flat on a desk or stand on the floor. Figure 3.8 shows a floor unit. The main parts of the processing unit are the central processing unit (CPU) and memory.

Central Processing Unit (CPU)

CPU Central processing unit; a microprocessor chip that is the central control for a computer.

The **CPU** (or **microprocessor**) is the "brains" of the computer. All instructions that a computer carries out must be understood and acted upon by the CPU. The input device, monitor, and printer depend upon the CPU in order to work. CPU chips are very powerful and are capable of performing certain commands at the rate of 6 million per second. Of course, like people and animals, the brain is nothing without the rest of the body. The brain may process the instructions for getting a chocolate sundae, but it needs arms and legs to carry it out. In the same way, the CPU needs the other chips, boards, and a power supply to function.

Figure 3.8
Processing Unit (Floor Unit)

Source: *Wang Laboratories, Inc.*

Individual brands of computers use their own kinds of CPU or microprocessor chips. IBM PCs use the Intel family of chips, and Apple computers use the Motorola family of chips. As new chips become faster and more powerful, the number of the chip is changed. The original IBM PCs used the Intel 8088 chip. Later chips were identified with numbers such as 80286, 80386, 80486, and 80586. A computer containing a 80486 chip is often referred to as a "486" machine.

Memory

Memory That part of the processing unit storing data and instructions.

Memory stores two types of information: data as it is entered and computer programs (application programs and operating system programs). When the CPU needs data or instructions, it retrieves them from memory.

Memory has two forms: ROM and RAM. Read-only memory (ROM) is permanent and cannot be changed or lost when the computer is turned off. Operating instructions are recorded on ROM memory chips. Similar to a printed book, you can read the text recorded in ROM but you cannot change it. Random-access memory (RAM) is temporary memory. As information is entered in the computer, it is temporarily stored in RAM. When the power is off, information in RAM is lost. To save the information, it must be stored onto a disk before the computer is turned off.

Figure 3.9
Internal Workings of a Computer

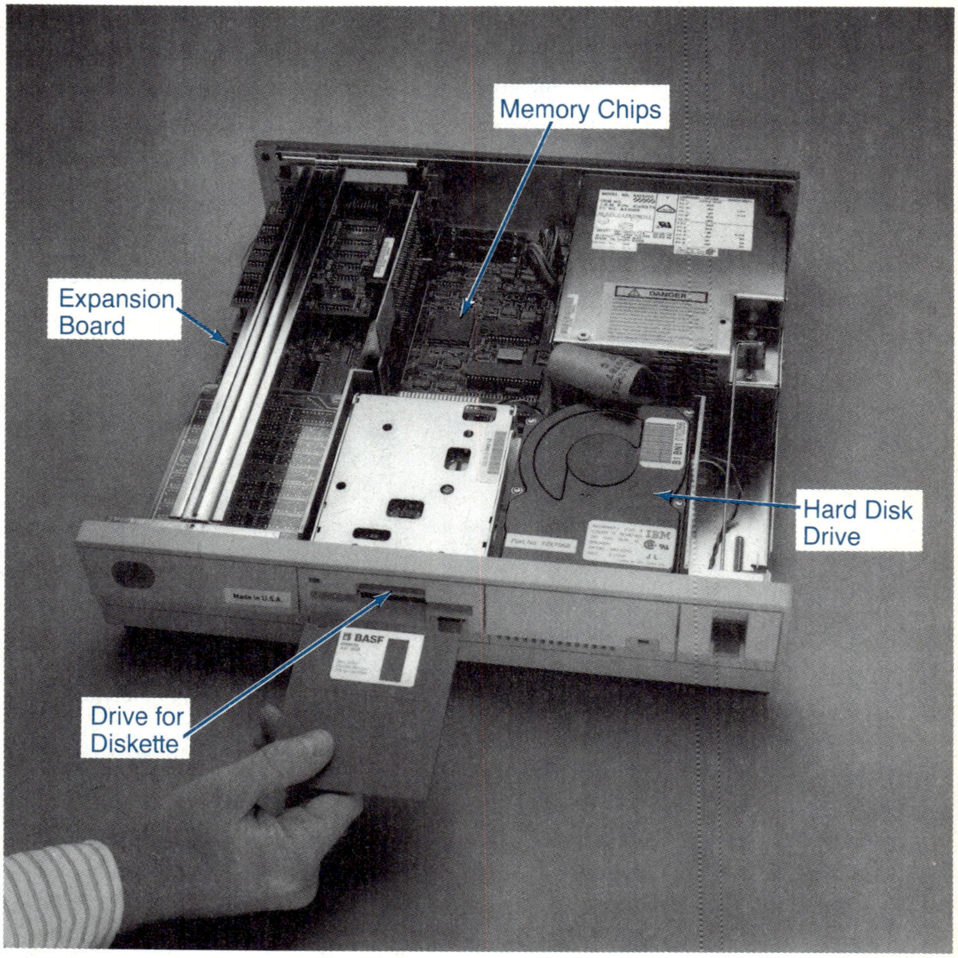

STORAGE DEVICES

A computer must be able to store information permanently. If information is not stored, it will be lost when the computer is turned off. The storage part of a computer saves and retrieves information. Common forms of storage devices are diskettes, hard disks, and optical disks (discussed in Chapter 2).

Disks are random access media, which enable text to be stored and retrieved rapidly. Information is stored on disks by a disk drive, which is the device that holds the disk. Computers generally have from one to three disk drives, but they may have more.

Storage on a computer can be either *removable* or *nonremovable*. As the terms suggest, removable storage can be taken from the computer. Nonremovable storage is built into the computer and cannot be easily removed. *Flexible disks* are removable and *hard disks* are nonremovable storage devices.

Removable Storage

Diskettes (sometimes called floppies or flexible disks) are plastic and coated with magnetic film. The two most popular diskette sizes are 5 1/4" and 3 1/2". The 5 1/4" diskette is flexible, and the 3 1/2" diskette is rigid and more durable. The advantages of using diskettes are that they are inexpensive and they can be removed from the drive for easy storage. However, compared with hard disks, they read and write data more slowly and their storage capacity is smaller.

Diskettes are available in double or high density. High density disks store more information. Storage capacity is generally expressed in terms of "K." One K equals 1,024 bytes of information. MB is the abbreviation for a megabyte, which is equal to one million characters. Table 1 shows the capacity of a disk.

Table 1 Disk Capacity

	Double Density	High Density
5 1/4"	360,000 (360K)	1,200,000 (1.2 MB)
3 1/2"	720,000 (720K)	1,400,000 (1.4 MB)

Care must be taken when using diskettes. Disks are damaged most often by heat and beverages or other liquids that are spilled on their surfaces. If a diskette is left in the sun or in a hot automobile, it may warp or melt. Likewise, spilling a hot liquid on a disk will warp its surface. Precautions should also be taken not to place a strong magnet next to a diskette or touch the surface of a diskette with your fingers. The oil from your hands can damage the surface. Dirt can also cause the disk to lose data or damage the disk drive.

Nonremovable Storage

Hard disks are the most common nonremovable storage medium. They work much the same as flexible disks, but they are made of steel, glass, or ceramic. A hard disk is sealed and cannot be handled.

Hard disks can store much more information than diskettes. A typical hard disk can store over 40 million characters. Some hard disks store 600 million characters. Typically a hard disk will hold 10, 20, or 40 megabytes of data.

■ PRINTERS

Printers provide the printed (hard) copy of a document. A printer is not part of the computer in the way that disk drives or a keyboard are, but it is linked to the computer with a cable. Sometimes a single printer is shared with several different computers. Each computer can use this single printer, but print jobs must first go through a print queue. The *queue* keeps each job in line and lets only one job print at a time.

Print size is measured in characters per inch (cpi) or in points. Most printers print in 10 or 12 cpi, although larger sizes (5 cpi) and smaller sizes (15 cpi) are available. Sophisticated printers are able to print using different type fonts (styles and sizes); sizes are then measured in points. Points sizes generally range from 8 - 36 points. (The smaller the point, the smaller the size.) Most printers produce fixed space or proportional space. Proportional spacing prints letters in varying widths, as in typeset copy. Text can be printed in two different formats: landcape and portrait. **Landscape** format is printed sideways, 11" x 8 1/2", while **portrait** format is the standard 8 1/2" x 11". All printers do not print in both formats.

Figure 3.10
Type Fonts (Styles and Sizes)

This is 18 point Helvetica

This is 24 point Bookman

This is 32 point New Century Schoolbook

This is 36 point Zapf Chancery

Printers are classified in various ways. *Page printers* produce a page at a time, *line printers* produce a line at a time, and *serial printers* produce a character at a time. Page printers, of course, are the fastest, and serial printers are the slowest. Printers are also referred to by their quality of print: *letter quality* (most like typed text), *near-letter quality (NLQ)*, or *draft quality*. Typically, however, printers are classified as impact or nonimpact printers. *Impact printers* transfer the image to the page by striking a ribbon against paper, while *nonimpact printers* do not.

Impact Printers

Impact printers typically used in offices include letter-quality printers (or daisy-wheel printers) and dot matrix printers. Of the two, dot matrix printers dominate the market.

Printers have evolved along with computers. Early letter-quality printers were designed with ribbons and printwheels or print elements (balls) similar to those found in typewriters. The output quality from letter-quality printers is about the same as that from a typewriter. These printers do not have the speed, quiet operation, or capability of printing graphics that today's state-of-the-art printers do.

Dot matrix printers are much faster than letter-quality printers, but the print quality is not as good. Dot matrix printers form characters by striking pins or wires against the ribbon. The sharpness of the print depends on the number of pins on the printhead. A 9-pin printer is considered to be a draft printer, and a 24-pin printer is near-letter quality. The most important benefit of dot matrix printers is that they can print graphics such as charts and pictures as well as text. If a graphic is very complicated, however, printing may take a long time.

Nonimpact Printers

Nonimpact printers are quiet because there is no contact between the printing element and the paper. These printers combine the best features of letter-quality printers and dot matrix printers: the print is of letter quality and graphics can be printed. The two most popular nonimpact printers are ink jet printers and laser printers. *Ink jet printers* form their characters by spraying ink onto a page in the shape of letters.

Recently, printer technology has made laser printers affordable. *Laser printers* form characters through the use of light and toner, much like photocopiers. Laser printers have these advantages:

- *High speed*: Speeds range from 6 ppm (pages per minute) for low-end desktop models to 10 to 90 ppm for high-end models. Print speeds are based on printing simple, double-spaced text documents. If the document contains several fonts or graphics, the printing time is much longer.
- *Quality*: Print quality is excellent, approaching typesetting quality. Laser output is becoming the standard in business. Most laser printers can print different fonts. These fonts must be downloaded from the computer to the printer, or a cartridge must be inserted into the printer.
- *Graphics*: Laser printers can print high quality text and graphics.

Resolution Clarity of the printed page or screen display.

Three trends are marking the next generation of laser printers: (1) higher resolution, (2) color, and (3) page description languages. **Resolution** describes the density of dots per inch (dpi). In the past, 300 dpi has been the standard. With the advent of desktop publishing and the need for higher quality printing, higher resolutions such as 600 dpi or 1000 dpi are possible. Color laser printers produce output by using a special thermal toner. A single page may cost a dollar, which is considered expensive by today's standards. *Page description language (PDL)* refers to software that allows the laser printer to output graphics as well as text. The higher the PDL, the higher the quality. PDL is important when producing sophisticated documents with several fonts and complex graphics. A commonly used page description language is PostScript.

Figure 3.11
Laser Printer

Source: Photo courtesy of Apple Computer, Inc.

SOFTWARE

Up to this point, you have been learning about computer hardware. The other vital part of a computer is software.

Software is divided into two categories: operating system software and application software. Operating system software is necessary to start up the computer and to get it ready for use. Application software enables the computer to perform specific tasks, such as word processing, spreadsheets, and graphics. Both kinds of software are necessary to operate a computer. In Chapter 1 you learned about many of the popular application software programs.

Operating System Software

Operating system software manages the operation of a computer. It performs three basic functions:

1. Manages files and runs other software.
2. Allows the user to enter commands to the computer.
3. Controls devices such as the printer, monitor, and disk drives. Without operating system software, a computer would be an expensive doorstop.

The operating system software can reside on a disk or it can be built into the computer. The IBM PC family of computers and others that are compatible with IBM computers have their operating system software on disk. The Apple Macintosh family of computers has their operating system built into the computer.

Compatible computers Computers that utilize the same operating system.

An operating system is normally designed to be used only on a specific computer. Computers are said to be **compatible** with one another if they can use the same operating system. Many computer manufacturers build computers that are designed to use the IBM operating system. Thus the term "IBM compatible" is often used. Compatibles can also run most of the same applications programs that IBM computers run.

When a computer is turned on, the first program that must be run is the operating system program, making it possible to run application programs. Turning on the computer and running the operating system program is called *booting the system.*

Operating systems, as well as most application software, have a name as well as a version number. The version number identifies the level of the software. The lower the number, the earlier the software was released. Later versions often have extra features that earlier versions lack. In addition, the same commands in later versions may work better or work slightly differently from earlier versions. Newer versions of application software must often be used with current versions of operating systems.

Multitasking Operating systems that allow more than one operation to be carried on simultaneously.

Some operating systems are **multitasking**, which means that more than one application program can run at the same time. The benefit of using a multitasking operating system is that you can do two or more things at once. For example, you could print documents in the background while continuing to work with an application program.

Graphical User Interface

Graphical user interface (GUI) Operating system that uses icons instead of words for directing the user.

Operating systems can be separated into two general kinds—those that use a **graphical user interface (GUI)** and those that use text characters. The difference between these two kinds of operating systems is in the way the user enters commands

Icon Symbolic picture

and in the way the application software operates. Character-based operating systems require the user to key commands from the keyboard. A GUI operating system accepts commands from pointing a mouse to icons. An **icon** is a picture that represents an object, such as a disk drive, a printer, or an applications program. Figure 3.12 illustrates a GUI operating system.

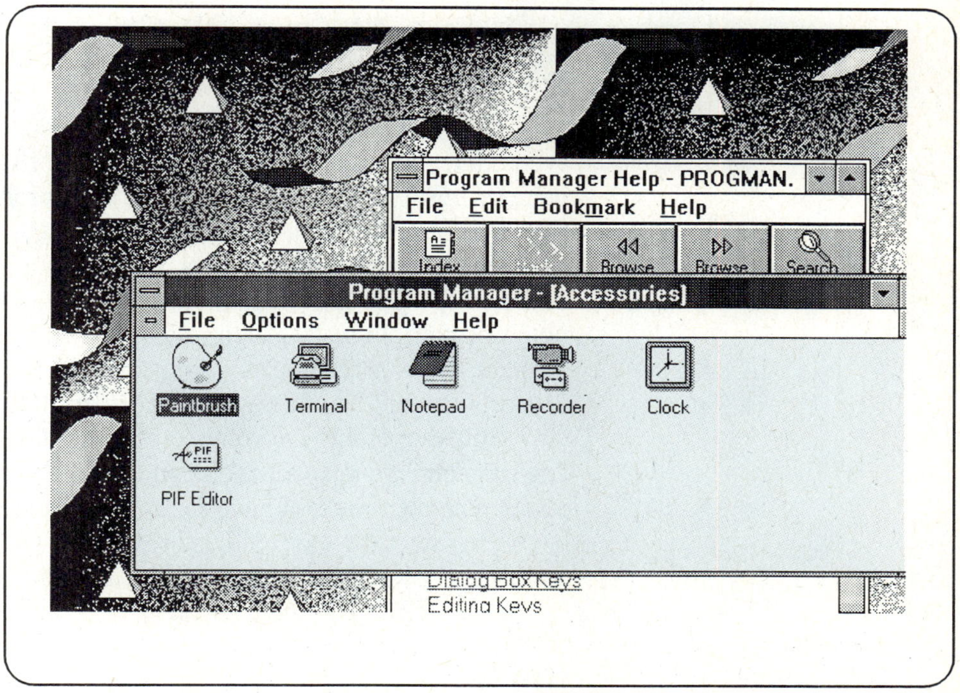

Figure 3.12
GUI Operating System

Names of Operating Systems

Examples of operating system programs available for IBM (and IBM compatible) personal computers are PC-DOS, MS-DOS, OS/2, and Unix. PC-DOS and MS-DOS are character-based operating systems written to run on IBM personal computers (PC-DOS) or on IBM compatible computers (MS-DOS). Apple Macintosh computers use the Apple OS or System 7 operating system. These operating systems perform the same basic tasks but differ in some of their other capabilities.

OS/2 is a GUI system that runs on IBM and compatible computers that have at least 4 megabytes of memory and a hard disk with more than 20 megabytes of storage. OS/2 is a multitasking system. Microsoft Windows is another GUI operating environment for the IBM family of computers. Like OS/2, it can perform more than one task at the same time. It does not require as powerful a computer as do computers running OS/2. It works well on a computer that has two megabytes of memory and a hard disk with six megabytes of storage. Unlike OS/2, Windows requires the computer to be booted with PC-DOS or MS-DOS first.

The Apple Macintosh was one of the first computers to use a GUI operating system. Its operating system, unlike the IBM operating system, is almost completely built into the computer. Like OS/2 and Windows, the Apple System 7 uses icons.

Application Software

Understanding how a computer works and what it can do is in large part knowing what application programs are available. Application software packages are used for specific purposes, such as word processing, database, spreadsheets, and graphics. Application software is loaded into the computer's memory after the operating system has been loaded.

Application programs must be compatible with the operating system. For example, you can purchase the application program Microsoft Excel in either an IBM version or in an Apple Macintosh version.

SUMMARY

A computer consists of both hardware and software. The hardware includes input devices, output devices, disk drives, and the processing unit. Input devices include the keyboard, mouse, touch screens, and light pen. Output devices include the monitor and printer. Monitors or displays may be either monochrome (one color) or colored. The most common classifications of printers include impact and nonimpact printers. Impact printers include letter-quality printers and dot matrix printers. The most common nonimpact printers are laser printers and ink jet printers. The processing unit of a computer consists of the CPU and memory.

Software makes the computer useful. Operating system software creates an environment; it manages the operation of the computer. Operating systems may be either character-based or have a graphical user interface that uses icons rather than words to direct the user. GUIs are usually controlled by a mouse. Application software allows specific applications such as word processing to be completed easily.

EXERCISES

KEY TERMS

Hardware	CPU
Function keys	Memory
Toggle key	Resolution
Cursor	Compatible
Cursor movement keys	Multitasking
Mouse	Graphical user interface
Monochrome screen	Icon

COMPLETION

1. ____________________ keys are defined by each application program to accomplish a certain task.
2. The __________ keys allow the user to move up, down, left, or right through text.
3. The ________________ key places all alphabetic keys in uppercase mode.
4. The _________________ is used to enter numbers rapidly.
5. The ______________ is an alternate input device used by operating systems with a GUI.
6. A _________________ monitor cannot display graphics, only text.
7. Flexible disks may be formatted as __________ or ________ density.
8. The two most used sizes of flexible disks are _______________ and _______________.
9. Print sizes are measured in ________________ or ________________.
10. An operating system that can run more than one application program at the same time is ___________________.

DISCUSSION QUESTIONS

1. Describe four methods of inputting information into a computer.
2. Describe the purpose of function keys.
3. Explain briefly the operation of each of these keys: insert key, delete key, Caps Lock, cursor movement keys, numeric keypad.
4. Identify the two parts of the processing unit.
5. What is the difference between ROM and RAM? What is stored in each?
6. List the advantages of laser printers.
8. List the purpose of operating systems software and application software.
9. What is the difference between a graphical user interface and a character-based operating system?

CHAPTER 4

MANAGING YOUR FILES

CHAPTER OBJECTIVES

After completing your study of Chapter 4, you should be able to:

1. Explain the importance of a good files management system and list those activities usually performed to maintain organized files.
2. Name files for easy retrieval according to file naming conventions.
3. List parts of a document summary and explain its usefulness to the user.
4. Perform basic DOS commands—format, label, directory, copy, delete, rename files, and make directories—as part of a files management program.
5. Explain how saving documents in directories contributes to organized files.
6. Discuss how word processing program utilities can simplify completing some of the DOS operations.
7. Discuss the need for document conversion, attributes of an ASCII file, and the importance of proofreading converted files.

WHAT IS FILES MANAGEMENT?

You have already learned that when a document is produced with word processing software, it is saved on some kind of magnetic media—generally a diskette or hard disk. Before a document can be saved, it must be given an appropriate filename. Also, a document summary should be composed to assist in a document's identification and retrieval. If the user has a choice, a decision must be made as to where the file will be stored so that it can be retrieved quickly when needed. The files management system for storing and retrieving files on disk is extremely important because these files cannot be read unless viewed on a monitor or printed.

Figure 4.1
Files Management Is an Important Skiill in Office Situations

Source: *Courtesy of International Business Machines, Inc.*

An organized files management program requires that you be able to perform the following operations:

1. Name files for storage so they can be located quickly.
2. Format disks.
3. Magnetically label diskettes to identify types or categories of files saved on them.
4. Display directories to assist in locating files.
5. Copy files from one storage media to another or from one directory to another and make backups of important files.
6. Delete files that are no longer needed.
7. Rename files if the need arises.

8. Organize files into directories and subdirectories on hard disk systems or a network fileserver.
9. Convert files so that they can be edited, printed, or manipulated in some way using other software or hardware systems.

The following sections describe the standard procedures and conventions for accomplishing the tasks listed above. Although computer software and hardware systems differ, most are similar in how these operations are completed.

LEARNING THE BASICS OF FILES MANAGEMENT

In order to save a document on disk, you must specify the drive containing the disk on which it is to be saved, name the file, and add an extension to the name when appropriate. Depending upon the software, you may be able to create a descriptive document summary to aid in retrieval.

Specifying Drives

Default drive Current drive that DOS will read or write to.

DOS prompt Drive letter followed by a > indicating the current drive.

Computers have one, two, or three disk drives. When you save a file, you must specify on which drive it is to be saved. If you do not specify a drive, the file will be saved on the default drive. The **default drive** is the current drive identified by the **DOS prompt** (A>, B>, or C>). For example, when you boot a hard disk computer, the default drive C will be indicated by the blinking cursor at C>. You may change the default drive by keying the drive specifier, a colon, and ENTER. For example, at C> key A:<Enter> to change the default drive to A.

Figure 4.1
A, B, and C Disk Drives

Source: *Reprinted with permission of Compaq Computer Corporation. All Rights Reserved.*

Naming Files

Every file saved on storage media must be given a name. All systems will prompt you to name the file either when it is created or when it is saved. Although guidelines for naming files vary, the name should clearly identify the file.

Filespec Complete name of a file.

Filename Name of a file.

The complete file name, called the **filespec** (file specification), consists of four parts: the drive specifier (letter), the path if filing in a directory, a **filename** (one word), and a filename extension with no spaces. [d:][path]filename[.ext] (Note: [d:] is used in this chapter to indicate the drive.) Figure 4.3 shows the four parts of the file name C:CLIENTS\91-TAXES.DOC. The directory path must be separated from the filename by a backslash (\).

Figure 4.3
Parts of a Filename

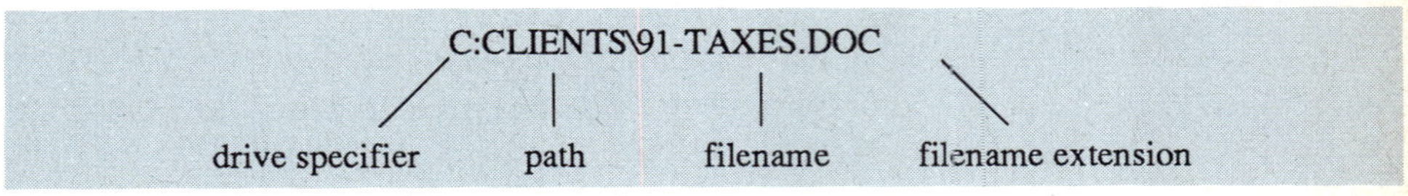

The filename is the only required part of the filespec if you are using the default drive, are not using directories, and are not adding an extension.

Drive

The first part of the filespec [d:] designates the disk drive on which the document will be saved. To specify a drive, key the drive letter followed by a colon and no space. A colon must always follow the drive letter.

Path

Path Directory and subdirectory where a file is saved.

The **path** is the second part of the filespec if you are saving files on a hard disk. The path indicates the name of the directory and any subdirectories. Since path names are usually used only with hard drives, the concept will be discussed in a later section (see page 65).

Filename

The filename is the file's specific name. All computers running under MS-DOS, PC-DOS, and OS/2 operating systems follow similar file-naming conventions. The following list shows these standard conventions. (If you are using a dedicated word processor or Apple Macintosh, however, many of these conventions may not apply.)

- There is a limit of eight characters—alphabetic (A-Z), numeric (0-9), and some symbols. Avoid using symbols, however, except for the hyphen (-), which is useful in making filenames easier to read. You may use fewer than eight characters. The drive specifier and extension are not counted in the eight characters. You may key in either lowercase or uppercase, but the system will convert to uppercase. Tip: you will be more efficient if you key in lowercase and avoid using the shift key when keying filenames.
- Do not key a space anywhere in the filespec; i.e., C:CLIENTS\91-TAXES.DOC.

If you violate the above conventions when keying a file name, you will receive a message such as "Invalid drive or filename," "Bad command or filename," or "Invalid parameter." If you key the name of a file already existing on the disk or in the directory, you will receive the message "File Already Exists," or you may be prompted with "Replace? (Y/N)."

No universal standards exist for naming document files. Being allowed only eight characters is very limiting. Some offices key the name of the receiver as the filename (example: B:RJONES.DOC). If other correspondence is likely to be addressed to this person, a numbering sequence might be incorporated into the filename (examples: B:RJONES2.DOC and B:RJONES3.DOC).

Filenames may consist of the subject or key word(s) in the file. If a subject line is not provided, the user must read the document to determine its subject. When one word will not suffice, two important words can be abbreviated and separated with a hyphen, as in B:CONGR-MD.DOC. This name identifies a document congratulating Michael Davis on an accomplishment.

Filename Extensions

Extension Three characters preceded by a period following a filename.

The filename **extension** is limited to three characters. An extension must be preceded by a period. Filename extensions can serve many important purposes: (1) to identify kinds of software files—word processing text files, spreadsheet files, graphics or desktop publishing files; (2) to designate DOS operating system files, such as .EXE or .BAT; or (3) to more fully describe files and organize records.

Some software automatically adds an extension. For example, ANNOUNCE.PM3 was produced with PageMaker 3.0. Lotus 1-2-3 adds WK1 or PIC, and Database IV adds DBF. Some word processing packages add the extension .TXT or .DOC. Users, however, may override the default extension and key their own. Other programs such as WordPerfect omit the extension, allowing users to compose their own.

Extensions may identify the department to which the file pertains. For example, the Tax Department might use .TAX, and the Accounting Department might use .ACT (example: B:ANNOUNCE.TAX).

Extensions can also be used to designate various versions of the same document as it is being finalized (examples: B:MGT-RPT.1 is the first version; B:MGT-RPT.2 is the second version). Notice that the filename can be the same if the file extension is different.

.BAT, .EXE, .COM, .PRN, and, .SYS are common extensions assigned by DOS and should be avoided when naming document files.

As you can see, identifying files for storage and retrieval takes careful thought and planning. Each office worker or word processing user should take time to identify the kinds of files produced and then design a logical and easy-to-follow plan for naming files.

Composing Document Summaries

Document summary Description of a WP document

A helpful technique for improving document files management is the **document summary**, comment, or description. Word processing programs such as DisplayWrite, WordPerfect, and Microsoft Word provide this feature either in a menu or as a prompt when you create or save a file. A document summary allows the user to key important information about the file to fully identify it. The summary may include the filename, date of creation, name of originator/author, subject, typist, and a text summary, as shown in Figure 4.4.

Figure 4.4
Document Summary for Word Processing Document

```
Document Summary

          Revision Date    07-19-90 08:00p

      1 - Creation Date    04-12-90 07:41p

      2 - Document Name    c:\text\corres\phelan-6.w51
          Document Type    letter

      3 - Author           c dolecheck
          Typist           lisa

      4 - Subject          Transmit Sec 3 Documents/Directions/Solutions

      5 - Account

      6 - Keywords         section 3; 15 documents; 7 functions

      7 - Abstract         TRANSMIT SECTION 3 DOCUMENTS/DIRECTIONS/SOLUTIONS
                           WS44CB; documents, their revisions, solutions and
                           directions for Section 3  Enhancing Text and
                           Adjusting Document Format of WS44CB.
```

The document summary is helpful to the user searching for a file. If the word processing system provides a Look feature, the user can read the document summary without accessing the file. Now let's learn how to manage files using basic DOS commands.

MANAGING FILES WITH DOS COMMANDS

DOS commands Instructions to the computer.

Internal command DOS instruction residing in memory.

External command DOS instruction that must be accessed from disk.

The most widely used computer operating systems today—MS-DOS, PC-DOS, and OS/2—allow users to manage their files with standard **DOS commands**. In fact, as shown in Figure 4.5, many newspaper classified advertisements for office workers and word processing operators specify that the applicant must have a working knowledge of DOS. Although many DOS commands are available, you will learn to use the most common ones. Most of these commands reside in memory when the computer is booted; these commands are called **internal** commands. For a few of the commands, the DOS files must be on a disk in a disk drive or accessible on the hard disk; these commands are called **external** commands.

Figure 4.5
Advertisement for Worker with DOS Skills

PART-TIME W/P: FEE PD. DOS, Word Star, accurate typist, good speller, professional communication skills. Morning or afternoon schedule available. Fast-paced environment. College students welcome! Call MARY 387-6090 Snelling and Snelling.

When you key DOS commands, key them exactly as shown since each keystroke and space is important. Omitting a space or including an extra space will result in a message such as "Bad command or filename." Also, you must key the correct drive specifiers so that the system looks at the correct drive to perform the operation. You should strike the ENTER or RETURN key after you key each command so that the system will accept it. (As you study the DOS commands that follow, you will not be reminded to press ENTER.)

Formatting a Disk

Command: FORMAT [d:]

Formatting Preparing a new disk for use.

Before you can save a document on a new disk, the disk must be prepared to accept data from your system since new disks are generic and can be used by many different microcomputers. This procedure, called **formatting**, does the following:

- Prepares the disk so that the system can read from it and record on it.
- Checks for any defects in the disk.
- Erases any previously saved files should you be reformatting a used disk.

Prompt Directions appearing on screen.

The command to format a disk is FORMAT [d:]; [d:] must be either A or B since you must never format a hard disk. The FORMAT command requires that the drive be specified. For example, if your new disk is in drive B, key FORMAT B:. The **prompt** "Insert new diskette for drive B: and strike ENTER when ready" will appear. Follow the prompt by inserting a diskette into drive B and pressing ENTER.

When formatting is complete, your system will display information about number of bytes/total disk space and number of bytes available. A screen prompt will ask "Format another? (Y/N)." Key an N for No, unless you need to format another. The disk is now ready to use. You will format a disk in Part 2, Section 1 of this text.

Labeling a Disk

Command: LABEL [d:]volume name

Label DOS command that adds a volume name to a disk.

DOS allows you to add, change, or delete a **label** or internal (volume) name on each disk; this label will appear each time you give the directory command to see the list of files.

To create a volume label on a disk, the DOS disk must be in drive A or DOS must be accessed from the hard disk. For this example, the data disk to be labeled is in drive B. If all files to be saved on the disk are related to the subject "sales," you might label the disk SALES. At A> or C> enter LABEL B:SALES. The volume label may contain a maximum of 11 characters.

You should then use a felt-tip pen and write the same name (label) on the paper label on your disk.

Listing Files on Disk (DIR Command)

Command: DIR [d:]

The directory command DIR is used to see a listing of files on a disk. These files may be document files, operating system files, or software program files. Your word processing program will also provide a special key or menu, such as List Files, for viewing the directory.

To see the directory of a disk in drive B, at A> enter DIR B:. However, if you enter DIR at A, you will see a directory of the disk in drive A. As with all DOS commands, if you do not specify a drive, DOS will use the default drive.

If you have many files on a disk, you will not be able to view all of them with the DIR command since the first ones will scroll off the screen. To see all the filenames, you may key either of two commands. The DIR/W command displays the filenames wide across the screen, as shown in Figure 4.6. The size of the file and the date created are not revealed with the DIR/W command.

Figure 4.6
Wide Directory Listing with the DIR/W Command

```
C:\> dir/w

 Volume in drive C is C DOLECHECK
 Directory of  C:\

COMMAND  COM     DW4              AUDIOHF  BAT     MODE     COM     DW4      BAT
EXCEL            GMK3             MOUSE            GOMOUSE  BAT     VINES
SPRINT   COM     PM               INSTALL  BAT     COPY             INSTALL
BIN              ETC              TMP              ATTUSR           CONFIG   BAK
TT               DOS              WINDOWS          EDLIN    COM     GMK2
ATTMENUS         AUTOEXEC BAT     CONFIG   SYS     ~CLP107B TMP     TT       EXE
TT200    CNF     TTFILE   EXE     TTHELP   TXT     {{_TT_}}         ADMENUS
AUTOEXEC BAK     HP               PCBACKUP LOG     WP50             WP5MAN   WP5
FASTBACK         BOOK             CIS101           OIS210           101
TEXT             OINS214          CORRES           WP51             OINS305
       50 File(s)   9586688 bytes free
```

The command DIR/P lists the filenames one screen at a time, pausing until you strike any key to continue. With the DIR/P command, the size of the file and date created are displayed, as illustrated in Figure 4.7.

Figure 4.7
Directory Listing with the DIR/P Command

```
C:\> dir/p

EDLIN     COM       7495   8-19-86   1:00p
GMK2          <DIR>        9-16-88   7:03a
ATTMENUS      <DIR>       10-12-88  11:35a
AUTOEXEC  BAT         32   4-13-89   6:27a
CONFIG    SYS         36  10-17-88  11:20a
~CLP107B  TMP          0  11-12-88  12:57p
TT        EXE     148236  10-28-88  10:26a
TT200     CNF        457  10-28-88   7:58a
TTFILE    EXE     134184  10-28-88  10:26a
TTHELP    TXT      37506  10-28-88  10:26a
{{_TT_}}      <DIR>       10-28-88   7:58a
ADMENUS       <DIR>       11-07-88  12:09p
AUTOEXEC  BAK        631  11-07-88  12:17p
HP            <DIR>        2-09-89   9:17a
PCBACKUP  LOG       6836   3-28-89  10:13a
WP50          <DIR>        3-28-89  10:05a
WP5MAN    WP5      96093  11-19-89   6:36p
FASTBACK      <DIR>        9-14-89   8:38p
BOOK               11716  12-20-89  12:28p
CIS101        <DIR>        3-17-90   3:25p
OIS210        <DIR>        3-17-90   3:26p
101                10402   3-21-90   3:07p
TEXT          <DIR>        7-19-90   7:38p
Strike a key when ready . . .
```

Copying Files

Commands: COPY [d:]filename [d:]; COPY [d:].* [d:]; DISKCOPY A: B:*

Many times you may have files on one disk that you want on another or files in one directory that should be in another directory. By using the DOS copy commands, you can duplicate one file, several files, or an entire disk.

Copying One File

To copy a file named LECTURE.TXT on a disk in drive A to a disk in drive B, keeping the same name (LECTURE.TXT), enter COPY A:LECTURE.TXT B:. When the copy process is finished, you will see the message "One file copied." If, however, you want to copy the file LECTURE.TXT on drive B to another file with a different name on the same disk, at A enter:
COPY B:LECTURE.TXT B:REVIEW.TXT.

Copying Files with *.*

Wildcard *.* Symbol representing all files and all extensions.

You may also copy all files on one disk simultaneously with one command using the **wildcard *.*** (star-dot-star). The symbol *.* represents all files and all extensions. To copy all the files in drive A to a disk in drive B, enter COPY A:*.* B:. The system will list each file as it is copied; it will not copy any directories you may have created on the disk. It will not erase those files that might already be saved on the disk in drive B.

The wildcard *.* may be used with other commands. In fact, you may see *.* when you list files using your word processing software. For example, with

WordPerfect you will see B:*.* when you strike the List Files key and specify drive B. That prompt means that you will see a listing of all files on drive B.

Copying Entire Disk

The DOS command DISKCOPY also allows you to copy all files on a disk to another disk. This powerful command, however, is quite different from the COPY *.* command:

- DISKCOPY will copy everything on the source disk (disk from which you are copying), including subdirectories and any hidden files.
- DISKCOPY erases any files that might be saved on the target disk (disk to which you are copying) and reformats the disk. COPY *.* does not erase the target disk.

The DISKCOPY command is used most often for making backups of diskettes. You cannot use the DISKCOPY command for copying the contents of a hard disk to a diskette. DISKCOPY is an external command; therefore, your DOS diskette must be in drive A or DOS must be accessed from the hard disk when you give the DISKCOPY command. Now let's learn the DISKCOPY command.

With DOS in drive A, at A> enter DISKCOPY A: B:. This command instructs your system to copy the files on the disk in drive A to the disk in drive B. Your screen will prompt you to "Insert SOURCE disk in drive A. Insert TARGET disk in drive B. Strike any key when ready." Place the disk that is to be copied (Source) in drive A, and insert a blank disk (Target) or a disk that contains no files that you want to save in drive B. Strike any key. Your screen will display the message "Copying 9 sectors per track, 2 side(s). Formatting while copying." After the copying is complete, you will be prompted, "Copy another diskette? (Y/N)." Strike N unless you want to copy another diskette.

Deleting Files

Command: DEL [d:]filename

The delete (DEL) command permits you to delete a file that is no longer needed. Files may also be deleted with the ERASE command, but DEL is used most often. To delete the file LECTURE.TXT from a disk in drive B, enter DEL B:LECTURE.TXT. You may use the wildcard *.* with DEL just as you did with COPY. To delete all files on a disk in drive B, key DEL B:*.*. You will be prompted "Are you sure? (Y/N)." Strike Y. As you can see, the wildcard *.* is a very powerful command and should be used carefully. As you work with documents in Part 2, Section 3 of this text, you will delete selected files using DOS or your software delete command.

Renaming Files

Command: REN [d:]filename filename

REN DOS command to rename a file.

Sometimes you will discover that you have named a file inappropriately. You can easily change the filename with the **RENAME (REN)** command. For example, if you wanted to change the name of the file LECTURE.TXT on drive B to SPEECH.TXT, you would enter the following command:
REN B:LECTURE.TXT SPEECH.TXT. You will be asked to rename a few files in Part 2, Section 3 of this text.

■ MAKING DIRECTORIES AND SUBDIRECTORIES USING DOS

Directory Named areas on disk for storing files.

Root directory Primary disk directory from which other directories are created.

Subdirectory Smaller subdivision of a directory.

Hard disks can store large amounts of information. In order for the computer to work efficiently, the hard disk storage space must be divided into manageable areas called **directories**. If you store related files within a directory, less time is required to locate a file.

Computers use a hierarchy, or levels, of directories. In DOS, the main directory is called the **root** directory. From it several **subdirectories** can be created. Most people, however, use the terms directory and subdirectory interchangeably. Therefore, directory will be used in this book unless specific clarification is needed. Although directories can be created on diskettes, it is generally not practical.

To help you understand the importance of organizing your files on hard disks, visualize an office with several filing cabinets filled with hard copy files. If these hard copies were not filed in an organized manner in file drawers and file folders within these drawers, records could not be located. The same situation would develop if files were stored randomly on a hard disk. You might compare the directories to file drawers in a filing cabinet. One directory contains the operating system, such as DOS. Another directory contains the word processing application software. Other directories might be made for spreadsheet software such as Lotus 1-2-3, a graphics package such as Harvard Graphics, and desktop publishing software such as PageMaker.

Within these application software directories, subdirectories are made for storing data files into groups of related files. Subdirectories can be compared to file folders in a drawer dividing the files into smaller groups. When you access the subdirectory, you can locate the file quickly. Also, if subdirectories are not made and data files are stored in the root directory, it will soon be filled since the root directory is limited to a fixed number of files—512 on a hard disk.

If you have many files related to a subject and you need more specialized categories, you may make subdirectories from a directory. In fact, common practice is to make more than one level of subdirectories. This type of file structure is called a **tree structure**, and it is shown in Figure 4.8.

Tree structure Listing of directories and subdirectories.

Creating Directories and Subdirectories

Command: MD [d:]directory name

Now that you have you learned why directories are important, let's learn how to create them. The naming conventions for filenames apply to names of directories—eight characters, no spaces, and selected symbols may be used. Extensions on directories are not used.

MD or MKDIR DOS command for creating a directory.

To create (make) a directory, you will key the Make Directory DOS command **MD** or **MKDIR**, a space, the drive specifier, and the directory name. Let's assume you want to make two directories.

At A> enter MD C:SALES. In this example, the default (current) drive is A and you place the directory SALES on drive C.

At C> enter MD TAXES. In this example, the default drive is C; therefore, you do not have to key the drive specifier to place the directory TAXES on C.

Subdirectories are often created from directories to make smaller groups of files. To create a subdirectory off the directory Sales, at A> you enter: MD C:SALES\SW-DIST. The backslash \ must be keyed to separate the subdirec-

Figure 4.8
Tree Structure Showing Directories and Subdirectories

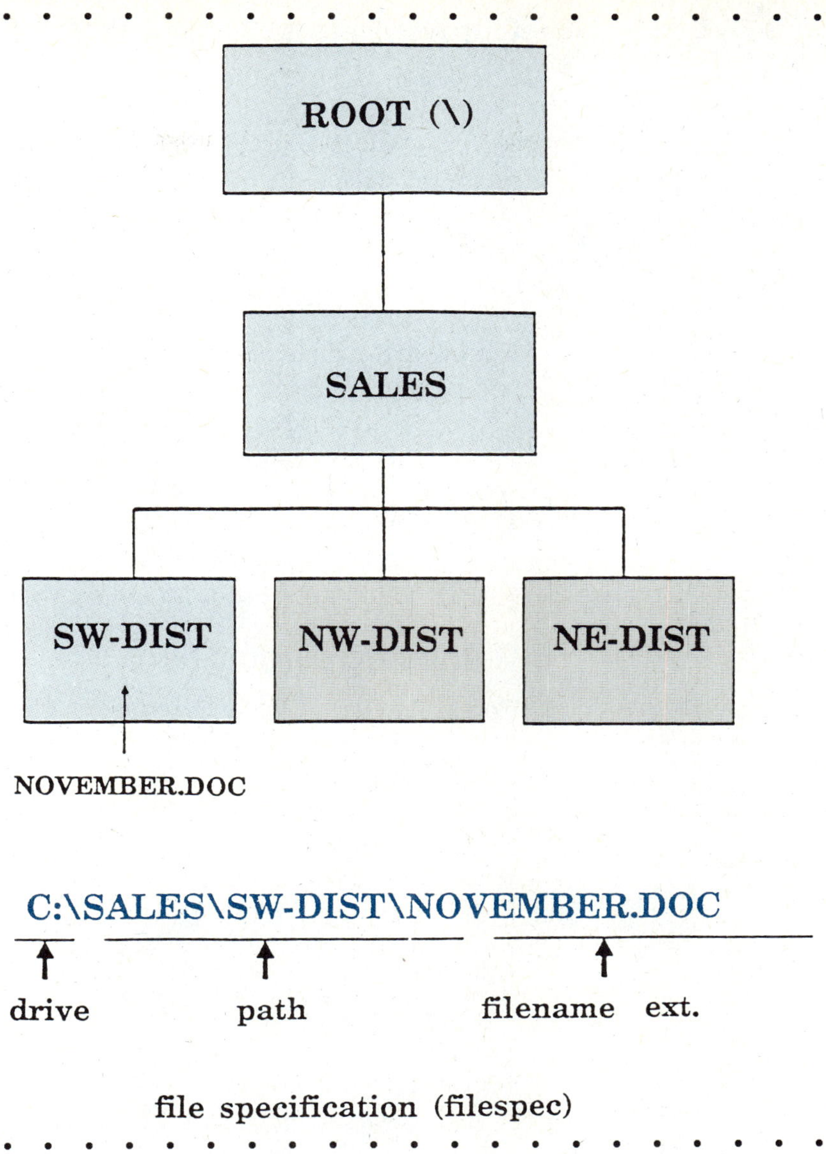

tory from the directory; no space is keyed between. By creating this subdirectory, you would be able to save files related to sales in the southwest district in its subdirectory.

Let's assume that you want to save a file named NOVEMBER.DOC in the SW-DIST subdirectory off the directory SALES on drive C. When prompted to key the file name (specification), you key the drive specifier, the path (directory and subdirectory), filename, and the extension as follows: C:SALES\SW-DIST\NOVEMBER.DOC. A \ separates the subdirectory and directory and another \ separates the filename from the subdirectory; no spaces are keyed in the filespec. The tree in Figure 4.8 demonstrates the structure of this filespec.

When you are ready to retrieve this file, you must key the entire filespec—drive specifier, path (directory and subdirectory), filename, and extension: C:SALES\SW-DIST\NOVEMBER.DOC.

The make directory command is easy to key; however, you will need much practice saving and retrieving files from directories and subdirectories to become proficient. Once you learn, however, your files should be well organized and easy to retrieve.

Changing the Current Directory

Command: CD [d:]directory name

Now that you have learned how to make directories and subdirectories, you need to know how to change from one directory or subdirectory to another. The examples given so far assumed that you were working from the root directory. As you can see from the example above, when you saved the file named NOVEMBER.DOC to the SW-DIST subdirectory of the directory SALES, you had to key the entire path name, SALES\SW-DIST.

If you are working with files in a directory, key the change directory command to move to that directory to make your work easier. When you create and save a file or perform any other commands related to files in that directory, you do not have to key the path. For example, to change from the root directory to the SW-DIST subdirectory, key the following: CD C:SALES\SW-DIST. If your DOS prompt has been set to show the current directory, it will look like this: C:SALES\SW-DIST> To retrieve or save a file from this directory, all you do is key the filename.

CD DOS command for changing directories.

To leave the SALES\SW-DIST subdirectory and to return to the root directory, key **CD** followed by the backslash (\), which represents the root—CD\.

Removing Directories

Command: RD [d:]directory name

RD or RMDIR DOS command for removing a directory.

If you want to delete a directory that you misnamed or no longer need, you can remove it with the **RD or RMDIR** command. For example, RD C:TAXES would delete the TAXES directory from C drive. If you have saved files in the directory, however, they must be deleted before you can remove the directory.

Figure 4.9 provides a summary of the most common DOS commands.

Figure 4.9
DOS Command Summary

Change the Default Drive	key drive designator [d:] <ENTER> A: or B: or C:
Format a Disk	FORMAT [d:] where [d:] is A or B
Label a Disk	LABEL [d:]volume name
List Files on Disk	DIR [d:]; DIR/W [d:]; DIR/P [d:]
Copy a Single File	COPY [d:]filename [d:]
Copy All Files	COPY [d:]*.* [d:]
Copy Entire Disk	DISKCOPY [d:] [d:] where [d:] is A and B
Delete a File	DEL [d:]filename
Delete All Files	DEL [d:]*.*
Rename a File	REN [d:]filename
Create a Directory	MD [d:]directory name
Change Directory	CD [d:]directory name
Remove a Directory	RD [d:]directory name directory must be empty

USING SOFTWARE UTILITIES FOR MANAGING FILES

The DOS commands you have just studied will always be useful because you do not have to use a software application program to perform them. Many word processing software applications programs, however, provide these DOS commands in easy-to-use utility menus or with special keys. Using these menus or keys simplifies completion of these commands; you do not have to remember and key the DOS commands. For example, if you want to delete an unneeded document file while you are using most word processing programs, you simply access the appropriate menu, either highlight the filename in the directory or key the filename, and select DELETE or ERASE.

These utility menus or keys also allow you to copy files, rename files, and perform other files management functions. Some even provide the capability to make directories and subdirectories with a menu. Instead of the DIR command, most word processing packages provide a DIRECTORY or LIST FILES key on the keyboard.

Another valuable aid for helping you manage your files is to print copies of the directories of each disk. By filing these printed directories in the paper jacket with the disk, you can quickly read the directory to see if a file is on that disk without having to insert it into a disk drive and display the directory.

As you continue your study of word processing in Part 2 of this text, you will be directed periodically to delete, rename, copy, print the directory, and perform other files management operations using your system's utilities menu.

CONVERTING FILES FOR USE WITH OTHER SOFTWARE

As you have already learned, thousands of computer application software packages are available; and workers within an organization often use the software of their preference. Files produced with one application cannot be shared with other employees who use another application unless the files are converted (made compatible). Also, if the organization changes word processing software programs, the existing files may not be compatible with the new software. For example, if an organization changed from DisplayWrite 4 to WordPerfect 5.1, the organization would have to convert its DisplayWrite 4 files to DCA format; then, using WordPerfect's conversion utility, the DCA files would be converted to WordPerfect.

Document conversion Make a file compatible for use with different software.

ASCII Format of basic text stored by computers.

Many of the word processing programs on the market, however, offer a **document conversion** utility that will change files to several other popular software formats or into a standard text format called **ASCII**. When a file is converted to be used with other programs, the formatting commands such as center, line spacing, underscoring, and margins are made compatible with the new program. Files that have been converted must be carefully edited to assure that all formatting commands have been converted.

If conversion to the desired program is not possible, you may convert the file to ASCII format, which can be used with any program. By comparing the ASCII document to the original in Figure 4.10, you can see that the underlining, bold, double spacing, page number, and right margin justification commands were lost in conversion. In addition, all returns are now hard returns and the indent commands are spaces. All of the text, however, is in the ASCII file; therefore, when an ASCII file is accessed by a software program, only the formatting commands must be reentered.

Because document conversion is often necessary, you will convert selected files (if your software permits) in Part 2, Section 7 of this text. The steps are usually simple; check your software manual for the procedure for converting files with that software.

Figure 4.10
Formatted Document

2

Steps for Preparing Primary File:
On a new document screen, position the cursor for the first line (date) of the letter.

WordPerfect has a wonderful command for inserting the date automatically if the

computer is on a network or has a hard disk with a calendar.

1. On the appropriate line, strike CTRL+D; ^D will appear. When you give the merge command, the current date will automatically be inserted! Key the appropriate number of hard returns between the date and the address.

2. At the point for the letter address which is made up of variables that will change, key Merge Codes made up of *field names.* Although you could use one field name for the complete address (name, street, city/state/ZIP), you will be wise to set up separate fields for each line in case you want to SORT by certain fields. See the section Conditional Statements for steps for including a conditional statement for fields which may not be used for all records, but you want to include when data is available. Follow the steps below for keying field names:

    a. For the first line of the address, position the cursor where the name is to print. Press **Shift+F9 (Merge Codes)**.

    b. Select **Field (1)**.

    c. Key the descriptive field name. For the first line of the address, key **name**. TIP: always key field names in lower case.

    d. Press ENTER. **name~** will appear. Press ENTER.

    e. For the second line of the address, Press **Shift+F9**. Select **Field**. Key **street**. Press ENTER. **street~** will appear.

    f. Set up appropriate fields for **city, state, ZIP** following the same steps.

3. After the ZIP, key two returns for the double space. If a salutation is used, key Dear(space) and then a field name: **sal~** representing the salutation.

4. Key the text of the document formatting it as you key. At each variable point, key a descriptive field name.

5. Check spelling and print primary document.

Figure 4.10 cont.
Formatted Document after Conversion to ASCII Format

Steps for Preparing Primary File:
On a new document screen, position the cursor for the first line (date) of the letter. WordPerfect has a wonderful command for inserting the date automatically if the computer is on a network or has a hard disk with a calendar.

1. On the appropriate line, strike CTRL+D; ^D will appear. When you give the merge command, the current date will automatically be inserted! Key the appropriate number of hard returns between the date and the address.

2. At the point for the letter address which is made up of variables that will change, key Merge Codes made up of field names. Although you could use one field name for the complete address (name, street, city/state/ZIP), you will be wise to set up separate fields for each line in case you want to SORT by certain fields. See the section Conditional Statements for steps for including a conditional statement for fields which may not be used for all records, but you want to include when data is available. Follow the steps below for keying field names:

   a. For the first line of the address, position the cursor where the name is to print. Press Shift+F9 (Merge Codes).

   b. Select Field (1).

   c. Key the descriptive field name. For the first line of the address, key name. TIP: always key field names in lower case.

   d. Press ENTER. name~ will appear. Press ENTER.

   e. For the second line of the address, Press Shift+F9. Select Field. Key street. Press ENTER. street~ will appear.

   f. Set up appropriate fields for city, state, ZIP following the same steps.

3. After the ZIP, key two returns for the double space. If a salutation is used, key Dear(space) and then a field name: sal~ representing the salutation.

4. Key the text of the document formatting it as you key. At each variable point, key a descriptive field name.

5. Check spelling and print primary document.

Whether you choose a career in word processing or use word processing for personal or business use, your files will be organized and easy to retrieve if you practice the principles taught in this chapter.

SUMMARY

For files saved on computer media to be organized for fast retrieval, a well-planned and organized program must be established. Users must be able to name files and compose document summaries for word processing documents. In addition, the skilled user can perform common DOS commands including format, label, directory, copy, delete, rename, and create, change, and remove directories.

Word processing users should be able to operate the word processing utilities program to complete some DOS operations. Also, since files created with different software often must be converted to be compatible with other software, users must use the conversion utilities of their software and carefully proofread documents after conversion.

EXERCISES

KEY TERMS

Default drive	DOS Commands
Filename	FORMAT
Extension	LABEL
Drive specifier	DIR
Document summary	COPY
Wildcard	DISKCOPY
Source disk	DEL
Target disk	REN
Directory	MD
Document conversion	CD
ASCII file	RD

COMPLETION

1. The filespec consists of four parts: ________________________________, ____________________, ____________________, and ____________________.
2. A maximum number of _____ characters may be used in a filename.
3. List three extensions reserved for DOS files. ____________, ____________ and ________________.
4. The information an operator can key to fully describe a document is called the____________________________.
5. Preparing a new disk for storing files on a computer is called ____________________.
6. When keying the LABEL command to name a disk, you may key up to ____________ characters in the name.
7. To view the listing of files on your disk in drive B using the DOS command, you would key ____________________.
8. The symbol *.*, which may be keyed to represent a filename and its extension, is called a ______________________.

9. The DOS command most often used to make backup copies of a disk is ____________________.

10. The DOS command to delete all files on a disk in drive B is ________________________________.

11. To organize files into related groups on a hard disk system, an operator should set up ____________________.

12. Write the entire file name including the path to save a file named PHOTO-A.DOC in a directory and subdirectory named TRIAL\JACKSON on drive C. ______________________________________

DISCUSSION QUESTIONS

1. List the major activities often completed as part of a files management system.
2. What information is typically recorded in a document summary?
3. How can word processing users perform files management activities such as delete, copy, and rename files rather than keying DOS commands?
4. How does making directories on a hard disk system contribute to good files management?
5. Why must files sometimes be converted using the conversion utilities of software?

CHAPTER 5

ERGONOMICS IN THE AUTOMATED OFFICE

CHAPTER OBJECTIVES

After completing your study of Chapter 5, you should be able to:

1. Discuss features of an ergonomically designed automated office and explain how these features affect worker performance.
2. Describe the furniture and accessories of an ergonomically designed workstation.
3. Explain the features of ergonomically designed monitors and keyboards of computer hardware.
4. Describe an ergonomic office environment in terms of controlling climate, noise, lighting, and glare.
5. List work guidelines for VDT users that many organizations follow.
6. Outline several causes of computer-related worker stress and list suggestions for reducing such stress.

As a student you have probably attended classes in which learning was hindered because you were uncomfortable in your surroundings. Imagine yourself in a situation similar to this one: You are taking a lecture class with 100 other students in a crowded classroom. You cannot see the chalkboard because it is too far away and the light from the window produces a glare that makes the instructor's handwriting impossible to read. In addition, your small arm chair is designed for a right-handed student while you write with your left hand, and your legs are cramped beneath the too-low desk arm. The air conditioning system is inadequate for the size of the room and everyone is too warm. Inattentive students are shuffling their feet, turning pages in their books, and whispering to others, making it impossible for you to hear the instructor's lecture. After a few class meetings, you convince yourself that you are not learning anything in class and do not attend the lectures.

Office workers often find themselves in a similar situation—their desks and chairs are not designed for computer work and cannot be adjusted, their VDT screens not only reflect glare but are improperly positioned, and the noise produced by printers and other workers is annoying. As a result, these employees often complain of headaches, backaches, eyestrain, stress, and reduced job satisfaction. They have higher absenteeism rates and work at a lower production rate than those employees who work in ergonomically designed offices.

WHAT IS ERGONOMICS?

In today's highly automated offices, workers are performing much of their work at computers. Yet, unless the office has been recently constructed or remodeled, it has not been designed for computer work. Very likely the furniture and lighting are designed for workers who perform their work handling paper and using typewriters and other traditional office tools.

Workstation Worker's immediate work area.

In contrast, the ergonomically designed office is one that provides a comfortable environment. **Workstations** and their accessories, lighting, and climate can be adjusted to suit the individual worker. The ergonomically designed office improves worker productivity and health.

Ergonomics Study of workers' performance and well-being in relation to jobs, equipment, and environment.

The science that studies workers' performance and well-being in relation to their jobs, equipment, and environment is **ergonomics**. Ergonomics involves designing furniture, hardware, lighting, and other aspects of the office so that workers can complete their work with a minimum of effort and stress.

Why You Should Study Ergonomics

Informal observations of some employees who use ergonomically designed workstations reveal that they do not realize that adjustments can be made to their workstations. Some employees do not know they have permission to change the position of anything at their workstation or their equipment.

By studying ergonomics as it relates to the automated office, you will be able to make some adjustments to your workstation so that it is compatible with your needs. In addition, you may be assigned to work with a committee to help select desks, chairs, hardware, and software and redesign the office for automation.

Factors Affecting Office Worker Performance

Because ergonomically designed offices significantly improve the worker's comfort and productivity, many changes have been made in the design of chairs, desks, and equipment, as well as in lighting, temperature, space, and noise control. Many vendors advertise their equipment and furniture as being "ergonomically designed," meaning it can be adjusted easily for maximum user comfort.

As a part of improving the work environment, firms are now considering important health-related issues; namely, the number of hours employees spend at VDTs, the number of rest breaks needed during the day, the need for periodic eye examinations, stress, and other issues. These health issues are so critical that several state legislatures have proposed legislation governing worker use of VDTs.

As you study the following material related to specific ergonomic features of the office environment, pay close attention to the simple adjustments that you can make to your present work area in the classroom and at work.

■ ERGONOMICALLY DESIGNED WORKSTATIONS

In today's automated office, the desk, work space, chair, and related workstation accessories are important to the worker's physical well being. In this book, the term **workstation** represents the area in which an individual works; it includes furniture, equipment, accessories, lighting, and storage modules. (Some vendors, however, market their computers as workstations; also, some marketers of ergonomically designed tables refer to their furniture as workstations.) Workstations are designed to be adjusted to the needs of the person.

Adjustable Furniture

If the workstation is designed for traditional paper-handling tasks and is not adjustable, workers performing most of their work at computers are uncomfortable and suffer from pain in the neck, back and shoulders. In addition, many complain of tingling and numbness in the arms, fingers and legs.

Desks

Desks or work surfaces designed for computer equipment are often multilevel and adjustable so that the height of the screen and keyboard can be changed for the individual worker. Since workers vary in size and shape—some are tall, others are short, and their arms and legs are of different lengths—the desks must be adjustable to accommodate these differences. Desks that are too low or too high place strain on the neck and back. As you can see in Figure 5.1, the shelf holding the keyboard can be raised or lowered and the computer monitor can be adjusted up or down and moved forward or backward. Also, sufficient space must be available not only for the computer but for other necessary items, such as software, reference manuals, and a mouse.

Figure 5.1
Ergonomically Designed Workstation

Source: *Photo Courtesy of Haworth, Inc.*

Seating

Chairs must be adjustable, also. You should be able to adjust the chair height to your leg length and adjust the backrest for optimum back support. The adjustable backrest should support the lower back to reduce spinal pain and increase blood circulation to the legs. It should provide tension that supports your back when you lean forward or backward in your chair. Also, the chair should have at least five legs to prevent its turning over. Many office workers prefer a chair with armrests for arm support. An ergonomically designed chair provides the flexibility of adding or removing the armrests for worker preference.

Figure 5.2
Ergonomically Designed Chair

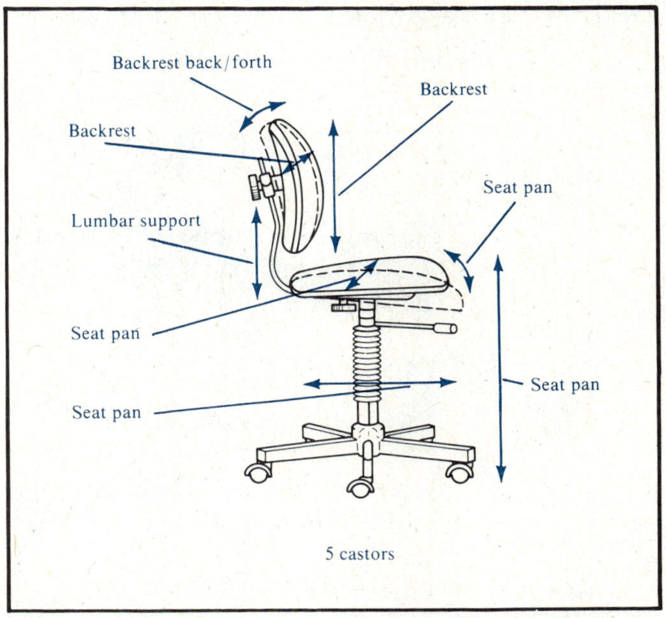

Helpful Accessories

Other workstation features can add comfort and improve worker performance. Some helpful accessories are copyholders, footrests, armrests, and antistatic mats.

Copyholders

Operators who must read from hard copy positioned to the side of their monitors often complain of neck aches, eyestrain, and losing their places in the copy because they have to turn their heads. Use of a copyholder can alleviate these problems since copyholders can be adjusted for the appropriate height and angle. Most operators find that placing copy directly in front of them between the screen and detached keyboard reduces neck aches and unnecessary eye movement. If copy is placed to the side, it should be positioned so that it is the same distance from your eyes as the monitor so that the eyes do not have to continuously readjust to distance.

Footrests and Armrests

Footrests and armrests reduce leg and arm fatigue. These appliances may already be built into the modern workstation, or they can easily be added to existing workstations. By raising the legs slightly with a footrest and supporting the wrists with a rest positioned at the base of the keyboard, VDT operators have discovered that they can work longer without their legs and arms becoming tired. Wristrests can help prevent tendonitis in the wrists, a complaint of some VDT workers who spend many hours a day at their computer.

Antistatic Mats

Low humidity (less than 40 percent) promotes static electricity. However, placing an antistatic mat under your chair will greatly reduce the static electricity that can damage a computer and cause loss of data. Antistatic carpet may also be installed to reduce static electricity.

Now that you have learned how office furniture and other workstation accessories can be adjusted to your needs and uses, take the time to make adjustments to your work area. You will be surprised at how much better you feel.

ERGONOMICALLY DESIGNED HARDWARE

Not only should you be able to adjust your desk, chair, and other accessories, but your computer should offer ergonomic features as well; namely, an adjustable monitor and keyboard.

Monitor

A well-designed monitor offers several features to provide maximum user comfort and flexibility. The screen should be adjustable for brightness and contrast and display legible text. The monitor should be separate from the keyboard to provide for tilting and turning or moving backward and forward.

Legibility of Text

Characters on the monitor should be sharp and clear, and they should be large enough to be seen from a viewing distance of 16 to 24 inches. Ideally, characters should be about one-fourth inch in height. Characters that are too large slow down reading. If characters appear too small, move the monitor a little closer to you, but not so close that you strain your eye muscles. Some monitors are marketed as *high resolution*, meaning they display text and graphics in sharp detail. The traditional screen size shows 25 lines of text, which is usually ideal for text documents. Larger screens are better suited to desktop publishing, spreadsheets, and graphics.

Cleanliness of the monitor greatly affects legibility. VDT screens attract dust and many operators touch their screens, leaving fingerprints that make viewing difficult. Screens should be wiped weekly. While office supply vendors sell special cleaning materials, you should find a clean soft cloth moistened with a glass cleaner or a dry tissue sufficient. Never spray anything directly onto the screen.

Brightness and Contrast

The user should be able to change the brightness of the characters and the contrast provided between the characters and the background. These adjustments reduce eyestrain. The image is made up of a series of light impulses; usually increasing brightness improves legibility of the text. Characters tend to flicker, however, if the brightness is turned too high. You will have to adjust the brightness and contrast to fit your vision and the lighting around you. The contrast and brightness knobs are usually located below or to the right side of the screen.

Figure 5.3
High-Resolution Monitor

***Source:** Photo Courtesy of Apple Computer, Inc.*

Viewing Angle

The monitor should be detached from the keyboard so that it can be tilted, turned, and moved forward and backward. If you work in natural light, you should turn your screen at a 90° angle to the light. If you work in artificial light, you should tilt your screen downward, away from the light. If the VDT does not tilt, you can purchase a stand for tilting and turning and place the VDT on it. Ideally, your eyes should look downward on the screen. If you wear bifocals or other reading glasses, you should adjust the screen by tilting it to a more comfortable angle and changing the distance between you and the screen. You might find glasses prescribed for use at a VDT helpful.

Color of Characters

Although many operators may prefer one screen color to another, research reveals that the color of the characters does not affect the VDT user's ease of viewing or performance. Studies have also found no significant differences in the use of light characters on a dark background or dark characters on a light background.

An interesting phenomenon sometimes occurs after operators have worked at a VDT screen for a length of time: they see a colored halo on objects around the work area. This experience, called **chromatic afterimage**, can occur whenever someone stares at a color for any length of time, so it is not limited to VDT users. When some

Chromatic afterimage Colored halo sometimes seen during VDT work.

VDT operators view green characters on a black background for a considerable length of time, they see a pink halo on objects around the work area. Operators viewing amber characters on a dark background have reported a blue halo. This phenomenon usually lasts a second or two and causes no harm.

Color monitors are very popular today with the increased use of desktop publishing and graphics programs. Some authorities report that viewing large color blocks is more tiring to the eyes than monochrome characters. Many word processing users, however, find the color monitor useful since several commands, such as underlining, bold, and font changes show the text in another color.

In addition to the adjustments you have already learned to make to your workstation and monitor, follow these suggestions to minimize eye fatigue and strain:

- Cup your hands lightly over closed eyes for one minute.
- Look into the distance from time to time at something at least 20 feet away.
- See an eye care specialist every one or two years; if vision correction is needed, be sure to tell the eye specialist that you work at a VDT.

Keyboard

A very important part of your computer is the keyboard. Its design can affect your production rate, your accuracy, and your attitude about your work. The keyboard should be detached to allow you flexibility in moving it to where it is most comfortable. To reduce neck and wrist fatigue, the keyboard should be slanted at a 10 to 15° angle. Most keyboards are equipped with small extensions on the bottom that can be released to provide the proper slant.

The alphabetic and numeric keys should be concave in shape to allow the round part of the fingers to rest in position. The matte, dull finish not only reduces glare but provides a nonslick surface so that fingers do not slide off the keys. The well-designed word processing keyboard provides a large return/enter key, large shift keys, and lighted caps lock and number lock keys. In addition, the delete key is placed far away from often-used keys to prevent accidental erasures. Other keys such as Ctrl, Alt, and Esc are positioned for easy access. The keyboard should be large enough to accommodate all the special keys without being crowded.

Keyboard template Keyboard guide identifying software functions.

Function keys should be labeled for easy reference. Always use the word processing program **keyboard templates** (as shown in Figure 5.4) or stick-on function key labels that identify the functions or operations performed by each key.

The numeric keypad is useful for entering numeric data. Most keypads are identical to those of the calculator (numbers 1, 2, and 3 are on the bottom row). Nevertheless, a change in the arrangement is being promoted to conform to the touch-tone telephone keypad (numbers 1, 2, and 3 are on the top row), since the touch-tone telephone is the adopted international telecommunication standard. You can usually specify which keypad arrangement you prefer when you select a keyboard.

The feel of the keyboard is also important to the user. Keys that are difficult to depress or are too sensitive to the touch may reduce keying speed and increase tension in the wrists. A few keyboards have been designed with "silent" touch-sensitive keys in order to reduce noise and save operator energy. Some systems give the operator the option of turning the click on or off. Most operators prefer to hear the keys click and feel them spring back after they are depressed.

Figure 5.4
Template Identifying Function Keys for Software

As you can see, the keyboard offers many ergonomic features that can reduce effort and increase keying performance. When you select a keyboard, check to determine if these important features are included.

ERGONOMIC OFFICE ENVIRONMENT

Although office workers may have ergonomically designed furniture and equipment, the overall environment must still be comfortable. Environmental factors that affect worker comfort and performance are the climate, acoustics, and lighting.

Climate

Employees who work in a room that is too warm, cold, dry or humid, or stale and stuffy do not perform well and often suffer from chronic illnesses. In addition, computer equipment functions best in a clean, temperature-controlled climate. Organizations, therefore, devote serious attention to climate control that includes temperature, humidity, and air quality.

Room temperature is usually maintained at a standard level of about 68°. If only authorized persons can make any adjustments and you find the temperature setting too cool, slip on a light jacket or sweater.

Various techniques such as installing dehumidifiers are used to adjust room humidity. Humidity, or the amount of moisture in the air, should be maintained in the range of 40 to 60 percent. High humidity in offices may cause paper jams in printers and malfunctioning disk drives. As you have already learned, antistatic mats should be installed if humidity is too low to prevent damage to computers and loss of data.

To help prevent stale and stuffy air and to protect expensive computer equipment, most organizations today restrict smoking to a designated area. Many companies prohibit smoking anywhere in the building. For windowless offices, firms often provide circulation of fresh air. Even those offices with windows often do not allow them to be opened because of air pollution.

Noise

Noise in the office hinders employee concentration and productivity. The ergonomically designed office reduces the noise level in several ways. Carpeting eliminates the sound of footsteps. Acoustic paneling around work areas or fabrics on walls absorb sound. Noisy equipment, especially printers, is housed in sound-reduction cabinets. Green plants not only help reduce noise but provide an inviting work environment. Many offices introduce music or other pleasing sounds via sound systems into the office to create a pleasant atmosphere and mask out some noise.

Figure 5.5
Pleasing Work Environment

Source: *Photo Courtesy of Haworth, Inc.*

A major contributor to noise in the office is the human voice. Even with all the ergonomic features to reduce noise listed above, an office can be too noisy if employees talk loudly and often. When conversation is necessary in your work area, strive to speak softly. Also, you will be wise to save your social conversation for breaks and lunch time. Your coworkers will appreciate your thoughtfulness.

Noise may also be controlled by careful space planning. For example, workers who must interact frequently should be positioned close to each other. Reference materials, files, printers, copiers, fax machines, and other resources should be placed close to the people who use them regularly. Many other factors must be carefully studied as offices are designed to reduce noise and contribute to a productive and comfortable work environment.

Lighting

Many of today's offices are still designed for working with white-paper tasks on a flat surface. Working from a computer screen, however, is different from working from paper. A computer screen is upright rather than flat, colored rather than white, emits light, and the surface is reflective rather than absorbent. As a consequence, the older lighting is inappropriate for computer work and causes screen glare, one of the most common complaints of VDT operators.

Glare Reduction

Glare Bright reflected light.

Glare, which is an uncomfortably bright light reflected from a surface, is a major problem for VDT workers. Because glare makes it difficult to read the characters on the screen, it can cause eyestrain and headaches and contribute to errors. If after adjusting the contrast of the VDT glare is still a problem, check for screen reflections. Glare produced by light from a window can be eliminated by closing blinds or drapes. Overhead lighting that often produces glare sometimes can be reduced by tilting or turning the monitor. A glare reduction screen or filter may be placed over the monitor. While this device will eliminate most of the glare, it may also reduce the readability of the text characters on the screen.

Figure 5.6
Glare Screen

Some users have noticed that white clothing causes a reflection from the monitor; therefore, they suggest wearing dark clothing when using a computer. The work surface of the workstation should be finished with a nonglare (not shiny) material. Be alert to adjustments you can make to your work area to reduce or eliminate the problem.

Light Sources

Although VDT workers can make minor adjustments to their work areas to reduce glare, other adjustments might be needed. Lowering the lighting level may help, but office workers also proofread and perform noncomputer tasks that require more light. Therefore, lighting must be designed for both tasks.

Ambient lighting Indirect light.

Task lighting Adjustable light source.

Newer offices are designed with **ambient lighting**, which is indirect light reflected from the ceiling. Ambient lighting reduces glare significantly. For those tasks such as reading and writing that require more light than working at the VDT, individual **task lighting** should be available. Task lighting is a small light built into the workstation furniture, such as under overhead cabinets. It can be directed to the work area where it is needed and away from the computer screen.

As you work with computers, be alert to the changes you can make to reduce glare and adjust the lighting to the task you are completing. By making the adjustments listed in Figure 5.7, your productivity should improve and the likelihood of physical problems related to computer use should be reduced.

Figure 5.7
Workstation Checklist

- Clean monitor for easier viewing.
- Adjust brightness and contrast.
- Determine correct distance of monitor—16 to 24 inches—depending on your vision and sharpness of characters.
- Tilt and turn monitor for best viewing angle.
- Slant keyboard 10 to 15° to provide proper angle for wrists.
- Affix software labels to function keys to facilitate their use.
- Adjust height of keyboard to prevent tension in wrists.
- Position hard copy between keyboard and monitor to reduce eye movement.
- Place hard copy and monitor the same distance from eyes to reduce amount of eye focusing.
- Adjust chair to proper height.
- Reduce glare on monitor by making simple adjustments.
- Adjust lighting for the task being performed.

CONCERNS AND GUIDELINES FOR VDT USERS

Several state legislatures, as well as the U.S. National Institute of Occupational Safety and Health (NIOSH), are studying or have introduced work guidelines for VDT users. Union contracts for office workers usually establish similar rules. At least fourteen other countries have similar rules.[1] The following guidelines give you an idea of the kinds of regulations and suggestions some organizations are following:

[1] "An Update: Computers and Your Health," The Secretary, Vol. 49, No. 8 (October 1989), p. 14.

- Although worldwide governmental health agencies have concluded that using VDTs has no adverse health effects,[2] many organizations suggest that pregnant women should have the right, if they desire, to be reassigned to other positions without loss of pay, seniority, and benefits.
- Maximum time limits are sometimes set for VDT operators. Working at a VDT for no more than five or six hours a day is usually recommended.
- Several rest breaks during the day are recommended. While some union contracts stipulate that a break should be taken each hour, some researchers recommend that the VDT operator be permitted to take a break whenever needed, depending on the task being performed.
- Individual workstations should be operator adjustable.

Although studies related to VDT safety issues have been completed and others are in progress, experts disagree on whether using a VDT for over 20 hours a week harms VDT workers in any way. Indeed, many users do experience eyestrain, headaches, and backaches. Continued improvements, however, in equipment, furniture, and accessory design should reduce these problems. If you make the recommended adjustments to your VDT and work area, follow the guidelines for rest breaks, limit your VDT work to five or six hours a day, and get periodic eye exams, you should be able to avoid many of these problems.

HANDLING COMPUTER WORKER STRESS

Stress Feeling of tension and anxiety.

Any work can cause **stress**, an emotional feeling that causes tension and anxiety. Unrelieved stress can result in physical and emotional problems. Let's examine some of the major causes of stress for workers in the automated office and learn how to handle or eliminate them.

Documentation Operating or training instructions.

Stress is sometimes caused by the introduction of automated equipment; some workers fear technology and therefore have difficulty adjusting to new equipment and software. They feel pressure to learn its operation quickly, sometimes with little or no training. The **documentation**, training manuals that accompany hardware and software, is often too technical and difficult to understand.

Some workers complain that their jobs are monotonous because they perform the same tasks over and over. Many believe that technology is controlling their work. Others state that working with equipment all day isolates them from other employees, thereby eliminating needed social interaction. In addition, physical ailments, such as headaches, backaches, and eyestrain, caused by poorly designed furniture and equipment and inappropriate lighting and climate control, also contribute to stress. You may be able to reduce stress in your work by following these suggestions:

1. If you believe you need additional training to perform your work, ask your supervisor about providing it. You may offer to take some personal time, such as evenings if necessary, to attend training sessions.
2. If software and hardware documentation is difficult to follow, check to see if simple, easy-to-read manuals have been written and are available for use. Usually the steps for completing a task are simple once you know what they are.

[2] R. F. Bettendorf, "Work-Station Comfort in the Computer Age," Office Systems '90, Vol. 7, No. 6 (June 1990), p. 50.

3. If your furniture and equipment are adjustable, determine what changes you should make to adapt to your body. You may need to experiment to determine the best settings.
4. Relax by taking a short walk during breaks and lunch time and performing simple stretch exercises at your desk, as shown in Figure 5.8.

Figure 5.8
Stretching Exercises Can Be Performed at Your Desk

Neck Stretch. Turn head slowly to the right side and hold for a few seconds. Turn head to the left side and hold. Drop chin to the chest slowly and then tilt head back. Repeat cycle five times.

Upper Back Stretch. With arm raised and elbow bent, grasp hand behind wrist and pull toward the opposite shoulder. Hold for a few seconds and relax. Repeat with other arm.

Upper Arm Stretch. Grasp hands behind head and pull arms back as far as possible. Relax and repeat five times.

Lower Back Stretch. Bend from waist and extend arms and head toward the floor. Hold for a few seconds and sit up straight. Repeat.

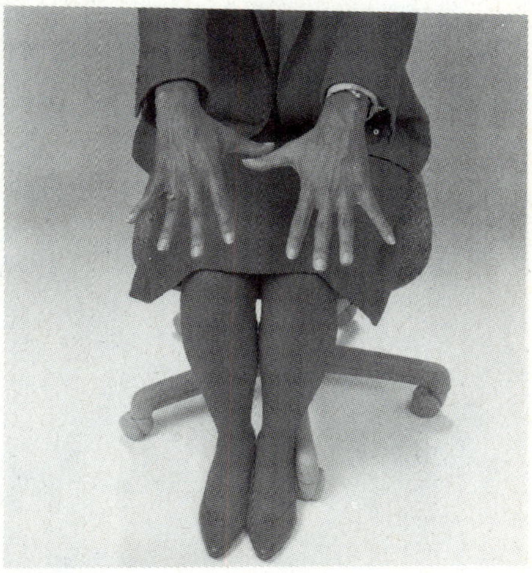

Hand Stretch. Spread fingers wide and hold for a few seconds. Make a tight fist and repeat finger and hand spread.

Wrist Stretch. Extend arms and raise and lower wrists several times. Then with fingers extended and knuckles facing up, turn wrists so that palms of hands are facing up. Repeat several times.

EXERCISES

KEY TERMS

Workstation
Ergonomics
Chromatic afterimage
Ambient lighting
Task lighting
Stress
Documentation

COMPLETION

1. _______________ is the science that studies workers' performance and well-being in relation to their job, equipment, and environment.
2. An ergonomically designed chair can help prevent ________ and ___________ pain.
3. The copyholder should be positioned the same distance from the eyes as the__________________.
4. A _______________________ may be placed under the chair to prevent static electricity that can harm a computer.
5. The standard viewing distance between the VDT monitor and the user is _____________________ inches.
6. Monitors that display text and graphics in sharp detail are called_________________________.
7. _______________________ monitors display the characters in one color on a contrasting background.
8. An operator who sees a colored halo on objects around the VDT work area after working at the screen for a period of time is experiencing ________________________________.
9. Direct light or light reflected from a surface is called ___________________.
10. ______________ hours a day is the maximum time limit set for VDT operators by some union contracts or proposed legislation.

DISCUSSION QUESTIONS

1. Why are automated offices installing ergonomically designed furniture and equipment and striving to control the office environment?
2. List the features of an ergonomically designed monitor and keyboard.
3. Discuss briefly how offices control climate, noise, glare, and lighting.
4. Identify four major work guidelines for VDT users established by many state legislatures, a federal government agency, and many office worker union contracts.
5. Study your classroom in terms of ergonomics. What features are not ergonomically designed for the work completed in the room?
6. Analyze your computer lab in terms of ergonomics. What features are not ergonomically designed for computer work?

GLOSSARY

Access rights. Computer protection settings in a multi-user environment such as a local area network for controlling which users may read or modify a file.

Ambient lighting. Indirect illumination that surrounds a work area.

Antistatic mats. Special polymer mats placed under chairs and computer desks for eliminating static electricity which can destroy data and damage equipment.

Application software. Software designed to do a certain kind of task such as word processing, desktop publishing, spreadsheets, database, graphics, or communication.

ASCII (American Standard Code for Information Interchange). Format of basic text which can be read by most software and DOS.

Backups. Duplicate copies of media (disks and tapes) containing files which contain valuable information.

CD. DOS command for Change Directory. This command is used when the user wishes to work in another directory.

CD-ROM. (Compact Disk-Read Only Memory) Optical disk for storing large quantities of data which can be read only.

Chromatic afterimage. A colored halo around an object which is sometimes seen by VDT workers after they have worked at their computers several hours. This phenomenon is not harmful to the eyes.

Compatible computers. Computers that utilize the same operating system.

Compound document. A document that combines information from two or more applications software.

Computer virus. A program written by an unethical programmer for the purpose of infecting software and operating systems; the virus spreads easily from disk to disk and can destroy or contaminate data and computer programs.

Copyholder. Adjustable workstation accessory for holding hard copy for reading while working at a computer.

CPU. Central processsing unit; a microprocessor chip that is the central control for a computer.

Cursor. Screen symbol that indicates where the next character will be displayed.

Cursor movement keys. Special keys that move the cursor to various points in a document.

Database applications. Software that stores and retrieves related data.

Dedicated word processor. Equipment programmed to do only word processing.

Default drive. The current drive which the computer will read or save to unless another drive is specified.

DEL. DOS command for Delete to erase a file.

Desktop publishing. Microcomputer-based publishing system that combines text and graphics on the page. Text may be set in different typestyles and sizes and the graphics moved and sized.

DIR. DOS command for Directory; the DIR command lists all files on a disk or in a directory.

Directory. A listing of all files on a disk or in a specific directory. A named section of a disk for storing related files.

DISKCOPY. DOS command for making a copy of all files including directories and subdirectories on a disk.

Document conversion. A process to make a file compatible (useable) with different software or DOS.

Document production cycle. A five-step process of originating, processing, printing and reproducing, distributing, and storing a document.

Document summary. An attachment to a word processing file listing information such as the date of creation, revision date, originator, typist, subject, and abstract of the document to assist in its retrieval.

Documentation. Software and equipment manuals with operating instructions.

DOS (Disk Operating System). DOS is an operating system used on IBM and IBM-compatible computers which must be loaded before the computer can operate.

DOS prompt. The drive letter (A, B, C) followed by a colon indicating the current drive and that DOS is waiting for a command.

Editing. Revising a document usually by inserting, deleting, moving, copying, or replacing text and modifying the format.

Electronic mail (E-Mail). A generic term for messages sent from one machine to another by electronic equipment.

Encryption. The process of coding a file with scrambled letters, numbers, and symbols so that it cannot be read until it is decoded.

Ergonomics. The science that studies workers' performance and well-being in relation to their jobs, equipment, and environment.

ET (electronic typewriter). Typewriter with many automated features such as centering, underlining, and indention. ETs may include a dsiplay for viewing text, error correction, and memory.

Facsimile (fax). A machine which transmits over telephone lines an exact copy to another fax machine or to a computer linked to a fax.

File server. A centralized computer with a large capacity, high-speed hard disk which is used for storing files and software and managing the network; a number of microcomputers are connected to the file server by cables or telephone lines.

Filename. A file's specific name containing one to eight characters.

Filename extension. One to three characters preceded by a period which follows the filename.

Filespec. The complete file name consisting of the drive specifier, path, filename, and extension.

Fonts. Sets of characters with the same type style, type size, and weight. An example is Palatino 12-point bold italic.

Format. The design of a document including side margins, top and bottom margins, tabs, line spacing, fonts, right margin justification, and other features.

Formatting. A step in the document processing stage in which the document design (margins, line spacing, et cetera) is set.

Function keys. Special keys on a computer that are programmed by the application software.

Glare. Unpleasant bright light reflected from a shiny surface.

Grammar checker. Computer software for checking a document for possible grammar errors such as subject and verb agreement, passive voice of verbs, pronoun antecedents, gender-biased terminology, and other troublesome writing areas.

Graphical user interface (GUI). Operating system that uses icons instead of words for directing the user.

Graphics. Charts, graphs, logos, and designs that are created by a computer.

Groupware. Software that runs on a newtwork and supports group activities such as electronic mail, scheduling, and group management.

Hard copy. Paper containing printed or handwritten material.

Hardware. Parts of a computer that include the monitor, keyboard, and processing unit.

High resolution. A term describing a monitor that displays material in sharp detail. Some high-resolution monitors also display different fonts.

Humidity. The amount of moisture in the air.

Icons. Symbolic pictures.

Import. To bring in. A file incorporated into another file is imported.

Information processing. Technologies involved with creating, processing, and distributing information.

Keyboard template. A software keyboard guide positioned around the keys which identifies the functions or operations performed by each function key; also lists most often used commands.

Label. DOS command for adding a volume name to a disk.

Local area network (LAN). An arrangement of microcomputers within a small radius (typically a building) linked together by cables or telephone lines and special software. A LAN allows users to share information and equipment such as printers and to communicate through electronic mail.

Machine dictation. The process of recording correspondence or other information by speaking into a microphone or telephone linked to a dictation machine which records the voice for transcription into printed words.

Magnetic tape. Storage medium used for backing up files on a hard disk or LAN file server.

MD. DOS command for Make Directory. This command is used when the user wishes to create a directory or subdirectory.

Memory. That part of the processing unit that stores data and instructions.

Microforms. Rolls or sheets of film containing exact duplicates of documents in miniature form; special equipment is required for reading them.

Monochrome. One color; a monitor is monochrome if the characters are one color on a contrasting background.

Mouse. A small handheld input device.

Multitasking. Operating systems that allow more than one operation to be carried on simultaneously.

Network. Group of computers linked together so that users can communicate or share devices such as printers.

Optical disk. A large capacity nonmagnetic disk which uses laser beams to read and write data on it.

Originator. The person who creates a document. Other terms include author or principal.

Password. A confidential code assigned to an authorized user; the code must be entered before the user can access a network or files protected with a password.

Path. The second part of the filespec. The path gives the location of a file in the directory and any subdirectory. The directory and subdirectory names are separated by backslashes (\).

Proofreading. Checking a document for accuracy of keyed text and format.

Queue. The order of jobs waiting for processing such as printing.

RD. DOS command for Remove Directory. The directory must be empty before it can be removed (deleted).

REN. DOS command to Rename a file. Only the filename and extension can be changed with the REN command.

Resolution. Clarity of the printed page or screen display.

Root directory. Primary disk directory from which other directories are created.

Scanner. A device commonly known as an OCR (optical character recognition) which reads a printed page of text or graphics and stores the information on a disk.

Scrolling. Moving the cursor on the screen line by line.

Software. Programmed instructions for a computer.

Spelling checker. Software that checks each word in a document by comparing it to those in a glossary or dictionary; words not found in the dictionary are marked for checking. Some spelling checkers offer a list of suggested spellings.

Spreadsheet applications. Electronic version of a worksheet that performs mathematical calculations. Spreadsheets are used to create and analyze financial records and determine sales forecasts, and other statistitcal activiites.

Stress. An emotional feeling that causes tension and anxiety.

Subdirectories. Smaller named subdivisions of a directory for storing files.

Task lighting. Individual adjustable light source at a workstation.

Telex. A written message sent over dedicated or telephone lines using a teleprinter; a form of electronic mail.

Thesaurus. A feature of some word processing software which lists synonyms and antonyms of selected words.

Toggle key. An on/off key.

Tree structure. A file structure of directories and their subdirectories; a special DOS command is keyed to display a tree structure.

Wide area networks (WAN). An arrangement of microcomputers located over long distances linked together by telephone lines, communication satellites, and special software. A WAN allows users to share information immediately and to communicate through electronic mail.

Wildcard *.*. The DOS symbol representing all files and extensions on a disk or in a directory. This wildcard is used for deleting and copying many files with one command.

Word processing. Entering, editing, storing, and printing text electronically. Word processing may be accomplished on a computer, word processor, or electronic typewriter.

Workstation. A worker's immediate work area including furniture, equipment, and accessories. Also, some computers as well as some ergonomically designed computer tables are called workstations.

WORM. (Write Once/Read Many) Optical disk which permits the user to save data on it, but the disk cannot be erased or rewritten. WORM disks are used primarily for library materials and other databases that must be updated.

PART 2

WORD PROCESSING APPLICATIONS

The ability to efficiently create, revise, and print business documents in a variety of formats using word processing is a necessary skill for everyone who produces written documents. Developing basic word processing, editing, and formatting skills, as well as setting specialized tabs, formatting tables, creating headers and footers and page numbers for multi-page documents, merging variables in form documents, and applying specialized features such as macros and a thesaurus, requires practice.

To provide the needed practice, seven sections in Part 2 introduce 36 word processing functions and operations along with short exercises and realistic business documents. By writing the steps to complete each function on your system and applying the functions in the many exercises and documents, you will develop suitable word processing skills for employment and personal use.

SECTION I

ENTERING AND SAVING TEXT

Objectives

After completing your study of Section 1 you should be able to:

- Load the operating system.
- Format a disk.
- Identify the version of the operating system on your computer.
- Identify the location of the special keys on the keyboard.
- Identify the version of your word processing software.
- Create a document using your word processing software.
- Save and print a document using your word processing software.
- Retrieve and edit a document with your word processing software.

You are about to begin an exciting adventure—learning to use your computer to process documents. With this knowledge, you will be able to prepare reports for your classes and develop a marketable skill.

Section 1 introduces you to features of your computer and software. In the space provided, you will write in specific information for your system. You will also load the operating system and software, enter, save, print, and retrieve text.

IDENTIFYING SYSTEM COMPONENTS

Diskettes, which are inserted into disk drives, may store varying amounts of information. The storage capacity of a diskette depends on whether information is stored on one or two sides and the density of the disk. A high capacity diskette stores about twice that of a double-sided, double-density disk. Hard disks store many times more information than a high capacity diskette.

Identify the size (3 1/2" or 5 1/4") and density of your disks (double or high). If you have a hard drive, indicate the storage capacity in megabytes.

	Size	Density/Capacity
Drive A:	____________	________ density
Drive B:	____________	________ density
Drive C:	Hard disk	________ MB
Drive D:	Hard disk	________ MB

The *keyboard* contains several keys not found on a typewriter. The following is a simple diagram of a computer keyboard. The sides are labeled as TOP, BOTTOM, LEFT, and RIGHT.

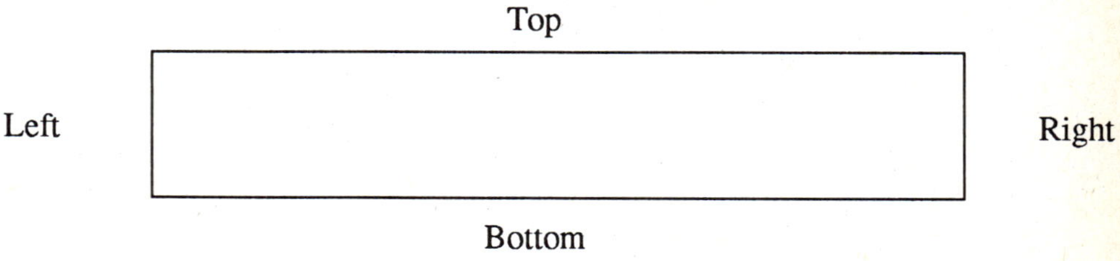

For each of the following keys, identify which side of the keyboard is closest. If a key is found on both sides of keyboard, identify both locations.

KEY	Location	KEY	Location
Alt	________	End	________
Ctrl	________	PgUp	________
Esc	________	PgDn	________
Enter	________	Up Arrow	________
Ins	________	Down Arrow	________
Del	________	Left Arrow	________
Tab	________	Right Arrow	________
Shift	________	Function Keys	________
Home	________	Num Lock	________
Caps Lock	________		

The *monitor* displays keyed information and prompts. Displays may be monochrome or color.

Identify the type of monitor of your computer. ______________________

If color, is it CGA, EGA, VGA? ______________________

How many lines does your monitor display? ______________________

LOADING THE SOFTWARE AND FORMATTING A DISK

As you recall, the operating system manages the operation of the computer, presents a way for you to enter commands in the computer, and controls the peripherals such as the printer. The operating system is required for the computer to run application programs. Turning on the computer and running the operating system program is called booting the system. The program is booted from either a hard disk or a floppy disk, depending upon the configuration of the equipment.

If a disk must be formatted, this step may be completed after the operating system has been loaded. Formatting a new disk prepares it to store files.

Formatting also erases documents on a disk that has been used previously.

Once the operating system has been loaded and a disk is formatted, the next step is to load the application software. Loading is the process of reading files from the disk into the computer's memory.

ACTIVITY 1 BOOTING THE SYSTEM

Follow the steps below to boot (load) the operating system.

1. If the power to your computer is not turned on, place an operating system disk in drive A. If you are on a network, put your network boot disk in drive A. If your computer has a hard disk, you may skip this step because the operating system will be on the hard disk.

2. Turn on the power to your computer. If the power is already on, reboot the computer with a warm boot. On an IBM PC or IBM compatible, a warm boot is accomplished by holding down the keys marked Ctrl and Alt with your left hand, and striking the key marked Del with your right hand.

   After the operating system is loaded, a DOS prompt will appear confirming that DOS is loaded and identifying the default (active) drive. On an IBM PC or compatible, the prompt will look similar to A> or C>. If you are on a network, you will be prompted to log in.

3. Record the prompt displayed on the monitor. ______________________

4. To learn which version of the operating system you are using, type the command **VER** and press ENTER.

   List the version of your operating system. ______________________

ACTIVITY 2 FORMATTING A DISK

To format a disk (5 1/4" or 3 1/2"), a disk containing the operating system files must be loaded. On an IBM PC or compatible this disk is called a **DOS** (Disk Operating System) disk. If your computer has a hard drive, DOS should already be loaded on the hard drive; DOS will start automatically when you turn on the computer.

The procedure for formatting a disk varies somewhat depending upon whether the DOS disk is in a disk drive or on a hard drive. Follow the procedures for the configuration of your equipment.

Two Disk Drives

1. Insert the disk containing the operating system in drive A. On most computers, this is the left (or top) drive. Turn on the computer.

2. Press Enter. Place a blank disk in drive B, which is normally the right (or bottom) drive.

3. At the A>, key **FORMAT B:** and press ENTER. A prompt will appear instructing you to place a disk in drive B.

4. After the formatting is completed, a prompt will ask if you want to format another disk. Key the **N** for no and press ENTER.

Hard Disk

1. If the computer is not on, press the power switch to on.

2. Place a blank disk in drive A, which is normally the left (or top) drive.

3. At the C>, key **FORMAT A:** and press ENTER.

4. After the formatting is complete, a prompt will ask if you want to format another disk. Key **N** for no and press ENTER.

ACTIVITY 3 LOADING THE WORD PROCESSING SOFTWARE

The procedures for loading application software will vary depending on whether you are working from a diskette drive or whether your software is already loaded on a hard drive or network. If you are loading software having more than one diskette and working from a diskette drive, you will need to insert the first disk (or Volume 1) and follow the prompts.

From the DOS prompt (C or A), key the name of your word processing program or the abbreviation required to load the software. Abbreviations for some of the common word processing programs are

DISPLAYWRITE	dw3 or dw4
MULTIMATE	mm
MICROSOFT WORD	word
WORDPERFECT	wp
WORDSTAR	ws

1. List the steps to load your software.

____

____

____

2. Identify the name and version of your word processing program from the opening screen. If the name and version are not on the opening screen, check your software manual.

Name ______________________________________

Version ____________________________________

• • • • • • • • • • • • • • • • • • • •

KEYING, SAVING, AND PRINTING DOCUMENTS

To key and save documents, you should become familiar with several basic features of your software. The monitor displays the **status line** or information line. The status line may include the margin settings, tab settings, document name, keying mode (insert or replace), line number, and page number. The status line is displayed at the top or bottom of the screen. Shown below is a typical status line of a word processor.

```
B:\REV-CMTS.WP5              Doc 1 Pg 1 Ln 23 Pos 12
```

What information is displayed on the status line of your software?

1. ________________ 4. ________________

2. ________________ 5. ________________

3. ________________ 6. ________________

Using Cursor Movement Keys

Cursor movement keys enable the user to move the cursor one position in the direction of the arrow: up, down, left, and right. Holding down one of these keys will cause the cursor to move rapidly. The cursor can also be moved very quickly to various points within a document by striking certain keys. List the keys you should strike to move the cursor quickly in the following manners:

1. Top of screen ____________ 5. Beginning of the line ____________

2. Bottom of screen ________ 6. End of the line ________________

3. Beginning of document ____ 7. Next page ____________________

4. End of the document _____ 8. Preceding page ________________

Using Defaults

Because changing formats such as margins or tabs is time-consuming, users frequently use the defaults to format documents. Defaults are automatically implemented unless the user changes them. Defaults include margins, line spacing, tabs, fonts, and paper size or page length. Some programs require that you access one or more format menus to locate the defaults. You will learn these procedures in Section 3. In Sections 1 and 2 you will format documents using the default settings of your software.

List the following defaults for your software.

Format	Default	Format	Default
1. Left margin	________	7. Page size	__________
2. Right margin	________	8. Tabs	__________
3. Bottom margin	________	9. Pitch	__________
4. Top margin	________	10. Type style	__________
5. Line spacing	________		
6. Right margin justification	________		

Word wrap, common to all packages, enables words that are too long to fit on the line to move automatically to the next line. When entering text, strike the ENTER key only at the end of the paragraph or short lines that do not extend to the right margin. The word wrap default is on for most programs.

Creating, Saving, and Retrieving Documents

To create a document and save it to disk, you must identify the document with a name. Depending upon your software, you will name the document either before keying it or while saving it. If necessary, review the procedures in Chapter 4, pages 57-59, for naming a document.

To store the document, you must save it onto the disk. When text is *saved*, it is copied from the computer's memory and written onto a disk. The file is saved under its file name. Documents should be saved 1) periodically as you are working on them so they are not lost in case of power failure, and 2) when you complete them. Documents saved onto disks are referred to as **files**.

Frequently, after completing one document you will want to create a new document. To create a second document, you must exit the first document. Later, should you want to work with the first document again, you ask the computer to read the text from the disk into the computer's memory. This process is called retrieving or loading a file.

1. Using your software, a file name may contain a maximum of ____________ characters, excluding the extension.

2. Does your software automatically add a three-character extension to the file name? __________ If it does, what is the extension? ____________

3. List the steps to enter the document (work) screen.

____

____

____

4. List the steps to save a document.

____

____

____

5. List the steps to exit a document and clear the screen.

____

____

____

6. List the steps to retrieve a document.

____

____

____

Printing a Document

To print a document requires either accessing a print menu or giving a command to print. You must check that the printer is turned on and loaded with paper.

1. Identify these facts about your printer

   a. Brand name and model number ____________________

   b. Type of printer (laser, dot matrix, or daisywheel) ____________

   c. Locate the power switch on your printer.

2. List the steps to print with your software.

____

____

____

Exiting the Software

A special command must be given to exit the word processing program. After exiting, you will be returned to a prompt such as A or C. If you are on a network, you will have steps to follow to log out.

Before turning your computer off, check with your instructor. Many experts believe it is better to leave the computer on and simply dim the screen. The screen is dimmed by either pressing the on/off button or turning the brightness control knob.

1. List the steps to exit your software.

____

____

2. How do you dim your screen?

____

S1-EX1

1. Prepare to create a document.
   a. Load the operating system.
   b. At the DOS prompt, load your word processing software.
   c. Insert the disk you formatted into either drive A or B, depending upon the configuration of your equipment.

   Note: You will not be reminded to follow these steps in later exercises.
2. Create a new document called Sl-EX1. In the exercises in this text, *S* represents *Section* and *EX* represents *Exercise*.
3. Key Sl-EX1 following these steps, using the default settings of your software:
   a. Press the Caps Lock key and key the title. You may see the status line change, indicating that Caps Lock is on. On some keyboards, the Caps Lock key is lighted when it is turned on. Press Caps Lock to turn it off after keying the title.
   b. Press ENTER four times after the title.
   c. Press the Tab key to indent paragraphs.
   d. Insert the appropriate information for your software for the information in parentheses.
   e. Word wrap should be on as you key each paragraph. Press ENTER twice at the end of the first paragraph to create a double space between the paragraphs.
   f. Correct errors as you key using the backspace key.

```
USING MY (NAME OF SOFTWARE) WORD PROCESSING SOFTWARE
     My computer can be used to process documents.
(Name of software) is a software program that I
can use to create different kinds of documents.
     To load the software, I must first boot the
computer and then enter the command (command).
```

4. Save your document with the name S1-EX1.
5. Print your document.
6. Clear the screen.

S1-EX2

1. Retrieve the document named S1-EX1.
2. With the document on the monitor, press ENTER two times to insert two blank lines before the title.
3. Using the up arrow key, move the cursor to the first line at the top of the document. Key your name on this line.
4. Save S1-EX1 again with the same file name. If prompted to replace the document, key **Y** for yes.

S1-EX3

1. Retrieve document S1-EX1.
2. Move the cursor to the end of the document by using the down arrow key or the PgDn key.
3. Add the following text:

```
Changing a document is not hard. You must retrieve the
document, make the changes, and save the document.  It
may be saved under the same file name.
```

4. Save your document and print it.
5. Clear the screen.
6. Exit the word processing program.
7. Either power down the computer or dim the screen.

SECTION 2

EDITING FILES

Functions

- Delete
- Insert
- Spelling Checker
- Block
- Move and Copy Block
- Hyphenation
- Required Space
- Search and Replace

DELETE

Delete erases characters, spaces, and instructional codes. Text can be deleted by use of either the backspace key or the delete (DEL) key.

In Section 1 you deleted using the backspace key by positioning the cursor one space to the right of the first character to be erased. Striking the backspace key erases the character to the left of the cursor.

To delete using the delete key, position the cursor on the first character to be deleted. Striking the delete key erases the character where the cursor is located.

Generally text may also be deleted by word, by line, to the end of the line or sentence, or to the end of the page. List the steps for deleting the various portions of text.

FUNCTION	STEPS REQUIRED
Character	____________________
Word	____________________
Line or to the End of Line	____________________
End of Page	____________________

S2-EX1

1. Key the following sentences. *Template users:* Retrieve the file S2-EX1 and proceed to Step 2.

```
Learning to use the backspace key to delete
unwanted text is easy.
Use the delete key to quickly delete text located
at the cursor.
Entire words can be deleted easily by using the
delete key.
```

2. Use the backspace key to revise Sentence 1. Position the cursor one space after the characters to be deleted. Do not delete the space between *Learn* and *to* or the period at the end of the sentence.

    Learn~~ing~~ to use the backspace key to delete unwanted text ~~is easy~~.

3. Use the delete key to revise Sentence 2.

    Use the delete key to ~~quickly~~ delete text ~~located at the cursor~~.

4. Revise Sentence 3 by deleting the words marked.

    Entire words can be deleted ~~easily by~~ using the delete key.

5. Delete Sentences 1 and 2 using the delete line/end-of-line feature.
6. Clear the screen.

S2-EX2

1. Key the following paragraph and save it as S2-EX2. *Template users*: Retrieve S2-EX2 and proceed to Step 2.

```
The department planned, funded, and implemented
this project within a two-month period.  The
purpose of the project was to automate a manual
system, which was no longer meeting our needs or
those of the customers.  The system was unreliable
as parts were often not available.
```

2. Delete the sentence marked using delete line or end of line.

```
The department planned, funded, and implemented
this project within a two-month period. The
purpose of the project was to automate a manual
system, which was no longer meeting our needs or
those of the customers. The system was unreliable
as parts were often not available.
```

3. Clear the screen.

S2-EX3

1. Key the following paragraph and save it as S2-EX3. *Template users:* Retrieve S2-EX3 and proceed to Step 2.

```
Several vendors were requested to demonstrate
their systems and discuss possible solutions to
the records retention problems.  Information was
obtained from various sources such as professional
associations, vendors, and other agencies as to
the types of systems available and what other
companies had installed.
```

2. Revise the paragraph by making the deletions marked. Correct any other errors you may have made. (NOTE: The paragraph is double-spaced below for ease in reading the revisions. Your copy will be single-spaced.)

```
Several vendors were requested to demonstrate

their systems and discuss possible solutions to

the records retention problems.  Information was

obtained from various sources such as professional

associations, vendors, and other agencies as to

the types of systems available and what other

companies had installed.
```

3. Save the revised document.

S2-DOC1

1. Open a new file. If the file must be named when opened, name it S2-DOC1. (Your software may automatically add an extension to the filename; example: S2-DOC1.TXT. If it does not add an extension, you do not have to key one.)

2. Review the simplified memo format illustrated in the Reference Section.

3. Use the default settings for margins and line spacing. If you must make these settings, ask your instructor for assistance or check the software manual. The following settings are recommended:

   Side and top margins = default margins
   Line spacing = single space
   Right margin justification off
   Word wrap on

4. Key S2-DOC1 following the directions marked on the document. With word wrap on, strike the RETURN key only at the end of short lines and twice at the end of each paragraph. If you make keying errors, correct them by backspacing and rekeying. You will learn to use the delete function later.

5. For the doc code at the end of the document, key your initials, a space, or a separator symbol such as the **:** or **/**, and the file name.
   Example: **xxx/s2-doc1**

   (The purpose of the document code is to help you retrieve the file; therefore, the document coding recommended for documents in this book will assist you in retrieving your documents for revision and will aid your instructor in recording the progress of your work.)

6. Save S2-DOC1 on your disk. You will retrieve it for revision.

TIPS TO OPERATOR

- When you see the — (in **19—**), key the current year.
- Ignore uneven right margins caused by word wrap. You will learn to hyphenate long words later.

Line 10 January 15, 19--

QS

Department Personnel

DS

ELECTRONIC MAIL SYSTEM FOR DEPARTMENT

DS

The departmental electronic mail system is now in operation. I will use the electronic mail system entirely for departmental communication. Unless we find a very serious deficiency in this mail system, this will be the last paper memo you will receive from me! In fact, you have an electronic message waiting for you now. By the way, the certification feature lets the sender know when the recipient has read the message.

When you log into the network at your computer each day, be sure to look for your mail messages. When you are logged in during the day, your system will beep and a note will appear on your computer screen indicating that you have a mail message. Please use our electronic mail system for all department correspondence.

QS

John Mayer

DS

doc code

1. Retrieve S2-DOC1 for revision.
2. Revise the document by deleting single characters, words, a line, or to the end of the line using the delete (DEL) key and special delete commands provided by your software. (You will learn to delete a block of text later.) Strive to use the most efficient methods of deleting text.
3. Proofread the document on screen. Check for correct spacing at each deletion point.
4. Save this revised document as S2-DOC1. (If your software requires you to respond to a question such as **Replace S2-DOC1? (Y/N)**, key **Y** for Yes. The changes you made will be saved in the original document.)
5. Print S2-DOC1r. Proofread. If you detect errors that can be corrected by deleting, make the needed corrections and reprint.

TIPS TO OPERATOR

- When you delete the last words in the subject line and the sentence at the end of the first paragraph, be careful that you do not delete the hard returns. If you delete the hard returns, you will lose the double space between paragraphs.
- Also, when you delete a word, check to determine if the space following the deleted word is also erased. Some software will automatically delete the space following a word if a word delete key/command is used. When you use the DEL key for deleting one character at a time, you must delete the space following the word.

January 15, 19--

Department Personnel

ELECTRONIC MAIL SYSTEM ~~FOR DEPARTMENT~~

The ~~departmental~~ electronic mail system is now in operation. I will use the electronic mail system entirely for departmental communication. Unless we find a ~~very~~ serious deficiency in this mail system, this will be the last paper memo you will receive from me! In fact, you have an ~~electronic~~ message waiting for you now. ~~By the way, the certification feature lets the sender know when the recipient has read the message.~~

When you log into the network ~~at your computer~~ each day, be sure to look for your mail messages. When you are logged in during the day, your system will beep and a note will appear on your computer screen indicating that you have a mail message. Please use our electronic mail system for all department correspondence.

John Mayer

doc code

S2-DOC2

1. Key S2-DOC2 as a simplified memo or retrieve it from the template and proceed to S2-DOC2r..
2. Proofread S2-DOC2 from the screen. Correct any errors by backspacing and rekeying. Do not attempt to make other corrections.
3. Save the document as S2-DOC2.

```
October 3, 19--


Arthur Sickels

CATALOG CHANGES DUE

Please read the enclosed catalog copy.  This draft incorporates
the changes you suggested last year.  Please note that it is a
draft, and it is intended to give us something concrete to talk
about.

The overstruck text is material in the current catalog which
would be deleted.  New material is in boldface.  I did not think
of doing the overstriking until I had deleted some of the
material.  When I put some of it back in, I may have forgotten
something; please read carefully.

Please respond by noon Thursday so that I can study your
suggestions.  Catalog copy must be submitted to Institutional
Research by Wednesday of next week.


Marsha Perera

doc code

Enclosure
```

INSERT

Insert allows text, space or instructional codes to be added to existing material or inserted to replace text that has been deleted. Text may be inserted in one of two ways: using the insert mode or using the typeover mode.

In the **insert mode**, text is inserted at the cursor, moving existing text to the right. To insert, place the cursor where new text is to begin and key. Any amount of text may be inserted.

In the **typeover/replace** mode, new characters replace or overwrite the previous ones. Use the typeover/replace mode when the text to be inserted has exactly the same number of characters as the text to be deleted.

Most software is automatically set in the insert mode. Changing to the typeover mode by striking the Insert key will require a special command with some software. When editing, remember to return to the insert mode or you will erase characters at the next revision point.

List the steps for inserting text.

FUNCTION	**STEPS REQUIRED**
Insert	______________________________
Typeover/Replace	______________________________

S2-EX4

1. Key the following sentences and save them as S2-EX4. *Template users:* Retrieve S2-EX4 and proceed to Step 2.

   ```
   You can insert a character or as much text as you need.
   Did the executives provide any directions?
   ```

2. Revise the first sentence in the insert mode. Revise the second sentence in the typeover/replace mode.

   You can insert a character[, a sentence,] or as much text as you need.

   Did the ~~executives~~ [management] provide any ~~directions~~ [guidelines]?

3. Clear the screen.

S2-EX5

1. Key the following paragraph and save it as S2-EX5. *Template users:* Retrieve S2-EX5 and proceed to Step 2.

   ```
   Today's workforce is different from yesterday's.
   Recent estimates show there is one computer for
   every twenty workers in this country.
   Predictions show that most industries will have a
   computer for every two employees.
   ```

2. Revise the paragraph using the insert mode.

   Today's workforce is [very] different from yesterday's. Recent estimates [now] show there is one computer for every twenty workers in this country. Predictions show that most industries will [soon] have a computer for every two [or three] employees.

3. Clear the screen.

S2-EX6

1. Retrieve S2-EX6 from the template, or key the following paragraph and save it as S2-EX6.

   ```
   Your interest in our organization is appreciated.
   The information you requested is provided for your
   convenience.  As a young and growing firm, we are
   excited about the programs and benefits we can
   offer our customers.  Ultimately, savings and
   productivity are our goals as reflected in these
   materials.
   ```

2. Revise the paragraph in the insert mode. Switch to the typover/replace to insert "enclosed" and "eventually."

   Your *recent* interest in our organization is appreciated.
   The information you requested is ~~provided~~ *enclosed* for your
   convenience. As a young and growing firm, we are
   extremely excited about the programs and *many* benefits we can
   offer our customers. ~~Ultimately~~ *Eventually*, savings and
   productivity are our *primary* goals as reflected in these
   materials.

3. Clear the screen.

S2-DOC2R

1. Retrieve S2-DOC2.
2. Read carefully the handwritten revisions for S2-DOC2r. Using the delete and insert functions of your software, make the requested changes in the order they appear on the document.

   Move the cursor to the end of the doc code and key an **r** to indicate that this is the revised version of S2-DOC2.
3. Proofread the document from the screen, checking spacing between words and lines. Correct any errors detected.
4. Save this revised document as S2-DOC2.
5. Print the document. Proofread the printed copy. If you detect errors, revise, save, and reprint. Clear the screen.

TIPS TO OPERATOR

- When proofreading, always read the document at least once to determine if the message makes sense. With this procedure, you often can detect omitted text or text that should have been deleted.
- Use the typeover or replace mode (strike the INS key) when revising the subject line for S2-DOC2r. (Remember to toggle the key off when you finish keying the subject line or you will erase desired text at the next revision point!)
- Always save a document before printing it. Sometimes a document can be lost from computer memory during the printing process. If lost from memory, the document can be retrieved from disk.

October 3, 19--

Arthur Sickels

~~CATALOG CHANGES DUE~~

Please read the enclosed catalog copy. This draft incorporates the changes you suggested last year. ~~Please note that it is a~~ draft, ~~and it is intended to~~ give us something concrete to ~~talk~~ about.

The overstruck text is material in the current catalog which ~~would~~ be ~~deleted~~. New material is in boldface. I did not think of ~~doing the~~ overstriking until I had deleted some of the material. When I ~~put some of it back in~~, I may have forgotten something; please read carefully.

Please respond by noon Thursday so that I can study your suggestions. Catalog copy must be submitted to Institutional Research by Wednesday ~~of next week.~~

Marsha Perera

doc code

Enclosure

S2-DOC3

1. Key S2-DOC3, a personal business letter, in block format. Refer to the Reference Section, which illustrates the personal business letter format.

2. Proofread from the screen. Correct any keying errors detected.

3. Save the document as S2-DOC3.

4. Print the document. Proofread the printed copy. If you detect errors, revise, save, and reprint.

```
P O box 1132
Silver Springs MD 20910 - 4162
January 12 19--   2 spaces



World Travel club
Attention Membership director
3110 Forbes Blvd
Lanham, MD 10706 - 3698     2 spaces
Ladies and Gentlemen:
Dear Membership Director:

Subject: Cancellation of World Travel Club Membership

Please do not renew my membership in your travel club.  I am
returning the World Travel club savings card and related
materials which your sent to me.  I do not wish to continue my
membership whioch expires in February.

          credit                        charge
Please do not charge anything to my credit card.

Sincerely yours


David T. Hotvedt
```

S2-DOC3R

1. Retrieve S2-DOC3.
2. Revise the document by deleting and inserting text. Key an **r** (for revised) at the end of the doc code.
3. Proofread carefully from the screen.
4. Save the document as S2-DOC3.
5. Print the document. Proofread the printed copy. If you detect errors, revise, save, and reprint.

```
P. O. Box 1132
Silver Spring, MD  20910-4162
January 12, 19--


World Travel Club
Attention Membership Director
3110 Forbes Blvd. ^ Suite 110
Lanham, MD  10706-3698

Ladies and Gentlemen:
```

~~Cancellation of~~ World Travel Club Membership No. T516X

Please ^cancel ~~do not renew~~ my membership in ~~your~~ World travel club. I am returning the World Travel Club Savings Card and related materials, which you sent to me. I do not wish to continue my membership which expires ~~in~~ (stet) February, 19--.

Please credit my ^Express charge card (for $50).

Sincerely yours,

David T. Hotvedt

doc code

Enclosure

SPELLING CHECKER

Spelling checker or **spelling verification** provides a proofreading capability that identifies misspelled words. Each word in a document is compared with a list of correctly spelled words from the software dictionary. Some software packages will also suggest correct spellings for words that have been identified as incorrect.

Generally you can personalize the dictionary by adding words to the dictionary such as proper nouns or technical words.

List below the steps for using the spelling checker.

STEPS REQUIRED

S2-EX7

1. Retrieve S2-EX7 from the template, or key the following paragraph exactly as shown (including errors) and save it as S2-EX7.

   This exercise is to demonstrate teh ability of software to check the accuracy of speling within a document. Most proper nouns, such as John Smith, will be marked for verficaton unless they have been aded to the dictionary.

2. Spell check the document and correct the errors (listed). Then save the revised document. Misspelled words: teh (the), speling (spelling), verficaton (verification), aded (added).

S2-EX8

1. Retrieve S2-EX8 from the template, or key the following paragraphs exactly as shown (including errors) and save them as S2-EX8.

   Training will be conducted in the user support centre located on the sixth floor at 125 East Jefferson Street. The instructor's microcomputer is connected to an overhead projecter so all material that needs to be demenstrated for the participents can be displayed on the screen. The projector can also be used to view transparencies.

   Before participants arrive for classes, all computor terminals and laser printers need to be checked to ensure that they are operating properly. If any assistence is required, please call the training coordinator at extension 1268.

2. Spell check the paragraphs to correct the misspelled words. Then save the revised document. Misspelled words: centre (center), projecter (projector), participents (participants), computor terminels (computer terminals), assistence (assistance).

S2-DOC4

1. Review the block letter format and open punctuation in the Reference Section.

2. Key S2-DOC4 in block format with open punctuation. As you key, correct any misspelled words you may detect and add any missing letter parts.

3. Save the document as S2-DOC4. Spell check the document, correcting any misspelled words.

4. Proofread the document from the screen, comparing it to the rough draft. Be sure you made all of the corrections.

5. Print the document. Proofread the printed copy. If you detect errors, revise, save, and reprint.

TIPS TO OPERATOR

- Did you find and key the one missing letter part?
- You should find and correct 12 misspelled words in S2-DOC4.
- The letter address is formatted correctly for you.
- Always save a document before spell checking in case your document is lost from memory during the process.

```
Mr. Anthony Deblieux
P. O. Box 5588
Place d'Armes
MONTREAL, QUEBEC H2Y 3L2
CANADA

Dear Mr. Deblieux;

You are invited to be among the first to subscribe to a new
computer magazine dedicated to users.  We have reserved an issue
for you FREE!  You know how hard it can be to keep up with
breakthroughs in personel systems.  You must realise that only a
dedicated publicaiton can accomplish the task.  BONUS COMPUTING
is the only publication that gives an objective apprasal of the
computer market.

BONUS COMPUTIG does a lot more than put hardware through its
paces; it also examines the ways to imrpove productivty.
```

Operator, please check spelling carefully. pth

(DOCUMENT CONTINUED ON NEXT PAGE)

Whether you're interested in computer systems, applications, operating systems or networking, you will find it in BONUS COMPUTING. You will find it here first. If you are a demanding profesional, you are going to like what you see.

To recieve you issue of BONUS COMPUTING, remove the label that says "I ACCEPT" from the envelope and afix it to the subcription form.

It contains useful and accurate information on computers that you have seen anywhere; you may keep it with our complimints. You won't be obligated in any way.

Don't delay. Be amoung the first to find out why Bonus Computing is the publications you'll turn to first every month.

Sincerly

Pearl T. Hershberger

Enclosure

S2-DOC5

1. Key S2-DOC5 as a simplified memo. Correct any misspelled words you may detect as you key.
2. Proofread from the screen by comparing the copy on the screen with the original. Correct any errors.
3. Save S2-DOC5 before using your spelling checker.
4. Using your spelling checker, verify spelling in this document. Correct any misspelled words.
5. Save the document again. Print two copies. Proofread the printed copy. If you detect errors, revise, save, and reprint.

TIPS TO OPERATOR

- Did you find and correct 10 originator spelling errors?
- One misspelled word will not be detected by your spelling checker software since it is written as two correctly spelled words.
- Always save a document before spell checking. Although a rare occurrence, the computer could lock during the procedure and the document would be lost from memory. If the system fails, reboot and retrieve the document, which is stored on disk.

All Employees

Operator: verify spelling, please. Jim

ACCOUNT PROGRAMS

To improve the speed of claims processing while complying with applicable federal laws and without increasing expense charges, the company is forced to require that all withdrawl or transfer requests be submited on forms approved by the company.

You must use one of the enclosed Request for Withdrawal forms whenever you wish to withdraw amounts from your account. Unless you submit this form properly completed, your withdrawal request can not be honored, and it will be returned to you.

Individual Account Programs are designed to provide flexable, effective ways you can save for your retirement while taking advantage of significant tax savings.

We regret any inconvience this new procedure may cause you, but we believe its implimentation will result in improved processing speed and continued low cost.

To request more information or to recieve copies of forms needed to request an anuity settlement of your account, call the Personel office, Extention 4077. Ask for Tina or allen; they will be happy to answer your questions.

James Cincone

pc Accounting Department

Enclosure

BLOCK

The **block** feature defines a certain portion of text. Once text has been blocked, it can be edited (deleted, moved, or copied) as one unit. Some software also uses the block feature with underline, bold, centering, and other operations.

A block may consist of a few words, sentences, or even pages. When a block is defined, it is set off from the rest of the copy in some way such as being displayed in a brighter mode or a different color.

Blocking text involves 1) positioning the cursor at the first character of the block, and 2) highlighting the block by moving the cursor to the last character.

An important part of blocking text is doing so efficiently. When the block involves more than one line, move the cursor *down* and then position the cursor on the appropriate character (rather than scrolling through each line). Similarly, if the block is several pages, use the Page Down key to move through the text quickly.

Complete the steps to use the block feature.

FUNCTION	STEPS REQUIRED
Block	Position the cursor at the first character of the block.
	Mark the beginning of the block by ______________________.
	Highlight the block by ______________________.
	Mark the end of the block by ______________________.
	Cancel the block command by ______________________.
	List the features such as copy and move that are used with block in your software.

______________________ ______________________

______________________ ______________________

______________________ ______________________

S2-EX9

1. Retrieve S2-EX9 from the template, or key the following and save it as S2-EX9.

```
Imaging is a technology that is designed to handle
the storage and transmission of graphic images.
Images may include photographs, signatures,
blueprints, or drawings.  Imaging technology
stores (and in some cases transmits) documents as
an electronic signal.
```

Facsimile, an imaging technology, may be explained as a copier equipped to transmit and receive graphic images. The original document is converted to an electronic signal and transmitted over a communications medium to another facsimile or receiving terminal, which in turns converts the signals back to a graphic image. Facsimile is less expensive and faster than overnight mail or courier service.

2. Use the block function to highlight Paragraph 1. Then cancel the block.

Deleting Blocked Text

Once text has been blocked, it can be deleted. Deleting a block is faster than deleting word by word.

FUNCTION	STEPS REQUIRED
Delete a block	____________________
	____________________
	____________________

S2-EX10

1. Retrieve S2-EX9.
2. Block Paragraph 1 and then delete it.
3. Block Sentence 2 of Paragraph 2, and then delete it. If necessary, adjust the spacing between the two remaining sentences. Clear the screen.

   Facsimile, an imaging technology, may be explained as a copier equipped to transmit and receive graphic images. The original document is converted to an electronic signal and transmitted over a communications medium to another facsimile or receiving terminal, which in turn converts the signals back to a graphic image. Facsimile is less expensive and faster than overnight mail or courier service.

4. Save the revised document.

S2-DOC4R

1. Retrieve S2-DOC4.

2. Revise S2-DOC4 using the block delete feature to delete blocks of text consisting of several words, a sentence, or a paragraph.

   Remember to key an **r** on the doc code line to show that this is the revised version of S2-DOC4.

3. Proofread carefully from the screen, paying close attention to the sections where deletions were made.

4. Save the document as S2-DOC4.

5. Print the document. Proofread the printed copy. If you detect errors, revise, save, and reprint.

TIPS TO OPERATOR

- You should not have to check spelling again for this document since very little new text was inserted.
- Be sure that you delete the hard returns following the deleted paragraph or too many lines will appear between the last paragraph and the closing.

```
Current date


Mr. Anthony Deblieux
P. O. Box 5588
Place d'Armes
MONTREAL, QUEBEC H2Y 3L2
CANADA
```

Dear Mr. Deblieux

You are invited to be among the first to subscribe to the new magazine dedicated to computer users. We have reserved an issue for you FREE!

You know how hard it can be to keep ~~up~~ with breakthroughs in personal systems. ~~You must realize that only a dedicated publication can accomplish the task.~~ BONUS COMPUTING is the only publication that gives an objective appraisal of the computer market including UNIX workstations and Macintoshes.

BONUS COMPUTING does more than ~~put~~ hardware ~~through its paces~~; it also examines ~~the~~ ways to improve productivity. Whether you are interested in computer systems, applications, operating systems or networking, you will find it in BONUS COMPUTING. ~~If you are a demanding professional, you are going to like what you see.~~

(DOCUMENT CONTINUED ON NEXT PAGE)

To receive your free issue of BONUS COMPUTING, remove the label that says "I ACCEPT" from the envelope and affix it to the subscription form.

BONUS COMPUTING

~~It~~ contains more useful and accurate information on personal computers than you have seen anywhere else; you may keep it with our compliments. ~~You will not be obligated in any way.~~

Don't delay. Be among the first to find out why BONUS COMPUTING is the publication you will turn to first every month.

Sincerely

Pearl T. Hershberger

doc code

Enclosure

MOVE AND COPY

The **move** feature, also called cut and paste, allows you to relocate a block of text. Text may be moved within a document or it may be moved (appended) to a new document. For example, the move function allows a paragraph from page 3 of a document to be moved to page 5. Only one block of text may be moved at a time.

Copying enables a block of text to be repeated in another location. During the copy process, the original text is not deleted. The difference between move and copy is that when you copy, the text will be located in more than one place; move deletes text from its original location and inserts it in the new location.

FUNCTION	STEPS REQUIRED
Move	____________________
Copy	____________________

S2-EX11

1. Retrieve S2-EX11 from the template, or key the following text and save it as S2-EX11.

   The keyboard is the main device for communicating with a computer, but with the advent of voice communications this may be changing. Soon, however, we will be integrating voice documents into our computing environments. Voice technology is relatively new and is still being refined, but the demand for it is great.

2. Revise the following paragraph by moving the sentence as indicated. Clear the screen.

The keyboard is the main device for communicating with a computer, but with the advent of voice communications this may be changing. Soon, however, we will be integrating voice documents into our computing environments. Voice technology is relatively new and is still being refined, but the demand for it is great.

S2-EX12

1. Retrieve S2-EX12 from the template, or key the following paragraph and save it as S2-EX12.

   ```
   When planning for the implementation of the
   overall strategy for each department, it will be
   necessary to determine the appropriate coverage of
   hardware and software for the users in the
   department.  Each department's needs will have to
   be analyzed to determine the office automation
   requirements of users.

   Price should be only one factor in the decision to
   buy one software package over another.  Although
   there are benefits to be gained in site licensing
   of microcomputer software, the initial cost of the
   software is only a minor part of the overall cost.
   Even more important to the decision is the
   extended cost of software maintenance,
   flexibility, connectivity, training, and vendor
   support.
   ```

2. Copy Paragraph 1 a double space below Paragraph 2. You should then have three paragraphs.
3. Revise Paragraph 2 as shown.

   ```
   Price should be only one factor in the decision to
   buy one software package over another.  Although
   there are benefits to be gained in site licensing
   of microcomputer software, the initial cost of the
   software is only a minor part of the overall cost.
   Even more important to the decision is the
   extended cost of software maintenance,
   flexibility, connectivity, training, and vendor
   support.
   ```

4. Block Paragaraph 3 and delete it. Save the revised document and print it.

S2-DOC4RR

1. Retrieve S2-DOC4. (Although revisions were made to S2-DOC4, it should still be saved on your disk as S2-DOC4.)
2. Revise the document using the block feature to move the sentence and paragraph.

   Be sure to key another **r** on the doc code line to indicate that this is the second revision of S2-DOC4. (Example: **xxx/s2-doc4rr**)
3. Proofread from the screen, checking that the moves are correct.

4. Save the document as S2-DOC4. Print the document. Proofread the printed copy. If you detect errors, revise, save, and reprint.

TIPS TO OPERATOR

■ Carefully check the spacing before and after text that has been moved, making sure two spaces follow a period and a double space follows a paragraph.

Current date

Mr. Anthony Deblieux
P. O. Box 5588
Place d'Armes
MONTREAL, QUEBEC H2Y 3L2
CANADA

Dear Mr. Deblieux

You are invited to be among the first to subscribe to the new BONUS COMPUTING magazine dedicated to computer users. We have reserved an issue for you FREE!

You know how hard it can be to keep pace with breakthroughs in personal computing systems. BONUS COMPUTING is the only publication that gives an objective appraisal of the computer market including UNIX workstations and Macintoshes. move

BONUS COMPUTING does more than evaluate hardware; it also examines ways to improve productivity. Whether you are interested in computer systems, applications, operating systems, or networking, you will find it in BONUS COMPUTING. software

move To receive your free issue of BONUS COMPUTING, remove the label that says "I ACCEPT" from the envelope and affix it to the subscription form. Return it in the enclosed postpaid envelope today.

BONUS COMPUTING contains more useful and accurate information on personal computers than you have seen anywhere else; you may keep your free ~~it~~ copy with our compliments.

Sincerely

Pearl T. Hershberger

doc code

Enclosure

1. Retrieve S2-DOC5.
2. Revise the document, using the block feature to delete and move text.
3. Proofread from the screen.
4. Save the document as S2-DOC5. Print two copies. Proofread the printed copy. If you detect errors, revise, save, and reprint.

TIPS TO OPERATOR

- Did you remember to key an **r** at the end of the doc code?
- Check carefully the spacing between paragraphs, special lines, and at the points where text was deleted and moved. Remember you should have a double space below the subject line and a quadruple space below the last line of the body.
- Revise text before moving it. When text is moved before changes are made, you may encounter some difficulty locating the text to be revised.

```
current date

     Salaried
All ^ Employees
INDIVIDUAL
^ACCOUNT PROGRAMS
                        must
To improve the speed of claims processing while complying with
applicable federal laws and without increasing expense charges,
the company is forced to require that all withdrawal or transfer
requests be submitted on forms approved by the company.

You must use one of the enclosed Request for Withdrawal forms
whenever you wish to withdraw amounts from your account.  Unless
you submit this form properly completed, your withdrawal request
cannot be honored, and it will be returned to you.

move
Individual Account Programs are designed to provide flexible,
effective ways you can save for your retirement while taking
advantage of significant tax savings.

We regret any inconvenience this new procedure may cause you, but
we believe its implementation will result in improved processing
speed and continued low cost.
                                                  the
To request more information or to receive copies of ^ forms needed
to request an annuity settlement of your account, call the
Personnel office, Extension 4077. Ask for Tina or Allen; they
will be happy to answer your questions.


James Cincone

doc code

pc Accounting Department

Enclosure
```

S2-DOC6

1. Key S2-DOC6 as a simplified memo.
2. Proofread from the screen, check spelling, and correct any errors.
3. Following the originator's request, use the block copy command to copy the memo to the bottom of the page. (Be sure that both copies fit on one page. If necessary, delete a blank line before the date.)
4. Print one copy. Proofread the printed copy. If you detect errors, revise, save, and reprint.

TIPS TO OPERATOR

■ The procedures to use the spelling checker (print, proofread the printed document, revise, save, and reprint) are standard procedures you should follow for each document. You will not be reminded to repeat these steps in text.

February 20, 19--

Operator:
Please key memo at top of page and copy it to bottom to make 2 copies on one page. I will make photocopies and cut in half. Key a dashed divider line between copies as shown.

Athletic Committee Members

ATHLETIC COMMITTEE MEETING AND HONORS LUNCHEON

The Athletic Committee will meet on Tuesday, March 6, at 3:30 p.m. in the Booster Room in Lang Stadium. Commissioner Scott Missett will speak to us about recruiting guidelines.

Also, you are encouraged to attend the honors luncheon on Monday, March 5, at noon in the Green Room. This luncheon will honor athletes with outstanding academic records. Tickets are $10 and can be purchased at the Athletic Ticket Office.

Quinton Seay, Chairperson

- -

Key S2-DOC7, a personal business letter, in block format. *Template users*: Retrieve S2-DOC7 and proceed to S2-DOC7r.

```
                                             Route 2, Box 36      IA
                                             Council Bluffs, Iowa 51501-1136
                                             January 18, 19--

Nation al Trust Assoc. iation
P. O. Box 6477 OH
Cleveland, Ohio 44101-1477

Dear Sir: Ladies and Gentlemen

Could you give me instructions as to what I need to do to get a
stock certificates for 13 shares of Jaguar common stock, which
evidently have been lost? ¶ You have my the power of attorney from my
mother, Colleen Jonish, which I sent you in September. 19. While
trying to get my mother's financial affairs in order, I have been
unable to locate all of the stock certificate s she owns for the her 48
shares of Jaguar.

I have in my possession Jaguar stock certificates C0827607 for 1 share,
N0527424 for 8 shares, and 044505 for 26 shares.  Therefore, I do
not have certificates for 13 shares.

I will shall appreciate you r sending me the needed information for
replacing these lost certificates.

Yours truly


Mark Stidham
```

S2-DOC7R

1. Revise S2-DOC7 as marked.

2. Since the address to be inserted at the end of the letter is the same as the return address, use the block copy function to copy it. Double-space above and below the inserted address.

copy

```
Route 2, Box 36
Council Bluffs, IA  51501-1136
January 18, 19--



National Trust Association
P. O. Box 6477
Cleveland, OH  44101-1477

Ladies and Gentlemen
LOST STOCK CERTIFICATES
Could you give me instructions as to what do I need to do to replace get a
stock certificates for 13 shares of Jaguar common stock, which
evidently have been lost?

You have the power of attorney from my mother, Colleen D. Jonish,
which I sent you in September.  While trying to organize get my mother's
financial affairs in order, I have been unable to locate all of
her the stock certificates for her 48 shares of Jaguar common stock.
I have the following in my possession Jaguar stock certificates: CO827607 for
1 share, NO527424 for 8 shares, and 044505 for 26 shares; therefore, I am missing do not have certificates for 13 shares.

Please I shall appreciate your sending me the needed information for
replacing these lost certificates to the following address:
DS
Yours truly


Mark Stidham

doc code
```

Operator: add subject line in ALL CAPS

Operator, add address shown above.

HYPHENATION

Hard Hyphen (Required Hyphen). When keying a word or group of words that must have a hyphen to be spelled correctly, a *hard hyphen* or *required hyphen* must be used. For example, the word *son-in-law* must be keyed with hard hyphens.

Soft Hyphen. A soft or syllable hyphen divides a word between syllables when the word is too long to print on a line. When text is revised and the line length changes, soft hyphens are automatically dropped. To use soft or syllable hyphenation with your software, you may first need to turn on the hyphenation feature.

Blocked Hyphen (Nonbreaking Hyphen). Words that should never be divided between lines must be keyed as a *blocked hyphen*, *hyphen character*, or *nonbreaking hyphen*. For example, blocked hyphens would be used to key a telephone number (254-6427) or Lotus 1-2-3 to ensure that they are not split between two lines. Also, *dashes* (formed by striking the hyphen twice) should be keyed as a blocked hyphen.

List the steps for hyphenation below.

FUNCTION	STEPS REQUIRED
Hard Hyphen	______________________________
	______________________________
Soft Hyphen	______________________________
	______________________________
Blocked Hyphen	______________________________
	______________________________

S2-EX13

1. Key the following sentences using a hard hyphen and save them as S2-EX13.

   His son-in-law required immediate medical attention.

   The in-service training program was very productive and interesting.

S2-EX14

1. Key the following sentences with dashes and save them as S2-EX14. Use the block hyphen feature.

   The Philadelphia Chamber of Commerce was very helpful- -particularly in the beginning with suggestions on business locations.

   These diskettes store more material- -20 pages more- -than previous diskettes of the same brand.

S2-DOC8

1. Key S2-DOC8 in block format with hyphenation on.
2. Correct misspelled or incorrectly written words as you key.

TIPS TO OPERATOR

- Remember that your spelling checker will not detect correctly spelled words that are used incorrectly. Examples: **it** for **if**; **you** for **your**; **from** for **form**; an omitted character such as an **s**.

Mr. Samuel Fincher
4003 Burdick Street
Kalamazoo, MI 49007-2177

Dear Mr. Fincher

YOUR REQUEST FOR INFORMATION

Thank you for your interest in Maritz office furniture. As a leader in quality and craftsmanship in the manufacture of bookcases, library shelving and filing systems, Maritz now offers you a full range of office furniture -- form computer media cabinets and lateral files to ergonomic gas lift chairs.

One of the features of Maritz lateral file cabinets is the chrome pull handle. This time-tested design allows for easy operation while blending with most office decor. In addition, Maritz file supports are used to convert a lateral file to popular front-to-back filing in either letter or legal depth drawers. Also, wood-grained laminate steel caps fit any model. As you can see from the enclosed brochure, these easy-to-assemble filing cabinet are attractive and space efficient.

Businesses today have more to store than just paper, and Maritz has a full line of storage products to suit your every need. We have products to store everything from paper clips to your corporate library.

Our area sales represientive, Tamitha Dunn, will call you soon. If your need is more immediate, please call me at our toll-free number, 1-800-555-7725. Your request will be given top priorty.

Sincerely

Christine Halperin
National Sales Manager

Enclosure: Brochure

HARD SPACE (REQUIRED SPACE)

A **hard space**, also known as a *required*, *nonbreaking*, or *forced space*, is used to prevent two words from being separated. For example, *March 15* should be keyed with a required space between *March* and *15* to prevent the month and date from being separated.

List the steps for keyboarding a required space.

FUNCTION	STEPS REQUIRED
Hard Space	______________________________
	______________________________

S2-EX15

1. Key the following sentences using required spaces after the bold characters.

```
She has a doctor's appointment at 8:30 a.m.
Mr. Smith lives at 243 South Madison Avenue in
Flagstaff, Arizona.
This particular brand of ice cream is 96 percent
fat free.
The recipe for chocolate cookies is on page 103.
Mrs. Jill Ball can be found in Room 300 of the
main building.
```

2. Save the exercise as S2-EX15.

S2-DOC9

1. Key S2-DOC9 in block format with mixed punctuation.
2. Be sure to key hard spaces between words where separation at a line ending would be undesirable, even if they do not currently appear near a line ending. During revision, separation could occur.

TIPS TO OPERATOR

- You should key at least 10 hard spaces in this document.
- When proofreading, check each line ending for words that may have separated during word wrap because a required space was not keyed. If you find such words separated, delete the normal space and then key a hard space; the two words should wrap together to the next line. Do not strike a hard return.

Mark Stidham
c/o Mrs. J. T. Hightower

Dear Mark Stidham

In response to you recent notice we advice that a stop transfer has been entered against certificate No. C07555586-2 for 13 shares of Jaguar common stock issued May 15, 1987.

Enclosed are forms of affidavit of lose and indemity agreement to be completed in order to secure issuance of a replacement certificate.

A check for $45.50 representing payment of the premium due the isurance company, made payable to The Henry Piatt Company should accompanie the 3 copies of the affidavits. The above premium includes a $10 non-refundable processing fee.
The instruments shoudl be ezecuted and acknowleged before a notary. All question must be answerd by completing the blank areas of items 1, 2, 3, and 7.All notiarzed copy must then be forwarded to The Henry Piatt Company, 1605 Bond Court, Cleveland, Ohio 44114-1105, for assumption of liability under lost security blanket bond No. 8847011.

IT IS IMPERATIVE THAT WE BE NOTIFIED IMMEDIATELY IF THE CERTIFICATE IS RECOVERED AT ANY TIME.

If you have any questions in regards to the above matter, please contact one of our shareholder representatives at (216) 555-7747 between the hours of 9 a.m. and 4:30 p.m. (EST).

Very truly yours

Ginette Evgenidi
Shareholder Communications

S2-DOC9R

1. Retrieve S2-DOC9.

2. Turn hyphenation on. Review word division (hyphenation) rules in the Reference Section before keying revisions.

TIPS TO OPERATOR

- As you insert text, be alert to words that should be joined with hard spaces.
- As words are hyphenated at line endings, be sure divisions occur at acceptable points according to standard word division rules.

Current Date

Mr. Mark Stidham
Route 2, Box 36
Council Bluffs, IA 51501-1136

Dear Mr. Stidham:

In response to your recent notice, ~~we advise that~~ a stop transfer has been entered against Certificate No. C07555586-2 for 13 shares of Jaguar common stock issued May 15, 1987.

The Enclosed ~~are~~ forms ~~of~~ affidavit of loss and indemnity agreement must ~~to~~ be completed by August 30, 19--, ~~in order~~ to secure ~~issuance of~~ a replacement certificate.

A check for $45.50 ~~representing payment of the premium due the insurance company,~~ made payable to The Henry Piatt Company should accompany the three copies of the affidavits. The above premium includes a $10 non-refundable processing fee.

move

The instruments should be executed and acknowledged before a notary public. All questions must be answered by completing ~~the blank areas of~~ items 1, 2, 3, and 7. All notarized copies must ~~then~~ be mailed ~~forwarded~~ to The Henry Piatt Company, 1605 Bond Court, Cleveland, ~~Ohio~~ OH 44114-1105, for assumption of liability under lost security blanket bond No. 8847011.

move

IT IS IMPERATIVE THAT ~~WE~~ CITY NATIONAL BANK BE NOTIFIED IMMEDIATELY IF THE CERTIFICATE IS RECOVERED AT ANY TIME.

If you have any questions ~~in~~ regarding ~~to the above~~ this matter, ~~please~~ call ~~contact~~ one of our stock shareholder representatives at (216) 555-7747 between ~~the hours of~~ 9 a.m. and 4:30 p.m. (EST).

Very truly yours,

Ginette Evgenidi
Shareholder Communications

doc code

Enclosures

S2-DOC10

Key S2-DOC10 in simplified block format with hyphenation on. Refer to the Reference Guide for correct letter format. *Template users*: Retrieve S2-DOC10 and proceed to S2-DOC10r after completing the exercises for the Search and Replace function.

Ms. Tricishaune Daniel
P.O. Box 1205
Marina del Rey, CA # 90295-1205
DS

Operator, please help with spelling.

TOWER CLUB SERVICES c/lc

DS

At Tower National Bank we take pride in bringing you quality products. Tower Club Service—our most popular account—combines a money market deposit account currently paying an impressive 8.30% annual yield/8.0% annual rate with a 12.9% A.P.R. no annual fee credit card. To make this a complete money management package, TNB offers a free interest-bearing checking account and discounts up to 10% on brokerage services and more. No service charges are payed when you maintain a $2,500 minimum balance in your money market account. Please look over the enclosed pamplet to learn more about TNB services.

TNB is commited to our customers. At TNB you can count on our stability and security. TNB is the only bank holding company in the state to earn Standard & Poor's highest ranking of A+ for earnings and dividend consistancy.

We invite you to visit your nearest TNB branch in Marina del Rey or call us at 555-2200 from 9 a.m. until 4 p.m. One of our friendly customer service representatives will be happy to tell you about TNB and the additional services we have available for you.

lc

WAI YAN HOANG
CUSTOMER RELATIONS MANAGER

Enclosure

SEARCH AND REPLACE

Search allows you to quickly locate each occurrence of a word or group of words (also called a *text string*) in a document without having to scroll through the document. The search function can also be used to locate punctuation marks, symbols, formatting, or instructional codes.

Replace will automatically replace a word or group of words with another word or group of words within a document.

Global Search and Replace will automatically locate every occurrence of a text string and replace it with a different text string throughout the document. **Selective search and replace** requires that you verify the change.

List below the steps for search and replace.

FUNCTION	STEPS REQUIRED
Search	______________________________
	______________________________
Replace	______________________________
	______________________________
Selective (Prompted) Search and Replace	______________________________
	______________________________
Global Search and Replace	______________________________
	______________________________

S2-EX16

1. Retrieve S2-EX16 from the template, or key the following paragraph and save it as S2-EX16.

```
All reports are due to Vickey by 10:30 a.m.  If
you cannot meet the 10:30 a.m. deadline, please
let Vickey know as soon as possible and Vickey
will request an extension for you.
```

2. Use selective search and replace to locate each occurrence of Vickey and replace it as shown below.

```
                             the director
All reports are due to ~~Vickey~~ by 10:30 a.m.  If

you cannot meet the 10:30 a.m. deadline, please
                                              she
let Vickey know as soon as possible and ~~Vickey~~

will request an extension for you.
```

3. Use global search and replace to change both occurrences of 10:30 to 8:30.

S2-DOC8R

1. Retrieve S2-DOC8.
2. Make all revisions marked on the copy including searching for and replacing text.

TIPS TO OPERATOR

- Complete search and replace after all other revisions are made since inserted text might need to be changed in the search and replace operation.
- Key necessary hard spaces.

```
Current date
  Sigstrom Company
Mr. Samuel Fincher, Office Manager
4003 Burdick Street
Kalamazoo, MI  49007-2177

Dear Mr. Fincher

YOUR REQUEST FOR INFORMATION

                                                      quality
Thank you for your interest in Maritz office furniture.  As a
leader ~~in quality and craftsmanship~~e in the manufacture of book-
cases, library shelving and filing systems, Maritz now offers you
a full range of office furniture--from computer media cabinets
and lateral files to ergonomic gas-lift chairs.
```

Operator, please revise as marked. Make maritz ALL CAPS each time it occurs. Thanks, Chris

(DOCUMENT CONTINUED ON NEXT PAGE)

One of the features of Maritz lateral file cabinets is the chrome pull handle. This time-tested design allows for easy operation while blending with most office decor. In addition, Maritz file supports are used to convert a lateral file to popular front-to-back filing in either letter or legal depth drawers. ~~Also, wood-grained laminate steel caps fit any model.~~ As you can see from the enclosed brochure, these easy-to-assemble filing cabinets are attractive and space efficient.

Businesses today ~~have more to~~ [should] store [more] than just paper~~, and~~ [.] [The] Maritz ~~has a~~ full line of storage products ~~to~~ suit your every need~~. We have~~ [—] products to store everything from paper clips to your corporate library. [move]

Our area sales representative, Tamitha Dunn, will call you [april 16] ~~soon~~. If your need is more immediate, please call me at our toll-free number, 1-800-555-7725. ~~Your request will be given top priority.~~

Sincerely

Christine Halperin
National Sales Manager

doc code

Enclosure: Brochure

S2-DOC10R

1. Retrieve S2-DOC10.
2. Make all revisions requested.

TIPS TO OPERATOR

- Remember to use the typeover or replace feature of your system when you change the address to ALL CAPS.
- Since the percent (%) sign prints after the number without a space, you must key a hard space before the word **percent** so that percent will print with a space after the number; otherwise, the percentages will print like this: **8.3percent**. The hard space is keyed to keep the number from separating from the word **percent**, should it appear at the end of a line.
- When you search for and replace the bank name, notice that the originator requested that you leave the bank initials in two places. Therefore, you must give the command when you search and replace that you want to verify each

change. When your system highlights or stops at text that should not be replaced, you must instruct your system not to replace the text. You may be prompted "Replace (Y/N)." Key **N** for No.

Operator - change % to percent. Also, spell out TNB to read Tower National Bank each time except where marked "leave."

Current date

Ms. Tricishaune Daniel
P. O. Box 1205
Marina del Rey, CA 90295-1205

Put in ALL CAPS with no punctuation.

TOWER CLUB SERVICES

At Tower National Bank we take pride in bringing you quality products. Tower Club Service--our most popular account--combines a money market deposit account currently paying an impressive 8.30% annual yield/8.0% annual rate with a 12.9% A.P.R. no annual fee credit card. To make this a complete money management package, TNB offers a free interest-bearing checking account and discounts up to 10% on brokerage services and more. No service charges are paid when you maintain a $2,500 minimum balance in your money market account. Please look over the enclosed pamphlet to learn more about TNB services.

(The; innovative and; services)

TNB is committed to our customers. At TNB *(leave)* you can count on our stability and security. TNB is the only bank holding company in the state to earn Standard & Poor's highest ranking of A+ for earnings and dividend consistency.

We invite you to visit your nearest TNB *(leave)* branch in Marina del Rey or call us at 555-2200 from 9 a.m. until 4 p.m. One of our friendly customer service representatives will be happy to tell you about TNB and the additional services we have available for you.

Wai Yan Hoang
Customer Relations Manager

Put in ALL CAPS.

doc code

Enclosure

SECTION 2

SOFTWARE FUNCTION SUMMARY

List the commands for the following:

Delete word ____

Delete line ____

Delete to end of line ______________________________________

Delete to end of page _____________________________________

Insert ____

Spelling checker ____

Block ____

Delete a block ____

Move a block ____

Copy a block ____

Hard/Required space ______________________________________

Search ____

Search and replace _______________________________________

(Selective/prompted) ______________________________________

Global search and replace __________________________________

SECTION 3

ENHANCING TEXT AND ADJUSTING DOCUMENT FORMAT

FUNCTIONS

- Displaying Formatting Codes
- Centering
- Underlining
- Bold
- Format Changes—Margins, Line Spacing, and Page Length
- Tabs
- Right Margin Justification
- Indent

DISPLAY INSTRUCTIONAL CODES

Instructional formatting codes for such features as underline, bold, center, line spacing, or any feature other than the default settings are hidden behind the text. For example, an underscored word will appear underlined on the screen or in a difficult color on a color monitor, but the code for underlining is not visible in the normal display mode.

At times you will want to reveal these codes so that you can see exactly why something is not working the way you think it should or to add or delete a code at the appropriate location.

List on the following page the steps for displaying instructional codes.

FUNCTION	STEPS REQUIRED
Reveal Codes	______________________
	______________________
Conceal Codes	______________________
	______________________

CENTERING

Centering automatically centers text horizontally between the left and right margins. Generally, you enter the center command before keying the text. Some software, however, may require you to position the cursor at the center point before you key the center command.

When editing text that is centered, you may want to display the instructional codes to insert the new text within the center codes. You should not have to reenter a new center command. Should the margins be changed after the text is centered, it will be centered automatically between the new margins.

FUNCTION	STEPS REQUIRED
Centering	______________________
	______________________
	______________________

S3-EX1

1. Center the following announcement and save it as S3-EX1.

```
                You are cordially invited to
  participate in a Departmental Liaison Briefing Session
                          to see
          the office automation system demonstrated
                        on July 19
                    Conference Room 601A
```

2. Move the cursor to the top of the document. Display the instructional code for centering. What is the code for turning on centering ______? for turning off centering _______?

3. Revise S3-EX1 as indicated; the document is double-spaced for ease in reading the revisions.

You are cordially invited to

participate in a Departmental Liaison ~~Briefing~~ Session

to ~~see~~ view

the office automation system demonstrated

on July 19

~~Conference Room 601A~~ Building A

S3-EX2

1. Retrieve S3-EX2 from the template, or key the following paragraphs and save them as S3-EX2. Center the heading.

HANDS OFF KEYBOARDING AND EDITING
What happens when you are asked to do the same tedious task again and again? If you are like most people, you get bored and your mind wanders which leads to mistakes in your work.

Word processing software isn't like most people. It never gets bored; it loves doing the same thing over and over again. When using word processing software to do tedious jobs, it completes them with speed and accuracy.

2. Revise S3-EX2 as indicated.

HANDS OFF KEYBOARDING, ~~AND~~ EDITING, AND PRINTING

What happens when you are asked to do the same

tedious task again and again? If you are like

most people, you get bored and your mind wanders,

which can ~~leads~~ lead to mistakes in your work.

Word processing software isn't like most people.

It never gets bored; it loves doing the same thing

over and over ~~again~~. When using word processing

software to do ~~tedious~~ routine jobs, ~~it~~ you can ~~completes~~ complete ~~them~~ the jobs

with speed and accuracy.

S3-DOC1

Key S3-DOC1 in simplified block format, centering specified lines as noted.

TIPS TO OPERATOR

- Refer to the Reference Section for the simplified block format, if you need to review it.
- Be sure to key hard spaces in dates.

Current date

Mrs. Elizabeth Chittenden
3800 Beach Blvd. Apt. C
Pascagoula, MS 39567-2250

VISIT THE BEAUTIFUL ORIENT

As a subscriber to DAILY LIVING, you have an opportunity to visit the beautiful Orient for 18 days and 17 nights for as low as $2,350. Flights from San Francisco depart October 15, November 20, and December 5.

During your 18 days you will visit these exciting oriental cities:

Singapore
Bangkok
Hong Kong
Taipei
Tokyo

Center each line

Your oriental vacation includes: round trip jet transportation via World Airlines; an escort accompanies every departure; baggage handling (except through customs areas); travel information; american breakfast daily.

For more details, read the enclosed four-page brochure which describes activities planned for each city. Call toll free 1-800-555-3321 for more information or to make reservations.

GEOK NG

Enclosure

S3-DOC1R

1. Retrieve S3-DOC1 and revise as marked.

2. Check the centered lines for correct placement.

Current date

Mrs. Elizabeth Chittenden
3800 Beach Blvd. Apt. C
Pascagoula, MS 39567-2250

VISIT THE ~~BEAUTIFUL~~ EXCITING ORIENT

As a valued subscriber to DAILY LIVING, you have an opportunity to visit the beautiful Orient for 18 days and 17 nights for ~~as low as~~ only $2,350. Flights from San Francisco depart October 15, November 20, and December 5.

During your 18-day visit you will ~~visit~~ tour these exciting oriental cities:

Singapore--4 days
Bangkok--3 days
Hong Kong--4 days
Taipei--3 days
Tokyo--4 days

Your oriental vacation includes: round-trip jet transportation via World Airlines; an escort on ~~accompanies~~ every departure; baggage handling (except through customs areas); travel information; American breakfast daily; and accommodations at first-class hotels.

For more details, read the enclosed four-page brochure which describes activities planned for each city. Call toll free 1-800-555-3321 weekdays from 8:30 a.m. to 9:00 p.m. (EST) for more information or to make your reservations.

Geok Ng
MARKETING MANAGER
doc code

Enclosure

Key S3-DOC2 as a simplified memo, carefully following proofreaders' marks.

current date

Ms. Vickie Westerburg, Head

Departmental Awards

The followig sutdents have been ~~chosen~~ selected to be recognized at the honors banquet on April 19.

OUTSTANDING OFFICE INFORMATION SYSTEMS MANAGEMENT GRADUATE

Mistie Clariec Presson

OUTSTANDING COMPUTER INFORMATION SYSTEMS GRADUATE

STEWART Sommerfeld

Would you please order plaques (from the same firm that we used last year) to be presented to these students. at the banquet

Also send ~~each~~ both student banquet reservations forms and ~~notify each student to attend the banq-uet~~ ask them to make reservations and . Each may bring one guest.

Center each line

Paul Ginter, Chair
Honors Committee

UNDERLINING

Underlining allows text to be underlined as it is keyed. Underlining is a toggle command that is turned on and off. Text can also be underlined after it is keyed. To underline existing text, some software requires that you block the text to be underlined and then key the underline command. With other programs, you simply turn on underlining at the beginning of the text and turn it off at the end of the text to be underlined.

Text can be inserted or deleted between the underline commands. By displaying the instructional codes when editing, you can add and delete underlined text easily. Do not underline any punctuation that may follow the underlined text.

List below the steps for underlining.

FUNCTION	STEPS REQUIRED
Underlining Text As It Is Keyed	________________________________
	________________________________
	________________________________
	________________________________
Underlining Existing Text	________________________________
	________________________________
	________________________________
	________________________________

S3-EX3

1. Key the following sentences and save them as S3-EX3.

   The book, Understanding Yourself, was well worth reading.
   They cannot exceed the manufacturer's recommended price.
   The purpose of this policy is to ensure that employees are informed.

2. Move the cursor to the beginning of Sentence 3. What code is revealed to begin underlining ______________? to end underlining ______________?

3. Revise these sentences as indicated. Reveal the instructional codes if necessary.

article
The ~~book~~, Understanding Yourself, was well worth reading.

They cannot exceed the manufacturer's recommended price.

~~The purpose of~~ this policy is to ensure that employees are informed.

S3-EX4

1. Key and save the following document as S3-EX4.

TECHNOLOGY MANAGEMENT STRATEGIES

Architecture. This function will be responsible for standards and hardware architecture ensuring compatibility among all users.
Network Management. This function will be responsible for effective and efficient voice and data communications.
Change Management. This function focuses on ensuring that the impact of new technologies on the organization are considered in all technology decisions.

2. Revise S3-EX4 as indicated.

Standards and
TECHNOLOGY MANAGEMENT STRATEGIES

Architecture. This function will be responsible for standards and hardware architecture ensuring compatibility among all users.

Network Management. This function will be responsible for effective and efficient voice and data communications.

Change Management. This function focuses on ensuring that the impact of new technologies on the organization are considered in all technology decisions.

S3-DOC3

Beginning with the date, key S3-DOC3 as a form letter or load S3-DOC3 from the template and proceed to S3-DOC3r. Position the salutation 6 lines below the date since the letter address is not included.

TIPS TO OPERATOR

- When underlining text, use the most efficient method for your system.
- Remember that terminal punctuation is not underlined (i.e., the period at the end of an underlined sentence).

Dear Investor:

The new USA tax exempt bond fund which is described in the Prospectus, was constructed for higher bracket tax payers who want an investment that pays not only a good rate of return but also has less risk than long-term bonds.

This is an Intermediate portfolio (not individual bonds) with an average life of four and ten years. The individual securities may be of a ten-year (or less-than-ten-year) maturity when purchased; or they can be bonds with maturities beyond ten years.

Why does USA concentrate on issues of this kind. with only a few year remaining util a bond can be redemmed at full value, the fluctuation in its price will be far less than that of a bond that will remain outstanding for a longer period of time. These bonds offer excellent yeidls.

Every dollar of this income is exempt from Federal income taxes. This fund also provides a unique feature--free redemption checks for amounts of $500.00 or more than will enable you to use this bond with complete liquididy.

You can open an account for only $1,500.00 and add to it at any time in amounts of $500.00 or more with no sales charge ever/ Form 8:30 a.m. to 5 p.m. (EDT) you may call toll free the number shown below:

1-800-555-1121

Sincerely,

Juan Gonzalez

enclosure

S3-DOC3R

1. Retrieve S3-DOC3 and revise as marked.

2. Proofread with careful attention to the points where underlining was deleted and inserted.

TIPS TO OPERATOR

■ When deleting formatting codes, such as the underline, reveal formatting codes to help you locate the commands.

current date

Dear Investor:

The new USA tax-exempt bond fund, which is described in the Prospectus, was constructed for higher bracket tax payers who want an investment that pays a good rate of return but has less risk than long-term bonds.

This is an intermediate portfolio (not individual bonds) with an average life of four and ten years. The individual securities may be of a ten-year (or less than ten-year) maturity when purchased; or they can be bonds with maturities beyond ten years.

Why does USA concentrate on issues of this kind? With only a few years remaining until a bond can be redeemed at full value, the fluctuation in its price will be far less than that of a bond that will remain outstanding for a longer period of time. These bonds offer excellent yields.

Every dollar of this income is exempt from Federal income taxes. This fund also provides a unique feature--free redemption checks for amounts of $500.00 or more that will enable you to use this bond with complete liquidity.

You can open an account for only $1,500.00 and add to it at any time in amounts of $500.00 or more with no sales charge ever. From 8:30 a.m. to 5 p.m. (EDT) you may call toll free the number shown below:

1-800-555-1121

Sincerely,

Juan Gonzalez

doc code

Enclosure

BOLD

The **bold** feature prints text darker than normal. It is used to emphasize key terms, headings, and other text. **This sentence is printed in bold to emphasize its importance.**

Bold is a toggle command that must be turned on and off. Text can be keyed in bold or bold can be added to existing text. Similar to underlining, some programs require you to block the existing text and then key the bold command.

FUNCTION	STEPS REQUIRED
Key Bold Text	______________________________
Turn Off Bold	______________________________
Bold Existing Text	______________________________

S3-EX5

1. Key and save the following sentence as S3-EX5.

   `This` **`word`** `is emphasized with bold text.`

2. Turn on formatting codes. What code is revealed to turn on bold ______________? to turn off bold ________________?

S3-EX6

1. Retrieve S3-EX4. Format the main heading and paragraph headings in bold.
2. Save and print the exercise.

S3-EX7

1. Retrieve S3-EX7 from the template, or key the following heading of a resume and save it as S3-EX7:

   CONFIDENTIAL RESUME

   OF

   MARY S. SHARPEN

   <u>Job Objective</u>: To secure a position as a financial analyst with a progressive and innovative company.

2. Revise S3-EX7 by making the entire heading bold.

1. Key S3-DOC4 as a form letter. Position the salutation six lines below the date.

2. When you print a hard copy, check to determine that each block of text to be bold is in bold print.

current date

Operator: Please key HOME REMODELING in bold each time.

Dear Former Subscriber:

FINAL NOTICE center

This is it! This is the last time we'll write you about your HOME REMODELING subscription; therefore, it's the last chance you will have to renew that subscription and get your name back on our active files.

All you have to do is return the enclosed renewal form with your instructions, and we will reinstate your HOME REMODELING subscription immediately.

That's important! When it comes to remodeling a home, it's not how much you do that matters, but how much you know!

No other magazine keeps you "in the know" like HOME REMODELING. Don't miss another issue of HOME REMODELING--the best home remodeling magazine in print. Return the renewal form today.

Sincerely,

Jean Laux-Baker
Circulation Director

Enclosure

S3-DOC2R

1. Revise S3-DOC2 as marked.

2. Print two copies.

current date

Ms. Vickie Westerburg, Head

DEPARTMENTAL AWARDS

The following students have been selected to be recognized at the honors banquet on April 19.

OUTSTANDING OFFICE INFORMATION SYSTEMS MANAGEMENT GRADUATE

Mistie Clarice Presson

OUTSTANDING COMPUTER INFORMATION SYSTEMS GRADUATE

Stewart Sommerfeld

Print in bold

Would you please order plaques (from the same firm that we used last year) to be presented to these students at the banquet.

Also, send both students' banquet reservation forms and ask them to make reservations and attend the banquet. Each may bring one guest.

Paul Ginter, Chair
Honors Committee

doc code

copy Dr. Zander

FORMAT CHANGES—MARGINS, LINE SPACING, AND PAGE LENGTH

Formatting a document involves setting line length (or changing left and right margins), line spacing, and top and bottom page margins. Formats are set when you want to use something other than the default settings.

Formats can be changed for an entire document or part of a document. In order for formats to affect an entire document, the cursor must be positioned at the beginning, before the first character in the document.

Formats can be changed at any point within a document. For example, within a report you could switch from double spacing to single spacing to format enumerated items or a long quotation. You would then reset the format back to double spacing. Format changes are stored with the document when it is saved. Changes in format do not affect any other documents.

List below the steps for making format changes.

FUNCTION	STEPS REQUIRED
Changing from Single to Double Spacing	______________________
	______________________
	______________________
	______________________
	______________________
Changing Left and Right Margins	______________________
	______________________
	______________________
	______________________
	______________________

Changing Top Margins

Changing Bottom Margins

S3-EX8

1. Set the margins at 2". Then key and save the paragraph below.

   ```
   The appearance of a document can be changed by
   changing the margins and spacing.  Because you
   have set 2-inch margins, the line length in this
   paragraph is 4 1/2 inches.
   ```

2. Move the cursor to the beginning of the document. Display the margin command with the display codes function. Delete the margin command. Reset the margins at 2 inches. The new margins should be displayed once again. Note: you may need to strike PgDn or scroll through the document to see the new margins.

3. Move the cursor to the beginning of the document. Delete the margin settings again. Reset the margins for 1 1/2 inches and change to double spacing. Revise the last sentence to read: Because you have set 1 1/2-inch margins, the line length for this paragraph is about 5 1/2 inches.

4. Save the revised document as S3-EX8 and print.

S3-DOC5

1. Key S3-DOC5 as a one-page report. Set line spacing to double-space; use default side margins; begin keying on line 10 by striking the Return key.

2. To indent the paragraphs, strike the Tab key once if default tabs are set every five spaces. If tabs are not preset for five spaces, strike the space bar five times to indent paragraphs.

TIPS TO OPERATOR

- If your default first line is line 7 and you set double spacing at the beginning of the document, you will not be able to begin keying on Line 10. Instead begin on line 11. You will learn later how to change the top margin (first keying line).

DESK TOP ORGANIZATION] center bold

by Don Abernathy, <u>The Secretary</u>, January 1990] center

(Operator: Please key double-spaced as shown.)

QS

Chances are you are one of the millions of office workers who has a personal computer. Chances also are that if you have had that computer for a while now, you have learned that keeping the information in your computer organized cna be quite a challenge.

In order to gain a competitive edge, you^r company may need to consider upgrading it's system of computers to a system of more sophisticated desk top work stations. Desk top organization is a systematic way of sorting desk top documents, folders, ^files, and other icon symbols. It is a system that allows a steady flow and control of information.

The ^computer industry appears to be heading toward ^m ore user-friendly screens, complete with symbols--or icons--that allow you to create and edit documents, write reports and memos, and deliver and recieve this information any where in the world. Keeping all this information organized means becoming well versed in desk top organization.

The ^best place to start is to define, categorize and code every document.

S3-DOC5R

1. Retrieve S3-DOC5 and revise as marked.
2. Use search and replace to replace each occurrence of *desk top* with *desktop*.

TIPS TO OPERATOR

■ Proofread carefully, making sure that *desktop* is one word each time it appears. Also, check that the title remained in all caps and bold after search and replace.

DESK TOP ORGANIZATION

by Don Abernathy, The Secretary, January 1990

Operator: Please make desk top one word each time it appears.

Chances are you're ~~are~~ one of the millions of office workers who has a personal computer. Chances also are that if you've ~~have~~ had that computer for a while now, you have learned that keeping the information in your computer organized can be quite a challenge.

In order to gain a competitive edge, your company may need to seriously consider upgrading its system of computers to a system of more sophisticated desk top workstations. Desk top organization is a systematic way of sorting desk top documents, folders, files, and other icon symbols. It is a system that allows a steady flow and control of information.

move

The computer industry appears to be heading toward more user-friendly screens, complete with symbols--or icons--that allow you to create and edit documents, write reports and memos, and deliver and receive this information anywhere in the world. Keeping all this information organized means becoming well versed in "desk top organization."

The best place to start is to define, categorize, and code every document.

Key S3-DOC6 as a one-page report. Format the report as follows:

Left margin:	1 1/2"
Right margin:	1"
Top margin:	1"
Spacing:	DS

DS > Office Lighting: Illuminating the Bottom Line } Center bold in all caps
Modern Office Technology, March 1990 } Center
QS

If you're involved in office management and make or influence decisions about lighting, ask yourself this question: Why did we install lighting in here in the first place? The answer is basic: So people can get their work done. Keep that answer firmly in mind before you allow anyone to tamper with the lighting for any purpose whatsoever, because changing the lighting can change people's ability to get the work done. It can affect productivity and/or error rates, either one of which can have substantial impact on the bottom line... not to mention ripple effects: e.g., better productivity can shorten turnaround time, which can enhance customer satisfaction and create a superior competitive position. It can also result in more output per unit of input, increasing profitability, and the like.

The National Lighting Bureau recently published a guide titled Office Lighting and Productivity. Its listing of benefits--primary and those derived secondarily--is impressive. The listing includes, in addition to productivity and error rate reduction, quality control, reduced absenteeism, inexpensive space differentiation, and accomodation of spatial changes.

S3-DOC6R

1. Retrieve S3-DOC6 and revise as marked on the printed draft.

2. Check to determine that all revisions were made.

TIPS TO OPERATOR

- For this revision, you will bold existing text, delete an underline, insert text into a centered line, and change existing text to all caps.

- To most efficiently make lower case text upper case, activate the Typeover (or Replace) command. Be sure to exit this command before making other revisions.

OFFICE LIGHTING: ILLUMINATING THE BOTTOM LINE

Excerpt from Modern Office Technology, March 1990

If you're involved in office management and make or influence decisions about lighting, ask yourself this question: Why did we install lighting in here in the first place? The answer is basic: So people can get their work done. It can affect productivity and/or error rates, either one of which can have a substantial impact on the bottom line . . . not to mention ripple effects: e.g., better productivity can shorten turnaround time, which can enhance customer satisfaction and create a superior competitive position. It can also result in more output per unit of input, increasing profitability, and the like.

Delete underline, key in all caps bold

The National Lighting Bureau recently published a guide titled Office Lighting and Productivity. Its listing of benefits--primary and those derived secondarily--is impressive. The listing includes, in addition to productivity and error rate reduction, quality control, reduced absenteeism, inexpensive space differentiation, ~~and~~ accommodation of frequent spatial changes, enhanced business image, effective mood setting, lower utility costs, and improved profitability.

doc code

Reprinted from the March issue of MODERN OFFICE TECHNOLOGY, and copyrighted 1990 by Penton Publishing, subsidiary of Pittway Corporation. → delete underlining, key in italic

S3-DOC7

1. Center the announcement and save it as S3-DOC7.
2. Omit the printed document code at the bottom of the document.
3. Proofread carefully, noting the correct spelling of names.

1½" top margin — 2" side margins

The Student Organizations of the
College of Business Administration
(Center, Bold, Single space, ALL CAPS)

Cordially Invite You to a ← Begin double spacing, center each line

Faculty & Staff Reception (& → and)

on Thursday, November 30, 19--

From 2-4 p.m. (insert p.m. after 2)

at the Alumni Center

Entertained by: (Bold)

Miss Heather Henann, Miss University

Mr. Karl Rubrecht, Pianist

Sponsored by: (Bold)

Collegiate Secretaries International

Pi Omega Pi

Pi Sigma Epsilon

Come and enjoy the food and entertainment!

S3-DOC7R

Retrieve S3-DOC7 and revise as marked.

TIPS TO OPERATOR

- Reveal formatting codes to quickly locate codes to be deleted.
- Check line spacing carefully since the originator prefers parts of the document single spaced and other sections double spaced.

THE STUDENT ORGANIZATIONS OF THE
COLLEGE OF BUSINESS ADMINISTRATION

Cordially Invite You to a

Faculty and Staff Reception

on Thursday, November 30, 19--

From 2 p.m. - 4 p.m.

at the Alumni Center

ENTERTAINED BY: Remove bold

Miss Heather Henann, Miss University

Mr. Karl Rubrecht, Pianist

SS

SPONSORED BY: Remove bold

Collegiate Secretaries International

Pi Omega Pi

Pi Sigma Epsilon

SS

Come and enjoy the food and entertainment!

S3-DOC8

Load S3-DOC8 from the template and proceed to S3-DOC8r or key S3-DOC8 as an advertisement following the format requested.

Word Processing Night Operations Supervisor) Center, all caps, bold

Warrner & Landrieu law firm, located in downtown San Francisco, has an immediate opening for a night operations supervisor in the WP Department.

This person will work Sunday through Thursday, 5 p.m.-1 a.m. The qualified canidate must have strong supervisery experience with a large WP center. Must have excellant written communications skills to interface with all personel. You'll need a good working knowledge of concepts and skills used by the department to include: typing, proofreading, WP and related software. You'll also need the ability to patiently and effectively give and recieve instructions. A professional appearance and attitude are required; a college degree is preferred. Law firm experience helpful, but not required.

You'll find exceptional rewards for your talents--excellent salary and a superior benefits package. For immediate consideration, please send resume to:

Warrner & Landrieu
WP Department
P.O. Box 2102
San Francisco, CA 91343-2102

Center each line, bold
Single space

1½" side and top margins.
DS
Check spelling.

Revise S3-DOC8 as marked on the printed draft. In addition, make these changes: spell out WP to word processing throughout; when WP is the department name, be sure to capitalize. Change side margins to 1-inch.

TIPS TO OPERATOR

- Reveal formatting codes to assist you in making revisions. While revising S3-DOC8, you will use the following commands: search and replace, reset margins, insert and delete text, remove centering commands.
- Double-check requested originator changes to make sure you have completed all of them.

WORD PROCESSING NIGHT OPERATIONS SUPERVISOR

Warrner & Landrieu law firm, located in downtown San Francisco, has an immediate opening for a night operations supervisor in the WP Department.

Operator: Spell out WP to read word processing each time.

Be sure name of department is in initial caps.

This person will work Sunday through Thursday, 5 p.m. - 1 a.m. The qualified candidate must have strong supervisory experience with a large WP center[and] ~~. Must have~~ excellent written communications skills to interface with all personnel. ~~You'll need a~~ [This applicant needs] good working knowledge of concepts and skills used by the department ~~to~~ include[ing]~~:~~ ~~typing~~ [keying], proofreading, WP and ~~related~~ [desktop publishing] software. You~~'ll also need~~ [must have] the ability to patiently and effectively give and receive instructions. A professional appearance and attitude are required; a college degree is preferred. Law firm experience helpful, but not required.

Change side margins to 1"

stet

You~~'ll~~ [will] find exceptional rewards for your talents--excellent salary and a superior benefits package[, including medical/dental and life insurance, and year-end bonus]. For immediate consideration, ~~please~~ send resume to:

Block at left

Warrner & Landrieu
WP Department
P.O. Box 2102
San Francisco, CA 91343-2102

doc code

TABS

Tab settings are used to indent text and align columns in tables. Default tabs, often set every five spaces, can be changed quickly and easily and reset at any point in a document. Tabs can also be cleared individually or all tabs can be removed at once.

You will learn to use other specialized tabs, such as decimal tab, later.

List below the steps for handling tabs.

FUNCTION	STEPS REQUIRED
Set Tabs	______________________________
	______________________________
Clear All Tabs	______________________________
	______________________________
Clear Individual Tabs	______________________________
	______________________________
Reset Default Tabs	______________________________
	______________________________

S3-EX9

1. Clear all tabs. Set tabs 5 and 9 spaces from the left margin.
2. Key and save the following outline as S3-EX9. Space forward once from the left margin to key Roman Numeral I. Key Roman Numeral II at the left margin so that both numerals align.

```
          ADVANCED WORD PROCESSING CONTENTS
 I.  TRAINING OBJECTIVES
     A.  OASIS Project Objectives
     B.  Training Session Objectives        ← 1st Tab
II.  REVIEW OF INTERMEDIATE WORD PROCESSING OPERATIONS
     A.  Revising Primary Format Line
     B.  Creating and Revising Alternate Format Lines
     C.  Copying and Moving Text
         1.  Deleting commands
         2.  Inserting text                 ← 2d Tab
```

S3-DOC9

Key S3-DOC9 following these steps:

1. Center the heading
2. Delete all tabs
3. Set these formats:
   Side margins: 1 1/2"
   Top margin: 2"
4. Set tab at position 50 (10 pitch) or 56 (12 pitch). The tab on some systems is called a Left Align Tab.
5. Key the first entry at the left margin; tab and key the first entry in Column 2, etc.

LISTING OF FIRMS ATTENDING
CPD TRAINING SESSIONS

2" Top margin
1½" Side margins
DS except for heading

Business Careers	MCI
Careers Unlimited	Midland Steel
DDS Telephone	Motor Supplies, Inc.
EGA Computers	Norton and White
Farm Insurance, Inc.	Rogers + Rogers
Gulf-South Transportation	Tel-Monitor
Holiday Homes	Western Credit Corp.
Industrial Linens	Xavier College

S3-DOC10

1. Key S3-DOC10 following these steps:
   a. Center the heading, spacing it as marked.
   b. Delete all tabs.
   c. Set format:

Side margins	1"	
Top margin	2"	
Tabs	10 pitch	12 pitch
	38, 61	45, 73
Line spacing	DS	

   d. Key body of table.
   e. Center the last three lines of the table using the center command.
2. Proofread names very carefully.

TIPS TO OPERATOR

■ If your software requires that you move the cursor to the centering point before you key the center command, you must delete the tabs for the table and reset default tabs or set a tab at the center point.

2" top margin
1" side margins

center bold

International Festival--Opening Ceremonies — all caps

Thursday, March 29, 19--
Burns Theater

DS

Welcome	Alvin Blakely	England
Introduction of Guests	Helga Kruger	Germany
International Song	Henry Cheung	China
Flag Presentation	Elefteri Evgenidis	Greece
International President	Hsin-Ginn Hwang	Taiwan
Ribbon Cutting	Vijaya Tammara Alena Sukova Yvette Benoit	India Czechoslovakia France

DS center each line

Special Entertainment
Food Fair and Cultural Exhibits
Fireworks Display

S3-DOC10R

1. Retrieve S3-DOC10 and revise as marked.
2. Check revisions carefully.

TIPS TO OPERATOR

■ When moving or copying a block of text keyed with tabs, you must be sure to move or copy the tab command along with the text. Note that the text to be copied in S3-DOC10r is a portion of a line; therefore, copy only that part marked but be sure to copy the tab command for correct placement.

INTERNATIONAL FESTIVAL--OPENING CEREMONIES

Burns Theater
Thursday, March 29, 19-- *6 p.m.*

Welcome	Alvin Blakely	England
Introduction of Guests	Helga Kruger	Germany
International Song	Henry Cheung	~~China~~ *Hong Kong*
Flag Presentation	Elefteri Evgenidis	Greece
International President	Hsin-Ginn Hwang	Taiwan
Ribbon Cutting *copy*	Vijaya Tammara	India
	Alena Sukova	Czechoslovakia
	Yvette Benoit	France

single space names in ribbon cutting

Special Entertainment

move Food Fair and Cultural Exhibits

~~Fireworks Display~~ *stet*

RIGHT MARGIN JUSTIFICATION

A **justified right margin** is perfectly aligned, similar to the typeset copy on this page. Justification of right margins is accomplished by the software automatically adding spaces during printing between words or characters to make the lines in a document end at the same point.

Lines that end with a required return, such as the last line of a paragraph, are not justified.

List below the steps for justifying right margins.

FUNCTION	STEPS REQUIRED
Right Margin Justification	______________________
	______________________
	______________________

S3-EX10

1. Retrieve S3-EX4 from your work disk.
2. Print the document with the right margin justified.

S3-DOC11

Key S3-DOC11 as an announcement following originator directions written on the handwritten draft. Note that the right margin is to be justified.

Just a Reminder . . .] Center in all caps, bold

Operator, justify right margin

1½" Revised forms were forwarded to all reporting agencies in March 19-- with the revisions to the Teachers' Retirement System Procedures Manual. Additional forms were mailed in May 19--. Agency personnel should compare the forms in use to those in the manual. Out-of-date forms should be discarded and the most recent revision placed in use. 1"

It is important that agencies use the new application for refund and notice of withholding forms. In most cases, contributions made after June 19-- are taxable when withdrawn unless rolled over into an IRA or another qualified plan. A "Notice of Withholding on Distributions from Annuities and/or Pensions" must accompany the application for refund.

S3-DOC11R

1. Revise S3-DOC11 as marked.
2. Proofread, noting particularly if text is readjusted between new margins.

TIPS TO OPERATOR

- When you revise margin settings for an existing document, you should scroll through the document before printing to make sure the text realigns within the new margins. Although many systems automatically adjust text within the new margins, some systems require that the operator key either an adjust line endings or paginate command.

JUST A REMINDER . . .

make right margin equal to left margin

Revised forms were ~~forwarded~~ sent to all reporting state agencies ~~in~~ March 15, 19--, with ~~the~~ revisions to the <u>Teachers' Retirement System Procedures Manual</u>. Additional forms were mailed ~~in~~ May 6, 19--. ¶ Agency personnel should compare the forms in use to those in the manual. Out-of-date forms should be <u>discarded</u> (bold) and the most recent revision placed in use.

~~It is important that~~ all agencies must use the new Application for Refund and Notice of Withholding forms. In most cases, contributions made after June 30, 19--, are taxable when withdrawn unless rolled over into an IRA or another qualified plan. A "Notice of Withholding on Distributions from Annuities and/or Pensions" must accompany the application for refund.

doc code

S3-DOC12

1. Retrieve S3-DOC5r (saved as S3-DOC5).
2. Revise by justifying the right margin.
3. Print and check the right margin to see if all lines except those ending with a hard return are evenly aligned. Save.
4. Rename the file S3-DOC12. Follow your instructor's directions as to whether you should use the DOS rename command (REN) or use your word processing software document utilities capability for renaming a file.

TIPS TO OPERATOR

- Although many systems will automatically adjust the right margin for justification when the command is given after the document is keyed, some systems will require the pagination command.
- Also, if any format changes were made within the document, the right margin justification command may have to be keyed at each format change.

DESKTOP ORGANIZATION

by Don Abernathy, <u>The Secretary</u>, January 1990

Chances are you're one of the millions of office workers who has a personal computer. Chances are also that if you've had that computer for a while now, you have learned that keeping the information in your computer organized can be quite a challenge.

In order to gain a competitive edge, your company may need to seriously consider upgrading its system of computers to a system of more sophisticated desktop workstations.

The computer industry appears to be heading toward more user-friendly screens, complete with symbols--or icons--that allow you to create and edit documents, write reports and memos, and deliver and receive this information anywhere in the world. Keeping all this information organized means becoming well versed in "desktop organization."

Desktop organization is a systematic way of sorting desktop documents, folders, files, and other icon symbols. It is a system that allows a steady flow and control of information. The best place to start is to define, categorize, and code every document.

1. Retrieve S3-DOC6r (saved as S3-DOC6).
2. Justify the right margin. Print and save.
3. Rename the file S3-DOC13.

(See S3-DOC12 Directions for Tips to Operator.)

OFFICE LIGHTING: ILLUMINATING THE BOTTOM LINE

Excerpt from Modern Office Technology, March 1990

If you're involved in office management and make or influence decisions about lighting, ask yourself this question: Why did we install lighting in here in the first place? The answer is basic: **So people can get their work done.** It can affect productivity and/or error rates, either one of which can have a substantial impact on the bottom line . . . not to mention ripple effects: e.g., better productivity can shorten turnaround time, which can enhance customer satisfaction and create a superior competitive position. It can also result in more output per unit of input, increasing profitability, and the like.

The National Lighting Bureau recently published a guide titled OFFICE LIGHTING AND PRODUCTIVITY. Its listing of benefits--primary and those derived secondarily--is impressive. The listing includes, in addition to productivity and error rate reduction, quality control, reduced absenteeism, inexpensive space differentiation, accommodation of frequent spatial changes, enhanced business image, effective mood setting, lower utility costs, and improved profitability.

doc code

DELETE FILES

Using the DOS delete (DEL) command or your word processing software document utilities capability, delete the following files from your disk:

S3-DOC3
S3-DOC4

Check your directory listing to verify that these two files were deleted.

INDENT

Indent, also known as a temporary margin, is used when more than one line of text needs to be indented from the left margin and/or right margin.

> The indent feature indents to the first tab stop, as in this paragraph. A required return on most systems will terminate the temporary margin and return to the original left margin.

List the steps for indenting text below.

FUNCTION	STEPS REQUIRED
Indent from Left Margin	______________________
	______________________
	______________________
	______________________
	______________________
Indent from Right Margin	______________________
	______________________
	______________________
	______________________
	______________________

S3-EX11

1. Key and save the following as S3-EX11.

```
This manual is designed to aid the supervisor in
solving  performance and behavioral problems.
Primary objectives of this manual follow:
1. To present some "human relation" ideas to
supervisors that they might find useful in raising
the level of morale in their department.
2. To provide guidelines for action that will avoid
the removal or dismissal of employees.
```

2. Revise S3-EX11 as indicated.

This manual is designed to aid the supervisor in solving performance and behavioral problems. Primary objectives of this manual follow:

1. To present some "human relation" ideas to supervisors that they might find useful in raising the level of morale in their department.

2. To provide guidelines for action that will avoid the removal or dismissal of employees.

S3-EX12

1. Key and save the following itinerary as S3-EX12.

ITINERARY FOR ROBERT ASHTON

July 25	Pick up Mr. Schmidt at airport at 9:30 a.m. and proceed to the main bank downtown.
July 26	Meet with Chamber of Commerce officials for breakfast meeting at 7:30 a.m.

2. Revise as indicated below.

ITINERARY FOR ROBERT ASHTON

July 25, 9:30 a.m.	**Pick up Mr. Schmidt at airport ~~at 9:30 a.m.~~ and proceed to the main bank downtown.**
July 26, 7:30 a.m.	**Meet with Chamber of Commerce officials for breakfast meeting. ~~at 7:30 a.m.~~**

S3-DOC14

Key S3-DOC14 following the proofreaders' marks and originator notations on the rough draft.

Use the indent command to indent the itemized paragraphs so that the text will align as marked.

TIPS TO OPERATOR

- To align numbers at the period, space once before numbers 1 through 9.

```
CINS 101 PERSONAL COMPUTER OPERATIONS

Purpose:  Personal Computer Operations has been designed to help
the student develop skills setting up and operating IBM PC-
compatible computers, keying dos commands, organizing file
directories, using the dos line editor, and working with
Mocrosoft Windows.

Course Objectives:  The student should be able to do the
following:

1.   Define, describe and explain hardware, software, floppy
     disks, and operating systems related to personal computers.

2.   Use the describe the functions of date, time, diskcopy and
     format commands.

3.   Use the basic DOS commands, DOS device names and DOS print
commands.

4.   Make directories and subdirectories, save files in
directories and remove directories.

5.   Use DOS redirection, filters and pipe command.

6.   Create and revise standard test files using DOS line editor
EDLIN.

7.   Use the local area network, MAIL and CHAT features.

8.   Use a mouse as well as the keyboard to use microsoft
windows.

9.   Delete, copy and rename files.

10.  Create and use batch files.
```

1. Revise S3-DOC14 as marked.

2. Proofread revisions carefully, especially itemized paragraph numbers and the spacing between paragraphs.

CINS 101 PERSONAL COMPUTER OPERATIONS

Delete underscore — Bold

Purpose: Personal Computer Operations was designed to help the student develop skills setting up and operating IBM PC-compatible computers, keying DOS commands, organizing file directories, using the DOS line editor, and working with Microsoft Windows. DS ¶

Delete underscore — Bold

Course Objectives: The student should be able to do the following:

1. Define, describe and explain hardware, software, ~~floppy~~ disks, and operating systems related to personal computers.

2. Use ~~and describe~~ the ~~functions of~~ commands: DATE, TIME, DISKCOPY and FORMAT ~~commands~~.

3. Use the basic DOS commands, DOS device names and DOS print commands.

4. Make directories and subdirectories, change directories, save files in directories, and delete and remove directories.

6 ~~5~~. Use DOS redirection, filters and pipe commands.

7 ~~6~~. Create and edit ~~revise~~ standard text (ASC II) files using the DOS line editor EDLIN.

8 ~~7~~. access ~~Use~~ the local area network, and operate MAIL and CHAT features.

10 ~~8~~. Use a mouse as well as the keyboard to manipulate ~~operate~~ Microsoft Windows.

move 5 ~~9~~. Delete, copy and rename files.

move 9 ~~10~~. Create and use batch files.

doc code

Key S3-DOC15 from the handwritten draft.

The ACCA Variable Contract Account-5
Notice of Annual Meeting--May 1, 19--) Center

justify right margin
1" margins

DS

You are hereby notified that pursuant to the Rules and Regulations of the ACCA Variable Contract Account-5 (VCA-5), the Annual Meeting of persons having voting rights in respect to VCA-5 will be held in the office of the ACCA Asset Management Company, Inc. at 1505 Meidinger Tower, Louisville, Kentucky, on Wednesday, May 1, 19--, at 10 a.m. (EDT) for the following purposes:

SS but DS between items

1. To elect the members of the ACCA VCA-5 Committee who shall serve until the next Annual Meeting of persons having VCA-5 voting rights.

2. To ratify or reject the selection of Capareti & Erlanger as the independent public accountant for VCA-5.

3. To transact such other business as may come before the meeting in accordance with the rules and regulations of VCA-5.

4. To approve or reject an amendment to the Rules and Regulations governing VCA-5 to include the ACCA Company as a person having voting rights.

DS

You are requested to specify your choices and sign, date and return the proxy as soon as possible in the enclosed self-addressed envelope, which requires no postage. If you attend, you may revoke the proxy and vote in person.

By order of the Committee

Secretary to the Committee

Revise S3-DOC15 as marked, changing each occurrence of VCA-5 to Variable Contract Account-5.

TIPS TO OPERATOR

- By completing S3-DOC15 and S3-DOC15r, you will have reviewed all commands studied except for copying text and deleting tabs.

THE ACCA VARIABLE CONTRACT ACCOUNT-5

Notice of Annual Meeting--May 1, 19--

Operator: change all VCA-5 to Variable Contract Account-5.

~~You are hereby notified that~~ according ~~pursuant~~ to the Rules and Regulations of ~~the~~ ACCA Variable Contract Account-5 ~~(VCA-5)~~, the Annual Meeting of persons having voting rights in respect to VCA-5 will be held in the office of the ACCA Asset Management Company, Inc. at 1505 Meidinger Tower, Louisville, Kentucky, on Wednesday, May 1, 19--, at 10 a.m. (EDT) for the following purposes:

SS

1. To elect the members of the ACCA VCA-5 Committee to ~~who shall~~ serve until the next Annual Meeting. ~~of persons having VCA-5 voting rights.~~

3 ~~2~~. To ratify or reject the selection of Capareti & Erlanger as the independent public accountant for VCA-5.

4 ~~3~~. To transact such other business as may properly come before the meeting in accordance with the rules and regulations of VCA-5.

move 2 ~~4~~. To approve or reject an amendment to the Rules and Regulations governing VCA-5 to include the ~~ACCA~~ Company as a person having voting rights.

~~You are requested to~~ Please specify your choices~~, and~~ sign, date and return the enclosed proxy by April 20 ~~as soon as possible~~ in the enclosed ~~self-addressed~~ envelope, which requires no postage. If you attend, you may revoke the proxy and vote in person.

SS

By order of the Committee

Secretary to the Committee

doc code

Enclosures

S3-DOC16

Key S3-DOC16 as a simplified memo from the rough draft or load S3-DOC16 from the template and revise as directed in S3-DOC16r.

TIPS TO OPERATOR

- Be sure to end the underlining command before the punctuation that follows the underlined word.

Current date

All Employee s

Reference Materials Available

The library in the Center for Business & Economic Research is open to all employees and the general public. The materials listed below are availalbe for you r use.

U.S. GOVERNMENT PUBLICATIONS--from the Departments of Commerce, Energy, Interior, Justice, Labor, State, Transportation , and Treasury. Some examples are CPI Detailed Report, County Business Patterns, Current Wage & ~~and~~ Development, and Economics Indicators. These materials include microfiche, diskettes , and tape data.

PERIODICALS--Magazines (e.g., American Demographics, Consumer Reports, Insight, Personal Publishing, PC World, and PC Computing); annual reports; newspapers (e.g., The Wall Street Journal, Barron's, The Chronicle, and PC Week); and journals (e.g., The Academy of Management Review and Journal, The Quarterly Review of Economics & Business , and The Dallas Federal Economic Review).

DATA RESOURCES--The center has access to several electronic databases through various "gateways". You are invited to discuss your database search needs with Ms. Cathy Ivanov.

The center invites you to take advantage of the services it ~~we~~ offer s. If you have questions or comments , please call me.

Delorise Kvaternik, Secretary

S3-DOC16R

Revise S3-DOC16 as marked.

TIPS TO OPERATOR

- This exercise reviews inserting and deleting text and underlining commands, bolding text, justifying the right margin of an existing document, and using the indent command to indent selected paragraphs.
- The paragraphs are indented for emphasis.

Current date

Operator, justify right margin

All Company Employees

REFERENCE MATERIALS AVAILABLE

The library in the Center for Business & Economic Research is open to all employees and the general public. The materials listed below are available for your use.

Delete underscore, then bold

U.S. GOVERNMENT PUBLICATIONS--from the Departments of Commerce, Energy, Interior, Justice, Labor, State, Transportation, and Treasury. Some examples are CPI Detailed Report, County Business Patterns, Current Wage & Development, and Economic Indicators. These materials include microfiche, diskettes, and tape data.

PERIODICALS--magazines (e.g., American Demographics, Consumer Reports, Insight, Personal Publishing, PC World, and PC Computing); ~~annual reports;~~ newspapers (e.g., The Wall Street Journal, Barron's, The Chronicle, and PC Week); and journals (e.g., The Academy of Management Review and Journal, The Quarterly Review of Economics & Business, and The Dallas Federal Economic Review).

DATA RESOURCES--The Center has access to many electronic databases through various "gateways." You are invited to discuss your database search needs with Ms. Cathy Ivanov.

The Center invites you to take advantage of the services it offers. If you have questions or comments, please call me at extension 1130.

Delorise Kvaternik, Secretary

doc code

insert: REFERENCES--publishing guides, statistical abstracts, data books, and various economics, business, and statistical references.

SOFTWARE FUNCTION SUMMARY

List the commands for the following:

Display instructional codes ____________________

Center ____________________

Underline ____________________

Underline existing text ____________________

Bold ____________________

Bold existing text ____________________

Change Formats ____________________

Change and set side margins ____________________

Change line spacing ____________________

Change page length ____________________

Tabs ____________________

Set tabs ____________________

Clear tabs ____________________

Clear individual tabs ____________________

Right margin justification ____________________

Indent ____________________

SECTION 4

SETTING SPECIALIZED TABS AND FORMATTING TABLES

Functions

- Left and Right Align Tabs
- Center Tab
- Decimal Tab
- Leader Tab
- Tables/Column Layout
- Moving and Deleting Columns and Rows in Tables

LEFT AND RIGHT ALIGN TABS

Left align tab, the most commonly used tab, aligns the left edge of the text with the tab stop.

Right align tab aligns the right edge of text with the tab stop. When the right align tab is set, keyed information will back up from the tab and will end where the tab is actually set. The right align tab is used primarily for keying whole numbers (without decimals).

	Left Tab	Right Tab
Left align tab	Monday	
	Tuesday	
	Wednesday	
Right align tab		Monday
		Tuesday
		Wednesday

List below the steps for setting left and right align tabs.

FUNCTION	STEPS REQUIRED
Left Align Tab	______________________________
	______________________________
Right Align Tab	______________________________
	______________________________

S4-EX1

1. Set 2-inch side margins.
2. Clear all tabs.
3. Set a left align tab at position 40.
4. Key *January* at the left margin. Press the tab, key *Garnet,* and press RETURN. Key the rest of the table in this manner and save it as S4-EX1. Notice that the left edge of Column 2 aligns at the tab.

January	Garnet
February	Amethyst
March	Aquamarine

S4-EX2

1. Move the cursor to the beginning of the first column.
2. Revise S4-EX1 by deleting the left align tab.
3. Set a right align tab at position 50.

January	Garnet
February	Amethyst
March	Aquamarine

S4-EX3

1. Clear all tabs.
2. Set a left align tab at 15 and a right align tab at 60.
3. Tab and key *First Quarter Profits*, tab, and key *$500,000*. Notice that the text in Column 2 moves to the left of the cursor as you key it.
4. Key and save this table as S4-EX3.

First Quarter Profits	$500,000
Second Quarter Profits	50,500
Third Quarter Profits	195,960
Fourth Quarter Profits	233,490

S4-DOC1

1. Set the following formats for S4-DOC1:

   1 1/2-inch side margins

   2-inch top margin

   left align tab 7 spaces to the *left* of the right margin

   block column heads at the left

   single space items; double space between them

2. Key Column 1 at the left margin. Press the space bar three times for indented items within Column 1.

3. Check spelling, proofread, and print.

TIPS TO OPERATOR

- Since this table is simple with only two columns, most word processing operators will delete all tabs and set a left align tab for the second column rather than using any column or table feature of their software. Do not set a tab for the first column since it begins at the left margin.

SOUTHLAND TOURS*

DS

Complete New Orleanst tours	Length
Nightclub tours includes drinks and admissions and tips	4 hours
Southern Plantations	6 hours
Garden Districk tour	3 hours
A day at the races	6 5 hours
Dining in New Orleans includes tips and taxes	3 hours
Golf and tennis tour	3 hours
A day in New Orleans	5 hours

1½" 1½"

*Rates will be furnished when the size of your group is determined.

S4-DOC1R

1. Revise S4-DOC1 as marked. Save, using the same file name.

2. Print.

SOUTHLAND TOURS*

Complete New Orleans Tours	Length
Nightclub Tours (includes drinks, admissions and tips)	4 hours
Southern Plantations (includes lunch)	5 ~~6~~ hours
Garden District Tour	3 hours
A Day at the Races (includes lunch)	6 hours
Dining in New Orleans (includes tips and taxes)	3 hours
Golf and Tennis Tour	3 hours
Antiquing in New Orleans	3 hours
A Day in New Orleans (includes lunch)	4 ~~5~~ hours

*Rates will be furnished when the size of your group and times of tours are ~~is~~ determined.

doc code

S4-DOC2

1. Set the following formats for S4-DOC2:

   1-inch side margins
   1 1/2-inch top margin
   right align tab at right margin
   single spacing

2. Key Column 1 at the left margin, press the Tab key, and key Column 2 at the right align tab. Check spelling, proofread, and print.

TIPS TO OPERATOR

- With most word processing software, you should key the table title before deleting and setting tabs.

- When setting the right align tab at the right margin, set the tab **one** space to the left of the right margin; some systems will not recognize a tab set on or outside the right margin.

- For indented items strike the space bar three times rather than setting a tab.
- To make the total line, use the underline feature of your software, not the underline key.
- The total lines must be as long as the longest item in the column excluding the $. To lengthen the line, key enough spaces before the number to produce the desired length. For example, to key the total line below **17** to extend over **51,004,** strike the space bar 4 times before keying **17**. If you have already keyed the number (**17**) and then want to add the underline, position the cursor on the **1,** strike the space bar as many times as needed, and then complete the steps for underlining existing text.

TRISLER, LEE & SAUNIER, INC.

Assets
December 31, 19--
($ amounts in thousands

Cash from operations	
Net income (loss)	$12,416
Noncash charges included in net income:	
Depreciation, depletion and amortzation	29,804
Amortization of restricted stock	517
Deferred income tax	6,271
Cash provided by operations	49,008
Cash from Other Sources	
Sales and retirements of properties and equipmenbt	237
Deferred revenues	(94)
Accounts recievable	(1,814)
Inventories	(474)
Accounts payable and accrue expense	(1,084)
Foriegn translation gain	1,473
Other items--net	(1,765)
Cash available before financing activities	45,487
Financing Activities	
Additions to debt	5,500
Issuance of common stock	17
Total cash available	51,004

CENTER TAB

The *center tab* is used to center text around a specified point. Center tab is most often used to center text in a column or to center headings over columns of text.

List the steps for setting the center tab.

FUNCTION	STEPS REQUIRED
Center Tab	______________________________
	______________________________
	______________________________

S4-EX4

1. Set a center tab at space 42 and set line spacing to double. Key the document, returning at the end of each line. In most software you will key a center command for each line. Save the announcement as S4-EX4.

```
             You are invited
               to attend
    a demonstration of the latest
          dictation systems
            at 6:00 p.m.
       Saturday, June 9, 19--
            Blackhawk Room
```

S4-EX5

1. Clear all tabs.
2. Center the heading over the longest line in the column using the center tab.
3. Set a left tab at position 20 to key the column.
4. Key and save this exercise as S4-EX5.

```
    Date
January 6
February 26
February 28
```

S4-EX6

1. Set 1-inch side margins.
2. Clear all tabs.
3. Center the headings for each column over the longest line using the center tab.
4. Set a left align tab for Column 2 at position 40.
5. Key Column 1 at left margin.
6. Save this exercise as S4-EX6.

Staff	Location
R. Vanegas	Monroe, Louisiana
K. Clifford	Phoenix, Arizona
T. Avent	Los Angeles, California
R. White	Seattle, Washington

S4-DOC3

1. Format S4-DOC3 to print at the top left quarter of standard-size paper by inputting the following settings:

   1-inch top margin
   default side margins*
   center tab at 21 on the 10-pitch scale or 25 on the 12-pitch scale
   (if using another point size or proportional fonts, you must determine where to set the center tab)

2. Key enough returns to leave the desired blank space between sections as noted on the handwritten copy.

3. Print and fold the hard copy into quarters; check for proper placement. Make any adjustments needed to improve placement and reprint.

4. Using a paper cutter or scissors, cut the program on the fold lines.

TIPS TO OPERATOR

- *Since you will key text from a center tab setting, side margin settings are not needed.

- Any text keyed at a center tab setting will automatically center from that point. (If you use the centering command, text will center between side margins.)

1" top margin

EMPLOYEE RECOGNITION BANQUET

½"

CRANE + CRANE COMPANY
West Coast Division

1"

The Chateau Restaurant
910 South Broadway
Tacoma, Washington

½"

Friday, May 15, 19--
7:00 p.m.

DECIMAL TAB

A *decimal tab* aligns columns of numbers at the decimal position. The decimal tab feature causes the computer to search for decimals and place all numbers keyed before the decimal to the left and all numbers keyed after the decimal to the right.

List below the steps for using decimal tabs.

FUNCTION	STEPS REQUIRED
Decimal Tab	______________________________
	______________________________
	______________________________

S4-EX7

1. Clear all tabs.
2. Set a decimal tab at position 25.
3. Key the following column of figures using the decimal tab and save it as S4-EX7.

```
100.00
 20.50
369.375
 96.20
240.125
```

S4-EX8

1. Set 1-inch side margins.
2. Clear all tabs.
3. Set a decimal tab at position 60.
4. Key the first column at the left margin, tab, and key Column 2 and save this as S4-EX8.

```
Arizona          16.3%
Nevada           22.0%
California       18.2%
Utah              1.9%
Washington       26.0%
Oregon           13.1%
```

5. Revise S4-EX8 as indicated on the following page. Remember to use the center tab for column headings.

State	Percent
Arizona	16.3%
Nevada	22.0%
California	18.2%
~~Utah~~ Arkansas	~~1.9%~~ 12.6%
Washington	26.0%
Oregon	13.1%

S4-DOC4

1. Key S4-DOC4 as a two-column table. Set a decimal align tab (command) for the second column three spaces to the left of the right margin.
2. Format: 1 1/2-inch top margin
   2-inch side margins
   single space

Cole & Killingsworth, Inc.
Pricing Schedule
Effective January 1, 19--

The items listed below are priced per unit for educational purposes. A 25 percent discount is extended for 12 or more identical orders.

Disk mailers #9921-x	$ 1.25
Letter-size swivel arm #8731-x	46.75
Black vinyl static mat #5342-x	140.00
Minifloppy file #1144	35.75
3½" disk HD, 2MB	5.40
5¼" disk 2D, 320K bytes, DS/DD	3.99
101 Enhanced Keyboard cover	21.95
Staticide liquid cleaner (32 oz.)	4.95
CP-50 polyester glare shield	49.95
Power strip #4543	29.50

S4-DOC4R

1. Revise S4-DOC4 as marked, making the necessary format changes.
2. Carefully proofread all stock numbers and prices.

TIPS TO OPERATOR

- A correction for the $ sign must be keyed as a result of moving text.

COLE & KILLINGSWORTH, INC.

Pricing Schedule
Effective January 1, 19--

The items listed below are priced per unit for educational purposes. A 25 percent discount is extended for 12 or more identical orders. *justify*

move to top / *move* / *DS*

Disk mailers #9921-x	$ 1.25
Letter-size swivel arm #8731-x	46.75
Black vinyl static mat #5342-x	140.00
~~Minifloppy file #1144~~	~~35.75~~
3 1/2" disk HD, 2MB	5.40
5 1/4" disk 2D, 320K bytes, DS/DD	3.99
101 Enhanced Keyboard cover	21.95
Staticide liquid cleaner (32 oz.)	4.95
CP-50 polyester glare shield	49.95
Power strip #4543	29.50
Silver mouse mat #8025	*9.90*

doc code

Desktop halogen lamp 127.00

LEADER TAB

Leader tabs automatically align dot leaders (periods) between text and the next tab stop. If the software has this function, it automatically inserts the leaders.

If your software does not automatically align leaders, you can manually key leaders by striking the period followed by a space enough times to join two columns (make sure the leaders align vertically). For example, the following utilizes leaders between columns one and two:

Cost of software	$1,000
Cost of hardware	3,000
Cost of communication	300

List the steps below for setting a leader tab.

FUNCTION	STEPS REQUIRED
Leader tab	______________________________
	______________________________
	______________________________

S4-EX9

1. Set 2-inch margins.
2. Clear all tabs.
3. Set a left align leader tab at space 50.
4. Key the following exercise and save it as S4-EX9.

Leader Tab

President	Nancy McCarthy
Vice President	Estella Brown
Secretary.	John Ball
Treasurer.	Bonnie Kline

S4-EX10

1. Set 1-inch margins.
2. Center the heading.
3. Clear all tabs.
4. Set a right align leader tab at space 60.
5. Key the following document and save it as S4-EX10.

TABLE OF CONTENTS

Chapter 1	Page 3
Chapter 2	Page 10
Chapter 3	Page 18
Chapter 4	Page 25

1. Format S4-DOC5 as two columns joined with leaders. Set a right align leader tab (if available on your system) one space to the left of the right margin. (If your software does not provide a leader tab, set a right align tab and manually key the leaders.)

2. Format: 1 1/2-inch side margins
   2-inch top margin
   single spacing

Contents

S4-DOC6

1. Format S4-DOC6 in two columns with the second column aligned at the right. Center section headings.*
2. Format: 1-inch side margins
   1 1/2-inch top margin
   single spacing

TIPS TO OPERATOR

- At the point in the document where leaders are requested, change the right align tab to a right align leader tab.
- *If the centering feature of your software requires a tab setting (i.e., you must strike the tab key to the center point before you key the center command), set a center tab for keying section headings. When you tab to that point, text will automatically center.
- DO NOT SET A CENTER TAB if your software automatically centers text between the side margins when the center command is given at the left margin.

COLLEGIATE SECRETARIES INTERNATIONAL (CSI) center

A DIVISION OF PROFESSIONAL SECRETARIES INTERNATIONAL (PSI) center

Central State University Chapter center

HONORING GRADUATING STUDENTS center

Miss Suzanne Scruggs	Mr. Joe Lightfoot
Ms. Gina Desouza	Miss Angelique Boyce
Miss Gretchen Bell	Ms. Dorothea Davis
Miss Carolus De la Salle	Mr. Benjamin Begnaud

CHAPTER OFFICERS center

President . . . . Ms. Shannon Zametto
Vice President - Programs . . . . Mr. Stelios Nicolaou
Vice President - Membership . . . . Miss Yolanda Gallardo
Secretary . . . . Mrs. Jana Bobo-Pesnell
Treasurer . . . . Mr. Karl Williams
Historian . . . . Miss Mei Yean Liew
Advisor . . . . Dr. J. R. Martinez

May 15, 19-- center

TABLES/COLUMN LAYOUT

Documents such as financial reports, budgets, and other statistical material presented in columns can be prepared easily with the tables or column layout feature available with many word processing software packages. Tables can be formatted using tab settings determined by the user; however, multicolumn material can be prepared and revised faster and easier using the tables feature. Tables must be created with a tables feature if columns are to be deleted, moved, copied, or inserted.

Multicolumn tables produced with word processing systems such as WordPerfect 4.2 and 5.0 as well as DisplayWrite 3 and 4 are formatted using tab settings. (For *text* columns, WordPerfect and DisplayWrite offer newspaper and parallel columns features in which margins are set for each column. Do not confuse those features with tables.) Some new versions of word processing software such as WordPerfect 5.1, however, offer a tables feature using the terminology and format of a spreadsheet. The user works with *rows*, *columns*, and *cells*.

Rows are horizontal lines of data. Columns are vertical lines of data. A cell is the intersection of a column and a row; a cell may be as small as one character or as large as a page.

Each cell and column can be formatted with center, left, right, or decimal align commands. Other attributes such as bold, change font, shading, and justification can be set for each cell or column. The WordPerfect 5.1 default of double-ruled lines around the table and single-ruled lines that separate each cell can be removed, if desired.

Although the tables or column layout features of each software package use different terminology and procedures, similarities exist. The following steps (not necessarily in the same order) may be completed when creating tables with numerical data or a combination of numerical and text data with the tables or column layout feature:

1. After selecting the Columns or Tables feature, the user must define the table format by identifying the number of columns and rows. Some software will require that the user identify the desired width (number of characters) in each column.

2. The command for alignment (center, right, left, decimal) should be selected for each column; these commands are typically offered in a menu. The appropriate command should also be selected for individual cells such as column heads.

3. If columns must be different widths, the default widths of each column and cell may be changed. (Text keyed within a cell will automatically wrap.)

4. After defining the table format, most software will require that the user exit to another screen before keying the data.

   The documents following this explanation can be formatted using operator-determined tabs; however, a tables/column layout feature should be used if available on your software.

   In the following space, write the commands to format a table using the tables/column layout of your software, if available. If the listed step is not necessary with your software, omit it.

FUNCTION	STEPS REQUIRED
Tables/Column Layout	____________________
Enter Table Feature	____________________
Set Number of Columns	____________________
Set Number of Rows	____________________
Set Column Width	____________________
Set Cell Width	____________________
Alignment Commands	
	Center ____________________
	Right ____________________
	Left ____________________
	Decimal ____________________
Add Double-Ruled Line	____________________
Add Single-Ruled Line	____________________
Delete Ruled Line	____________________
Delete All Ruled Lines	____________________
Exit Table Feature	____________________

S4-DOC7

1. Key S4-DOC7 as a three-column ruled table using the tables feature of your software, if available. Set the following tabs (commands) for each column: center for each column heading; left align for Column 2; and right align for Column 3.*

2. Format: 1 1/2-inch top and side margins
   single spacing

3. For the ruled lines, use the underline key on your keyboard. (In WordPerfect 5.1, Tables offers a Lines feature for creating ruled lines.) The line spacing before and after the ruled lines is marked for you.

TIPS TO OPERATOR

■ *Some word processing software packages do not set tabs in their tables feature; however, the user must determine how each column is to be aligned—right, left, center, decimal—and key the appropriate commands.

Qualifying Transpacific Flights

Origin] center	Destination] center	DS Flight SS
Minneapolis/St. Paul	Tokyo	DS 7
Tokyo	Minneapolis/St. Paul	8
Seattle/Tacoma	Seoul	30
Seoul	Seattle/Tacoma	31
Detroit	Seoul	35
Seoul	Detroit	36
Seattle/Tacoma	Hong Kong	65/75
Hong Kong	Seattle/Tacoma	52/62 SS

S4-DOC8

1. Key S4-DOC8 as a two-column ruled table using the tables feature of your software.

2. Align Column 1 at the right and Column 2 at the decimal. Since the Column 1 heading is much wider than the column, the right align tab (command) should be set about 14 spaces from the left margin so that the column is centered below the heading.

3. Format: 2-inch top margin
   2-inch side margins
   single spacing

TIPS TO OPERATOR

- The tables feature of most software automatically determines the number of spaces between columns. If you want fewer spaces between the two columns, you will have to make the side margins slightly wider, i.e., set 2.25-inch margins.

Refund Based on Electricity Actually Used
During Past Year

Refund factor of $.002201268 per kwh

Total kwh used in 19--	Refund
500	$ 1.10
1,000	2.20
2,000	4.40
5,000	11.01
10,000	22.01
12,000	26.42
15,000	33.02
20,000	44.03
30,000	66.04
50,000	110.06
100,000	220.13

S4-DOC9

1. Format and key S4-DOC9 as a three-column table using the tables feature of your software.*
2. Format: 2-inch top margin
   1-inch side margins
   single spacing

TIPS TO OPERATOR

- *This document will be revised by moving a column; therefore, the table must be keyed using the tables feature of your software. (Columns can be moved only if they have been formatted as columns within a table.)
- The kinds of column tabs (commands) needed for each column will no longer be identified for you.

FELLOWES & SONS, INC.

CONDENSED INCOME STATEMENT

Amts. in millions, except per share	1991	1990
SALES	$3,667.5	$3,122.7
Income before taxes	97.5	105.3
Income taxes	29.6	35.6
Income from continuing operations	67.9	69.7
Income from discontinued operations	16.7	0.0
NET INCOME	84.6	69.7
EARNINGS PER SHARE OF COMMON STOCK		
Primary earnings per share		
Continuing operations	$ .51	$ 1.50
Discontinued operations	.18	0.00
	$ .69	$ 1.50

MOVING AND DELETING COLUMNS AND ROWS IN TABLES

Columns and rows in multicolumn documents that are formatted with the tables or column layout feature may be easily moved or deleted. To modify the table format, the operator typically must access the table editor by selecting Tables or Column Layout and Edit. The column or row to be deleted or moved is identified (usually with a block command); then the command to delete, move, or copy is keyed. (The commands block and move/delete may be reversed with some software such as DisplayWrite 4.) After a column or row has been deleted from a table, another command to edit the number of columns or rows in the table or to adjust the remaining columns between the margins must be given.

Rows (but not columns) may be easily deleted and moved even if formatted with operator-set tabs rather than the tables feature.

In the space below, write the commands to move and delete columns and rows, if available with your software.

FUNCTION	STEPS REQUIRED
Move and Delete Columns and Rows	
Edit Table	______________________
Move Column Within Table	______________________
	______________________
	______________________
Delete Column	______________________
Move Row	______________________
Delete Row	______________________
Adjust Table	______________________
	______________________
Exit Edit Table	______________________

S4-DOC9R

1. Revise S4-DOC9 by moving Column 3 into the Column 2 position.

2. Verify that all data in the columns were moved correctly. Always check to see that the column headings were moved with the columns.

TIPS TO OPERATOR

- When moving (transposing) two adjacent columns, move right to left, i.e., block the right column for moving. Most software will not accept the move command of left to right for two adjacent columns.

FELLOWES & SONS, INC.

CONDENSED INCOME STATEMENT

Amts. in millions, except per share	1991	1990
SALES	$3,667.5	$3,122.7
Income before taxes	97.5	105.3
Income taxes	29.6	35.6
Income from continuing operations	67.9	69.7
Income from discontinued operations	16.7	0.0
NET INCOME	84.6	69.7
EARNINGS PER SHARE OF COMMON STOCK		
Primary earnings per share		
Continuing operations	$ .51	$ 1.50
Discontinued operations	.18	0.00
	$ .69	$ 1.50

doc code

S4-DOC10

1. Format S4-DOC10 as a five-column table setting the necessary align tabs (commands) using the tables feature of your software.* Set 1-inch side margins, a 1 1/2-inch top margin, and single spacing.

2. The braced heading (Labor) is centered over the last three columns.

3. Carefully proofread all numbers.

TIPS TO OPERATOR

- *If you are using software that requires that you identify the number of columns and rows in the table as you format it, count only **one row** for the column heads although two columns have three-line headings. The words in the headings will wrap to the next line in the same cell. (All the other text lines should be counted as rows.)

- Remember that column heads align at the bottom.

RATING SMALL BUSINESSES IN
ARKANSAS, LOUISIANA, AND MISSISSIPPI

		Labor		
State	Year	Average Weekly Wage	% Union	Value Added Per Worker ($000/yr)
National Median	1988	$ 325	24	$46.6
	1989	348	24	40.1
	1990	380	25	43.7
Arkansas	1988	$ 256	17	$ 38.4
	1989	270	17	39.3
	1990	300	17	38.9
Louisiana	1988	375	17	71.1
	1989	387	17	70.3
	1990	408	17	77.8
Mississippi	1988	255	16	45.8
	1989	267	16	49.0
	1990	289	16	50.1

S4-DOC10R

1. Revise S4-DOC10 by deleting a column, inserting two rows, and deleting four rows.
2. Adjust the table between the margins.*

TIPS TO OPERATOR

- *Word processing software packages vary significantly in how this adjustment is accomplished.
- Notice that the braced heading must be adjusted over the last two columns after one column is deleted.

RATING SMALL BUSINESSES IN
ARKANSAS, LOUISIANA, AND MISSISSIPPI, TEXAS

shorten line over 2 col. | Labor | adjust over 2 columns

State	Year	Average Weekly Wage	% Union	Value Added Per Worker ($000/yr)
National Median	~~1988~~	~~$325~~	~~24~~	~~$46.6~~
	1989	$348	24	$40.1
	1990	380	25	43.7
Arkansas	~~1988~~	~~$256~~	~~17~~	~~$38.4~~
	1989	$270	17	$39.3
	1990	300	17	38.9
Louisiana	~~1988~~	~~375~~	~~17~~	~~71.1~~
	1989	387	17	70.3
	1990	408	17	77.8
Mississippi	~~1988~~	~~255~~	~~16~~	~~45.8~~
	1989	267	16	49.0
	1990	289	16	50.1

insert

doc code

Texas	1989	335		58.7
	1990	352		59.9

S4-DOC11

1. Format S4-DOC11 as a five-column table. If your software supports horizontal and vertical ruled lines in the tables feature, key this table with lines; if not, omit vertical and double-ruled lines and set up as a standard table with horizontal lines before and after the column headings and at the end of the table before the source note.

2. Format: 1-inch side margins
   2-inch top margin
   justify text in Column 1, if software permits
   center column heads
   decimal align numbers and center them within each cell

TIPS TO OPERATOR

- S4-DOC11 as shown was created with the latest release of a very popular word processing software package. The ruled lines for tables are automatically created, but lines can be turned off or modified in many ways. As you can see, this table looks very much like a spreadsheet.

TABLE 1

PERCENT RESPONSES TO STATEMENTS CONCERNING ATTITUDES OF ETHICAL CONDUCT IN BUSINESS

Statements	Strongly Agree	Agree	Disagree	Strongly Disagree
A reputation for ethical conduct is less important in a manager's chances for promotion than a reputation for making money.	7.5	37.5	44.4	10.6
I find that sometimes I must compromise my personal principles to conform to my organization's expectations.	3.1	37.5	41.9	17.5
Business ethics is simply operating the firm in such a way as to stay within the law.	1.3	10.0	66.5	22.2
Additional government regulation will increase the likelihood of ethical conduct and fairer treatment of consumers.	1.9	20.1	51.0	27.0

SOURCE: Maynard M. Dolecheck, James Caldwell, Carolyn C. Dolecheck, "Ethical Perceptions and Attitudes of Business Personnel," American Business Review (January 1988), p. 49.

1. Retrieve S4-DOC11; make the requested revisions, which include making the column heads bold, moving a row, and shading a column.*

2. Check your revisions carefully before printing.

TIPS TO OPERATOR

- *You should be able to make all revisions requested **except shading the column** with any word processing software. Omit the shading if not supported with your software.

- If your software supports the ruled lines as shown, check the last row when you move it; if the double-ruled line moved with the row, change it to a single line. Make the last line of the table double-ruled.

TABLE 1

PERCENT RESPONSES TO STATEMENTS CONCERNING ATTITUDES OF ETHICAL CONDUCT IN BUSINESS

Operator – make column heads bold. Shade Column 1 10% if you can.

Statements	Strongly Agree	Agree	Disagree	Strongly Disagree
A reputation for ethical conduct is less important in a manager's chances for promotion than a reputation for making money ^for the organization^	7.5	37.5	44.4	10.6
~~I find that~~ sometimes I must compromise my personal principles to conform to my organization's expectations.	3.1	37.5	41.9	17.5
Business ethics is simply operating the firm ~~in such a way as~~ to stay within the law.	1.3	10.0	66.5	22.2
Additional government regulation will increase the likelihood of ethical conduct and fairer treatment of consumers.	1.9	20.1	51.0	27.0

move row

SOURCE: Maynard M. Dolecheck, James Caldwell, Carolyn C. Dolecheck, "Ethical Perceptions and Attitudes of Business Personnel," American Business Review (January 1988), p. 49.

doc code

SOFTWARE FUNCTION SUMMARY

List the commands for the following:

Left align tab ______________________________

Right align tab ______________________________

Center tab ______________________________

Decimal tab ______________________________

Leader tab ______________________________

Tables/Column Layout ______________________________

Edit column

- **Move column** ______________________________
- **Delete column** ______________________________
- **Move row** ______________________________
- **Delete row** ______________________________
- **Adjust table** ______________________________

SECTION 5

FORMATTING AND EDITING MULTIPAGE DOCUMENTS

Functions

- Page Breaks/Pagination
- Page Numbering
- Headers and Footers
- Subscripts and Superscripts

PAGE BREAKS/PAGINATION

A **page breaks** (also known as pagination) divide a multipage document into pages. A page break is usually executed automatically by the software. Using standard size paper containing 66 lines, on most software you will be able to print 54 lines, leaving both a one-inch top and bottom margin. Most software permits the user to specify the page length or the number of lines on each page. If you add or delete a line, the page break readjusts automatically. An adjustable page break may be called a **soft page break**.

You may break the page or begin a new page at any point in the document by inserting a **required page break,** sometimes referred to as a **hard page break.** The required page break causes the printer to begin printing on a new page.

Text that should never be split between two pages during pagination should be **block protected**. For example, a small statistical table should not be split between two pages. The table should be block protected.

At least two lines of a paragraph should be printed on each page when dividing a paragraph. An **orphan** is the first line of a paragraph at the bottom of a page. A **widow** is the last line of a paragraph appearing at the top of a page. Single orphan and widow lines should be avoided. Software may have a widow and orphan default. If not, you will need to scroll through each page to check the paragraph division.

List below the steps for pagination, block protect, and widow/orphan protect.

FUNCTION	STEPS REQUIRED
Page Break (Hard)	______________________
	______________________
	______________________
Block Protect	______________________
	______________________
	______________________
Widow/Orphan Protect	______________________
	______________________
	______________________

S5-EX1

1. Set 1-inch side margins and page length at 54 lines (or 1" top and 1" bottom margin).
2. Set widow/orphan protection to "on" if available on your system.
3. Strike RETURN to position the cursor on line 48 (or 8" from the top).
4. Set line spacing to double.
5. Key, save, and print the following paragraph as S5-EX1. Text should be divided between the two printed pages with three lines printed on the first page and two lines printed on the second page.

   Companies are competing to see who can give the best service. The faster applications are processed and customer inquiries are answered, the more likely a company is to beat the competition. Imaging systems excel at retrieving customer records quickly, enabling orders to be filled quickly.

6. Insert a required page break after the first line.
7. Delete the required page break.

PAGE NUMBERING

Page numbering allows you to print a page number on each page at the location you select. Some software allows you to choose Arabic numbers (1, 2, 3) or Roman numerals (i, ii, iii, or I, II, III). Some software allows words such as Page to become a part of the page number.

Page numbers do not usually display on the screen, only on the printed copy. Pages are automatically numbered according to your selections.

List the steps below for numbering pages.

FUNCTION	STEPS REQUIRED
Page Numbering	______________________________
	______________________________
	______________________________
	______________________________

S5-EX2

1. Retrieve S5-EX1.
2. Add the command to number the pages consecutively beginning with page 1. Place the page number at the right margin on line 6. Save this exercise and print it.

S5-EX3

1. Retrieve S5-EX1 and revise the document so that the page number will print only on page 2.
2. Save the exercise and print it.

1. Following the directions in the Reference Guide, key S5-DOC1 as an unbound two-page report. Set the following formats and commands:

   1" margins
   double spacing
   hyphenation on
   right margin justification off
   widow/orphan protection on

2. Do not key a page number command until the next exercise, S5-DOC1r.

TIPS TO OPERATOR

- If your system does not automatically paginate this document, key the pagination command before printing.

Document reprinted by permission of the Peed Corporation, 120 West Harvest Drive, Lincoln, NE 68521.

YOUR POWER SUPPLY: MORE IMPORTANT THAN YOU KNOW

Excerpt from PC TODAY, July 1990, by Rachel Pred

QS

Always suspect the power supply. If your personal computer is acting up, there's a good chance it will be the power supply. The power supply affects all hardware, software,^ and extras you add to your personal computer. It is an important component in your computer and should be a factor in your personal computer purchasing decision.

Different types of computers require different power supplies. An 8088, or XT generally uses a 150-200 watt power supply. An AT (286) or 386 will need a 200 to 230 watt power supply unless your AT is using a lot of expansion slots, then you'll want to lean toward the 250 watt range and look for a more powerful fan.

A power supply has other functions, too. The power supply runs a Power-On Self Test (POST), when you turn on your computer. The drives in your computer run on a 12 volt current and the cards run on a 5 volt current. The POST makes sure the computer won't start up until all the power levels are just right for the different components of the computer. Then it sends a "power good" signal to the motherboard so the computer knows it's OK to boot up. It's sort of an "all systems go" for your computer.

Although the power supply is one of the most important components in your system, it is also one of the components most likely to fail. There are ways, though, to protect yourself from power supply failure and damage to your system from power supply malfunctions.

The ~~most~~ simpl~~e~~est way to prevent problems is to make sure you have enough power for your system. Take the power supply into account when you purchase a system or add to your existing personal computer.

Leaving your system running between uses can prevent damage and prolong your computer's life. Turning your system on and off causes fluctuations in the temperature of your system. The fluctuations result in expansion and contraction of the metal, plastics and even the hard disks of your system.

1. Revise S5-DOC1 as marked.
2. Key the command to number page 2 in the upper right corner on line 6 (1 inch from the top edge). Suppress the page number on page 1.

TIPS TO OPERATOR

- If your system does not automatically repaginate as you make revisions, remember to paginate before printing.
- If your software offers the View Document feature, turn it on before printing to verify that the page number on page 2 appears in the desired place and that no page number appears on page 1.

YOUR POWER SUPPLY: MORE IMPORTANT THAN YOU KNOW

Excerpt from PC TODAY, July 1990, by Rachel Pred

says Bob Roark of PC Power and Cooling

"Always suspect the power supply." If your personal computer is acting up, there's is a good chance it will be the power supply. The power supply affects all hardware, software, and extras you add to your personal computer. It is an important component in your computer and should be a factor in your personal computer purchasing decision.

Different types of computers require different power supplies. An 8088, or XT generally uses a 150-200 watt power supply. An AT (286) or 386 will need a 200 to 230 watt power supply unless your AT is using a lot of expansion slots, then you'll want to lean toward the 250 watt range and look for a more powerful fan.

to

(DOCUMENT CONTINUED ON NEXT PAGE)

A power supply has other functions, too. The power supply runs a Power-On Self Test (POST), when you turn on your computer. The drives in your computer run on a 12 volt current and the cards run on a 5 volt current. The POST makes sure the computer won't start up until all the power levels are just right for the different components of the computer. Then it sends a "power good" signal to the motherboard so the computer knows it's OK to boot up. It's sort of an "all systems go" for your computer.

Although the power supply is one of the most important components in your system, it is also one of the components most likely to fail. There are ways, though, to protect yourself from power supply failure and damage to your system from power supply malfunctions.

The simpiest way to prevent problems is to make sure you have enough power for your system. Take the power supply into account when you purchase a system or add to your existing personal computer.

Leaving your system running between uses can prevent damage and prolong your computer's life. Turning your system on and off causes fluctuations in the temperature of your system. The fluctuations result in expansion and contraction of the metal, plastics and even the hard disks of your system.

doc code

S5-DOC2

Key S5-DOC2 as an unbound two-page report using the following formats:
1" margins
double spacing
right margin justification on
hyphenation on
page number in upper right, 1" from top edge

TIPS TO OPERATOR

- To keep the side heading on the page with the text that follows, key a block protect or begin keep/end keep command.
- Key an indent tab before each enumerated paragraph so that the text will wrap under the number.

Guideline for Working at Video Display Terminal

Employers must provide video display terminal operators and all employees with a safe, comfortable, and productive working enviroment.Effective use of VDTs stem from a basic understanding of what equipment is best for both the work and the employee, how the equipment is being used, and how it is to be set up for maximum employee comfort.

The principles that follow hav beeen developed as a aid to employers in establishing the work station environmet where office automation is being used or introduced.

Flexible Workstations

Since most equipment has many uses and many users, flexibility is a major advantage. Therefore employees hsould be encourag to take advantage of this flexibiliy.

1. Detachable key boards and contrast screen controls enhance the employee's comfort and productivity.

2. The chair should allow the employee to assume a comfortable position. When it is adjustable, the employee should be encouraged to take advantage of those adjustments.

3. The employee should be able to fit his or her legs comfortably under the desk.

Location

VDT operators seem more comfortable in areas with lighting levels that are lower than the office lighting levels of the past. Recommended levels range from 400 to 800 lux, with lower

(DOCUMENT CONTINUED ON NEXT PAGE)

levels being prefered by many full time operators. Individual task may be ehlpful for hard copy work.

VDTs should be positioned to minimize glare from windows and lighting sources. Terminals should be arranged so that air currents and heat distribution from VDTs do not cuase discomfort.

Routine Changes

Where job design requires long periods of very routine duties, employees may benefit from a change in routine such as performing stretch exercises, changing eye focus, moving around, or taking a break.

HEADERS AND FOOTERS

Headers and footers are used to print the same information at the top or bottom of each page. For example, you may want to print a chapter title or a company name at the top or bottom of each page. A **header** is a block of text designated to print at the top of one or more pages; a **footer** prints at the bottom of the page.

Generally to key a header or footer you must enter a special screen. The header or footer is keyed only once and is printed on the designated pages automatically. Headers and footers are not displayed on the screen, but most software allows you to view the header or footer to verify that it is correct.

Commands for headers and footers affect only text from the point the header or footer is inserted. For the header command to take effect on the current page, the command must be inserted ahead of any text or spaces. A footer command takes effect at the bottom of the page on which it is entered. Page numbers may be included within a header or footer.

List below the steps for keying headers and footers.

FUNCTION	STEPS REQUIRED
Header	______________________________
	______________________________
Footer	______________________________
	______________________________

S5-EX4

1. Create the header FIRST DRAFT so that it will appear at the left margin. Use the header default for vertical placement.
2. View the header for accuracy but do not save it.

S5-EX5

1. Create the footer FIRST DRAFT so that it will appear at the left margin. Use the footer default for vertical placement.
2. View the footer for accuracy but do not save it.

S5-EX6

1. Retrieve the file S5-EX1.
2. Add a header consisting of CHAPTER 1 and the page number. Position CHAPTER 1 at the left margin and the page number at the right margin. Insert the header so that it will print on both pages. Save this exercise and print it.
3. Revise S5-EX1 so that the header and page number print only on page 2.

S5-EX7

1. Retrieve S5-EX1.
2. Delete the header and page number.
3. Add the footer DRAFT and the page number so that it will print on both pages. Save and print the exercise.

S5-DOC2R

1. Revise S5-DOC2.
2. Add the following header to begin at the left margin on page 2 and aligned with the page number:
   GUIDELINES FOR WORKING AT VIDEO DISPLAY TERMINALS
3. Reformat enumerated items: single space items with a double space between each item.

TIPS TO OPERATOR

- After adding the header, use the View feature (if available on your system) to determine if the header will print in the desired position on page 2 only.

S5-DOC3

1. Key S5-DOC3 as a left-bound report. Set the following formats:
   1 1/2" left margin; 1" right margin
   double spacing
   right margin justification on
2. Print References on a separate page. Key each reference listing in hanging indent format (first line at the left margin and all following lines indented 5 spaces). Align the following header with the page number on page 2:
   SMOKING IN THE WORKPLACE

TIPS TO OPERATOR

- You will use the following functions to produce this document: change formats (line spacing and margins), centering, bold, underscoring, forced space, right margin justification, header, page number, hanging indent, pagination, and forced page end.

SMOKING IN THE WORKPLACE] Bold

Should smoking be allowed in the workplace? This is one of today's biggest controversies in many organizations. In spite of the U.S. Surgeon General's warnings and the findings of medical researchers world-wide, approximately 3 of every 10 adults in the U.S. (Mackay, 1988, 9) and, according to some estimates, 6 of every 10 male adults in Asia (Magnusson, 1989, 61) and 9 of 10 in China (Schmeisser, 1988, 16) continue to smoke cigarettes regularly. ~~In Hong Kong, estimates are that 2 out of 10 adults smoke (Ko, 1988).~~

Smoking at work is of major concern because its effects are so pronounced and profound. Smokers are known to suffer chronicbronchitis, emphysema, lung cancer, and other serious illnesses. Unfortunately, the smoker is not the only person effected by cigarette, cigar, or pipe smoking. Also affected is the side stream or secondary smoker--the person who is near as the smoker iights up, inhales, exhales and spreads smoke

(DOCUMENT CONTINUED ON NEXT PAGE)

throughout an inclosed work area. The side stream smoker, in fact, may actually be affected more than the principle smoker. A report issued by Action on Smoking and Health (ASH), states that an idling cigarette generates as much as four times the toxic agents given off by a cigarette being puffed by a smoker. In addition, toxic agents go into the air without being filtered (ASH Special Report, 1990, 104).

The cost of having smokers as employees is significant. The most authoritative estimate of the cost effect of having a smoker in the work place was completed by Weis in 1981 (Weis, 1981, 46). Weis estimated that each smoking employee costs the employer approximately $4,600 a year more than the nonsmoking worker.

At least 15 states and more than 100 municipalities in the U.S. have laws regulating smoking at work. A survey performed by the Administrative Management Society in 1987 discovered that 42% of the organizations sampled had some type of smoking policy. Of the 336 participating organizations, 22% regulated smoking in meeting rooms, 20% controlled smoking in storage areas, and 19% managed smoking in reception areas. Other areas and the percentages of organizations regulating smoking were hallways and aisles (18%), open office areas (15%), cafeterias (14%), security areas (10%), and all areas (8%). Four percent of the respondents in this U.S. survey said they hired only nonsmokers and 24% indicated that they had a smoking cessation program to assist their employees in stopping their smoking habit (Employee Health and Fitness, 1987, 85).

Place References on separate page. Print header (use title) and pg. # on Reference page.

References

ASH Special Report: The Economics of Smoking Washington, D.C. Action on Smoking and Health, 1990.

(DOCUMENT CONTINUED ON NEXT PAGE)

Mackay, Judith. "The Tobacco Epidemic Spreads," World Health, October 1988.

Magnusson, Paul. "Uncle Sam Shouldn't Be A Traveling Salesman for Tobacco," Business Week, Number 3127, October 9, 1989.

Schmeisser, Peter. "Pushing Cigarettes Overseas," The New York Times Magazine, July 10, 1988.

Weis, William L. "Can You Afford To Hire Smokers?" Personnel Administrator, Vol. 27, Number 4, May 1981.

"Smoking Is Costly for Employers," Employee Health and Fitness. Vol. 9, Number 6, August 1987.

S5-DOC3R

1. Revise S5-DOC3.

2. Prepare a title page following the directions shown below. The header and page number should not print on the title page.

TIPS TO OPERATOR

- To prevent the header and page number from printing on the title page, discontinue, suppress, or delete the header and page number for that page. Check your software manual for directions.

- Key the title page as the last page of the document so that you will not have to change the page number for the first page of text.

Operator: Prepare a title page with information shown below. Center each line. Print bold.

2½"

SMOKING IN THE WORKPLACE

3"

Prepared by:
DS
Art Bethke, Ph.D., SPHR
College of Business Administration
Northeast Louisiana University
Monroe, LA 71209-0100
FAX number: 318-555-1133

1½"

June 15, 19xx

S5-DOC4

1. Key S5-DOC4 as a two-page letter in block format with mixed punctuation.
2. Set the following formats:
   1" side margins
   dateline on line 14
   block header at left on page 2
   hyphenation on
   key company name a DS below closing in all caps
   key copy notation (key a **c**, one space, and the name a DS below the Enclosure notation)
3. Key the following three-line header at the top of page 2: Dr. Magrit Loomis
   Page 2
   January 5, 19--

TIPS TO OPERATOR

- When keying the header that contains the page number, you will not be able to select the page number command from the menu. Instead, you may key a special command (^B in WordPerfect) for inserting the page number at the desired point.

January 5, 19--

Dr. Margrit Loomis, Professor
New Hampshire College
2500 River Road
Manchester, NH 03104-2211

Dear Dr. Loomis:

MANUSCRIPT REVIEW PROCESS

Would you be interested in reviewing a manuscript for our textbook Word Processing, Stock No. WP002?

WP002 is a generic word processing applications book. Its purpose is to present the concepts which underlie word/information processing and provide practical hands-on experience producing business documents using any word processing software. The primary market would be junior colleges, postsecondary vocational schools, and AICS schools.

We will follow this procedure in the reviewing process:

1. The authors will submit first-draft manuscript. I will photocopy the materials and send them to you on the day that I receive them. You will then have two weeks to prepare your critique of the unit. You should concentrate on evaluating the content of the chapter. You will not be asked to check mechanics such as grammar, punctuation, or spelling. [mechanics — bold]

(DOCUMENT CONTINUED ON NEXT PAGE)

2. When your critique and manuscript are received, I will prepare a composite review for the authors, incorporating your critique comments with mine. The authors realize there will be reviewers, but they will be unaware of specific individual's comments. In this way, more objectivity will be achieved. I will be reviewing the manuscript at the same time that you are.

3. The authors will review the composite critique comments and revise as appropriate to achieve second-draft manuscript.

4. The manuscript and critique is to be returned by the date that will be specified in the cover letter. If your critique is not received by the date specified, your comments and fee will be eliminated for that unit.

For your assistance in this project, the following is enclosed:

1. a table of contents for WP002.
2. a PSI curriculum guide.
3. a guideline to use when critiquing the manuscript.
4. a projected time frame to help you in your planning.

If you want to be involved with this project, please contact me by January 15.

Please call me if you have any questions or concerns related to this project. You may reach me at 817-555-7733. I look forward to hearing from you.

Sincerely,

FOSS-DAY PUBLISHING

Lawrence Larason
Editor

Enclosures

c Tony Fazio

1. Revise S5-DOC4 as marked.

2. The facsimile (FAX) number is keyed in all caps a DS below the copy notation or enclosure line.

January 5, 19--

Dr. Margrit Loomis, Professor
New Hampshire College
2500 River Road
Manchester, NH 03104-2211

Dear Dr. Loomis:

MANUSCRIPT REVIEW PROCESS

Would you be interested in reviewing a manuscript for our textbook Word Processing, Stock No. WP002?

WP002 is a generic word processing applications book. Its purpose is to present the concepts which underlie word/information processing and provide practical hands-on experience producing business documents using any word processing software. The primary market would be junior colleges, postsecondary vocational schools, and AICS schools.

We will follow this procedure in the reviewing process:

1. The authors will submit first-draft manuscript. I will photocopy the materials and send them to you on the day that I receive them. You will then have two weeks to prepare your critique of the unit. You should concentrate on evaluating the **content** of the chapter. You will not ~~be asked to~~ check mechanics such as grammar, punctuation, or spelling.

2. When your critique and manuscript are received, I will prepare a composite review for the authors, incorporating your critique comments with mine. The authors realize there will be reviewers, but they will be unaware of a specific individual's comments. In this way, more objectivity will be achieved.

3. I will be reviewing the manuscript at the same time that you are.

5 ~~3~~. The authors will review the composite critique comments and revise as appropriate to achieve second-draft manuscript.

move stet ~~4~~. The manuscript and critique ~~is~~ are to be returned by the date that will be specified in the cover letter. If your critique is not received by the date specified, your comments and fee will be eliminated for that unit.

(DOCUMENT CONTINUED ON NEXT PAGE)

Dr. Margrit Loomis, Professor
Page 2
January 5, 19--

For your assistance in this project, the following items are ~~is~~ enclosed:

1. A table of contents for WP002?
2. A PSI curriculum guide.
3. A guideline to use when critiquing the manuscript.
4. A projected time frame to help you in your planning.

~~If you want~~ to ~~be involved with~~ participate in this project, please call ~~contact~~ me by January 15.

one ¶

~~Please~~ call me at 817-555-7733 if you have any questions or concerns related to this project. ~~You may reach me at 817-555-7733.~~ I look forward to hearing from you.

Sincerely,

FOSS-DAY PUBLISHING

Lawrence Larason
Editor

doc code

Enclosures

c Tony Fazio

FAX number (603)555-7100

S5-DOC5

Key S5-DOC5 as an unbound report. Set the following formats:
1" side margins
1 1/2" top margin
justify right margin
DS body; SS tables
left align columns in tables
center page number at bottom of page

TIPS TO OPERATOR

- Set single spacing for title lines, but double-space between them; change to double spacing at the beginning of the first paragraph.

Document reprinted by permission of the National Business Education Association, 1914 Association Drive, Reston, VA 22091.

justify right margin

Business Curriculum Models from Professional Organizations) center

DS

by W. Clark Ford, C. Steven Hunt, and Roy W. Hedrick) center

DS

Excerpt from Strategic Planning for the 1990's, NBEA Yearbook No. 28) center

QS

The school curriculum is like a glacier--massive, rough and craggy on the surface; slow-moving, constantly changing; and with parts often disappearing. Glaciers are uncontrollable. Educational curriculums often appear to be the same.

The information presented in this material focuses on curriculum models developed for business education. The data are from select groups and should not be considered all-inclusive.

Association for Information Systems Professionals (AISP)

In response to the needs of business and industry, the Information Systems Curriculum for Postsecondary Institutions was developed in cooperation with the Association for Information Systems Professionals. This model curriculum was designed to prepare entry-level employees to be able to

(DOCUMENT CONTINUED ON NEXT PAGE)

understand and operate the information-based technology of today's business environment. At the collegiate level the curriculum provides the basis for programs in systems management, information management, systems design, and systems analysis. These are the courses of the Information Systems Curriculum:

DS

1. Computer Business Applications I
2. Computer Business Applications II
3. Telecommunications/Networking
4. Database Systems
5. Applied Information Systems
6. Human Behavior in Organizations
7. Integrated Information Systems
8. Information Systems Administration
9. Communication for the Automated Office

Office Systems Research Association (OSRA)

With encouragement from business and industry to develop collegiate programs to address more specifically office systems education, OSRA accepted the challenge and sponsored the development of a Model Curriculum for Office Systems. The structure of the curriculum is presented within a framework of 10 three-semester-credit courses:

SS

Core Courses	Optional Courses
OS1-Office Systems + Technologies	OS6-Telecommunications
OS2-Office Systems Planning	OS7-Administrative Communications
OS3-Office Systems Implementation Strategies	OS8-Training/Development in Office Systems
OS4-Office Systems Applications	OS9-Special Topics in Office Systems
OS5-Integrated Office Systems	OS10-Professional Practice in Office Systems

DS

This framework is flexible, and course content may be included

(DOCUMENT CONTINUED ON NEXT PAGE)

in programs in other forms. Content may be split between courses or within courses with other titles.

Professional Secretaries International (PSI)

The Postsecondary Model Curriculum for Office Professionals was designed for adaptation in all postsecondary-level programs. Specifically, it has been designed for programs in independent colleges, junior/community colleges, vocational-technical schools, adult education, and two-year programs in colleges and universities. The courses within the curriculum are shown by semester.

Year One

Semester 1	Semester 2
Document Formatting	Document Production/Word Processing
Administrative Systems and Procedures	Business Communication
Fundamentals of Communication	Advanced Word Processing Applications
Information Processing Concepts and Applications	Advanced Information Processing Applications

SS

DS

The second year of study can integrate the third and fourth semesters of study to meet institutional scheduling and the student's career objectives.

SUPERSCRIPTS AND SUBSCRIPTS

A **superscript** is a character that is above the normal line of type; a **subscript** falls below the normal line of type. Equations and footnotes require superscripts and subscripts.

The 3 in the following is an example of a superscript:

$10^3 + y$

The 2 in the following is an example of a subscript:

H_2O

Some software will display the superscript or subscript in the proper position on the screen; others will display a special symbol or the superscript or subscript aligned with the text.

List below the steps for keying superscripts and subscripts.

FUNCTION	STEPS REQUIRED
Superscripts	______________________________
	______________________________
Subscripts	______________________________
	______________________________

S5-EX8

1. Key and print the following sentences using superscripts and subscripts.

The temperature was 90° yesterday.

She had trouble in math class with the equation $3^3 = 27$.

CO_2 was on the chemistry exam again.

Water, also known as H_2O, is necessary to sustain life.

S5-DOC5R

1. Revise S5-DOC5 as marked.

2. Major revisions:

   a. Add text footer
   b. Move page number to right margin
   c. Key ENDNOTES on separate page
   d. Turn hyphenation on; do not divide words in tables
   e. Single space enumerated items; double space between them
   f. Add superscripts where marked

BUSINESS CURRICULUM MODELS FROM PROFESSIONAL ORGANIZATIONS

by W. Clark Ford, C. Steven Hunt, and Roy W. Hedrick

Excerpt from Strategic Planning for the 1990's,
NBEA Yearbook No. 28

The school curriculum is like a glacier--massive, rough and craggy on the surface; slow-moving, constantly changing; and with parts often disappearing. Glaciers are uncontrollable. Educational curriculums often appear to be the same.

The information presented in this material focuses on curriculum models developed for business education. The data are from select groups and should not be considered all-inclusive.

Association for Information Systems Professionals (AISP)

In response to the needs of business and industry, the Information Systems Curriculum for Postsecondary Institutions was developed in cooperation with the Association for Information Systems Professionals. This model curriculum was designed to prepare entry-level employees to be able to understand and operate the information-based technology of today's business environment. At the collegiate level the curriculum provides the basis for programs in systems management, information management, systems design, and systems analysis. These are the courses of the Information Systems Curriculum:

(DOCUMENT CONTINUED ON NEXT PAGE)

↙SS items; DS between them

1. Computer Business Applications I (reinforce and enlarge existing skills in working with integrated software)
2. Computer Business Applications II (build skills in comparing, evaluating, selecting, and manipulating software and hardware)
4 3. Telecommunications/Networking
3 4. Database Systems
5. Applied Information Systems
6. 9 Human Behavior in Organizations
7. 6 Integrated Information Systems
8. 7 Information Systems Administration (capstone course)
9. 8 Communication for the Automated Office

Office Systems Research Association (OSRA)

With encouragement from business and industry to develop collegiate programs to address more specifically office systems education, OSRA accepted the challenge and sponsored the development of a Model Curriculum for Office Systems.[1] The structure of the curriculum is presented within a framework of 10 three-semester-credit courses:

Core Courses	Optional Courses
OS1-Office Systems & Technologies	OS6-Telecommunications
OS2-Office Systems Planning	OS7-Administrative Communications
OS3-Office Systems Implementation Strategies	OS8-Training/Development in Office Systems
OS4-Office Systems Applications	OS9-Special Topics in Office Systems
OS5-Integrated Office Systems	OS10-Professional Practice in Office Systems

This framework is flexible, and course content may be included in programs in many other forms. Content may be split between or among courses or within courses with other titles.

Chapter 7 2 2

(DOCUMENT CONTINUED ON NEXT PAGE)

Professional Secretaries International (PSI) [2]

has been

The Postsecondary Model Curriculum for Office Professionals ~~was~~ designed for adaptation in all postsecondary-level programs. Specifically, it has been designed for programs in independent colleges, junior/community colleges, vocational-technical schools, adult education, and two-year programs in colleges and universities. The specific courses within the curriculum are shown by semester.

YEAR ONE

*Semester 1	Semester 2
Document Formatting	Document Production/Word Processing
Administrative Systems and Procedures	Business Communication
Fundamentals of Communication	Advanced Word Processing Applications
Information Processing Concepts and Applications	Advanced Information Processing Applications

*The first semester requires a prerequisite of keyboarding skills.

The second year of study can integrate the third and fourth semesters of study to meet institutional scheduling and the student's career objectives.

doc code move to end

Operator: Put endnotes on separate page; 1½" top margin

1½"

Endnotes

QS

[1] Office Systems Curriculum Group. The Office Systems Research Association Model Curriculum for Office Systems Education. Cincinnati: South-Western Publishing Co., 1986, pp. 1-3.

[2] Professional Secretaries International (PSI). PSI Postsecondary Model Curriculum for Office Careers. Kansas City, MO: PSI, 1988, pp. 1-5.

Chapter 7

3 3

S5-DOC6

Set the following formats for S5-DOC6.
1 1/2" left margin; 1" right margin
single space block indented text; double space between indented blocks
footer on first page, align at left margin
header on all pages except first, align at left margin
begin page numbering with page number 41 at right margin
hyphenation on
left align Column 1 in tables; center Columns 2 and 3

TIPS TO OPERATOR

- Assume that this document is a unit from a long report; therefore, the page numbering does not begin with one.
- This unit from a multipage report is formatted with a footer and page number at the bottom of the first page and headers with page numbers at the top of the following pages.
- You must turn off the footer when you set the header for pages following the first.
- Be sure pages are numbered sequentially.
- Omit the document code since this is a portion of a longer document.

Excerpt reprinted from the NCAA Guide to Financial Aid, 1990-91 by permission of the National Collegiate Athletic Association, Mission, Kansas.

SECTION 5. Understanding Institutional Limits on Financial Aid

Overview

NCAA regulations set limits on the financial aid that institutions in Divisions I and II can award for various intercollegiate sports. This chapter describes the limits and answers these quesiton:

What NCAA legislation applies?
What financial is counted toward institutuional limits?
What aid is not counted toward institutional limits?
Which student-athletes are counters or noncounters?
Where are student-athletes who participate in more than one sport counted?
What certification is required for noncounters?
What two categories of sports are used to determine sport by sport limits?
What are the head count sportS?
What is an initial counter?
What are the equivalency sports?

What NCAA legislation applies?

Bylaw 15.5 is the most relevant for understanding institutional limits on finanial aid.

What financial aid if counted toward institutional limits?

As a general rule, institutional financial aid includes any aid that evokes a "Yes" answer to any of these questions:

Does your institution administer the aid? This adi include scholarships, grants, loan, workstudy program, on campus employment, and tuition waivers.

Does your institutions provide matching or supplementary aid for a previously selected recipient?

Did your institution's athletic department or athletcs interests help the student-athlete obtain a job off campus or some other source of income during the academic year that lead to this aid?

Was participation in athletics a major criterion for this aid?

What aid is not counted toward institution limits?

Theee types of institution financial aid are exempt from your institutions limits, The three are:

Understanding Institutional Limits 41

(DOCUMENT CONTINUED ON NEXT PAGE)

Understanding Institutional Limits 42

1. homorary academic awards for outstanding academic achievement or research grants [Bylaw 15.01.5] with these characterics:
they are described in your institutions catalog

the honorary academic awards are part of ongoing scholarship programs; the research grants are through well-established programs

They are based on acadeic achievement

recipients are determined by competition among students in a specific class or college at your institution

2. academic honors awards (in Division II only) that are

part of your institution;s normal arrangements for academic scholarships

awarded independently of athletics interests

in amounts that are consistent with the pattern for all such awards that your institution makes

3. loans that have regular repayment schedules and are made available and administered on the same basis to all students. Examples are Perkins and Stafford Student Loans.

The following chart, Financial Aid to Be Counted Toward Maximum Limits, lists various types of aid and indicates whether each type is counted toward individual and institutional limits.

(DOCUMENT CONTINUED ON NEXT PAGE)

Understanding Institutional Limits 43

FINANCIAL AID TO BE COUNTED TOWARD MAXIMUM LIMITS

Type of aid	Included in individual limits?[1]	Included in institutional limits?
Academic honor award, Division II	Yes	No
Aid based on athletics ability	Yes	Yes
Athletics grant	Yes	Yes
Athletics participation compensation	Yes	No
Disabled veterans award	No	No
Employment, on-campus during term	Yes	Yes
Employment during vacation period	No	No
G. I. Bill of Rights	No	No
Gift following completion of eligibility	Yes	No
Government grant that is administered by your institution	Yes	yes
Honorary academic award	No	no
Institutional grant or scholarship	yes	yes
Loan	No	No
Military reserve training program	No	No

[1]Individual limits apply only if the student athlete meets any of the criteria described in Chapter 4.

S5-DOC6R

Revise S5-DOC6 as marked. Make these format changes:
justify right margin
bold footer, header, page numbers, and title
key bullets (small o's) where shown; align the bullet with the text above; block indent the text following the bullet
move columns two and three in the table as marked

TIPS TO OPERATOR

- You may key the bullet with a small **o**. (If your word processing software provides a special command for a bullet, your instructor may suggest you use that command.)

- Turn off right margin justification for table.

SECTION 5. UNDERSTANDING INSTITUTIONAL LIMITS ON FINANCIAL AID

Overview

NCAA regulations set limits on the financial aid that institutions in Divisions I and II can award for various intercollegiate sports. This chapter describes the limits and answers these questions:

What NCAA legislation applies?

What financial aid is counted toward institutional limits?

What aid is **not** counted toward institutional limits?

Which student-athletes are <u>counters</u> or <u>noncounters</u>?

Where are student-athletes who participate in more than one sport counted?

What certification is required for noncounters?

What two categories of sports are used to determine sport-by-sport limits?

What are the head-count sports?

What is an initial counter?

What are the equivalency sports?

What financial aid is counted toward institutional limits?

As a general rule, institutional financial aid includes aid that evokes a "Yes" answer to any of these questions:

Does your institution administer the aid? This aid includes scholarships, grants, loans, workstudy program assistance, on-campus employment, and tuition waivers.

Does your institution provide matching or supplementary aid for a previously selected recipient?

(DOCUMENT CONTINUED ON NEXT PAGE)

Did your institution's athletics department or athletics interests help the student-athlete obtain a job off-campus or some other source of income during the academic year that led to this aid?

Was participation in athletics a major criterion for this aid?

What aid is not counted toward institutional limits?

Three types of institutional financial aid are exempt from your institution's limits. The three are:

1. **honorary academic awards** for outstanding academic achievement or research grants [Bylaw 15.01.5] with these characteristics:

align bullets under text above; indent text following bullet

- they are described in your institution's catalog
- the honorary academic awards are part of ongoing scholarship programs; the research grants are through well-established programs
- they are based on academic achievement
- recipients are determined by competition among students in a specific class or college at your institution

2. **academic honors awards** (in Division II only) that are part of your institution's normal arrangements for academic scholarships

- awarded independently of athletics interests
- in amounts that are consistent with the pattern for all such awards that your institution makes

3. **loans** that have regular repayment schedules and are made available and administered on the same basis to all students. Examples are Perkins and Stafford Student Loans.

The following chart, Financial aid to Be Counted toward Maximum Limits, lists various types of aid and indicates whether each type is counted toward individual and institutional limits.

All other types of aid not administered by your institution, such as Pell Grants, are not counted in institutional limits.

(DOCUMENT CONTINUED ON NEXT PAGE)

Understanding Institutional Limits 43

FINANCIAL AID TO BE COUNTED TOWARD MAXIMUM LIMITS

Type of aid	Included in individual limits?[1]	Included in institutional limits?
Academic honor award, Division II	Yes	No
Aid based on athletics ability	Yes	Yes
Athletics grant	Yes	Yes
Athletics participation compensation	Yes	No
Disabled veterans award	No	No
Employment, on-campus during term	Yes	Yes
Employment, off-campus during term ~~Employment during vacation period~~	Yes ~~No~~	Yes ~~No~~
G. I. Bill of Rights	No	No
Gift following completion of eligibility	Yes	No
Government grant that is administered by your institution	Yes	Yes
Honorary academic award	No	No
Institutional grant or scholarship	Yes	Yes
Loan	No	No
Military reserve training program	No	No

[1]Individual limits apply only if the student athlete meets any of the criteria described in Chapter 4.

S5-DOC7

1. Key S5-DOC7 as an unbound report. Set the following formats:
   1" side margins
   double spacing
   page numbers at top right margin
   justify right margin

2. Tables should be SS; if text wraps within a column, DS between items. Key a double-ruled line above the column heads if your software and printer provide the capability.

TIPS TO OPERATOR

- If you need assistance formatting the title page, refer to S5-DOC3r.

- The page number should be turned off for the title page. If you key the title page as the first page of the document, you must reset the page number to one for the first text page.

Reprinted from American Business Review, January 1988, by permission of the College of Business, University of New Haven.

An Excerpt from

ETHICAL PERCEPTIONS AND ATTITUDES OF BUSINESS PERSONNEL

Published in

American Business Review

January 1988

by

Maynard M. Dolecheck
James Caldwell
Carolyn C. Dolecheck

College of Business Administration
Northeast Louisiana University
Monroe, LA 71209

(DOCUMENT CONTINUED ON NEXT PAGE)

ETHICAL PERCEPTIONS AND ATTITUDES OF BUSINESS PERSONNEL

Recent events in financial communities have raised sharp questions about unethical conduct and moral leadership. A prominent financial entrepreneur was fined $100,000,000 for illegal insider trading in stocks involved in take-over actions. A leading defense contractor was found guilty of fraudulently overcharging the U.S. Government for military supplies. A producer of baby food admitted selling colored, flavored water as pure apple juice.

A New York Times/CBS News Poll conducted in June 1985, revealed that 55% of the American public believed that most corporate executives are dishonest; 59% thought white-collar crime occurs very often.[1] The implication is that fraud and lying are typical of American business policy.

Counsel for Ethical Situations

Because extreme value conflicts can be a result of today's rapidly changing environment, counseling with others about ethical situations in the workplace can provide perspective, understanding, and comfort. Recently, an accountant in an accounting firm knowingly approved another firm's false financial statements and is now facing a prison sentence. He stated in retrospect, "If I had sought counsel from someone that I had respect for, if I had even talked to my wife . . . ."[2]

To determine with whom or if respondents have discussed an ethical dilemma occurring at work, the respondents were asked to mark one of seven choices they

(DOCUMENT CONTINUED ON NEXT PAGE)

would make when confronted with an ethical dilemma. The list of choices selected for inclusion is one established by Posner and Schmidt and other researchers.[3] Percentage responses are shown in Table 1.

TABLE 1

Percent Responses to Statement: When You Are Confronted with an Ethical Dilemma in Performing Your Job, Whom Do You Usually Consult?

Source	Percent
Boss	41.7
Colleague or Friend at Work	21.7
No One	17.7
Spouse	10.2
Friend Outside Work	6.0
Legal Staff	1.7
Clergy	1.0
Total	100.0

Reasons for Engaging in Unethical Conduct

With the fact of unethical conduct clearly established as an occurrence, the question remains as to why persons engage in such activities. Various studies have attempted to determine the relative importance of various factors that could contribute to unethical conduct. In 1961, Raymond Baumhart surveyed Harvard Business Review readers asking them to rank a list of five factors.[4] Barry Posner and Warren Schmidt reported on their similar survey in the California Management Review in 1984.[5] The authors' study (labeled as the 1986 study in Table 2) of business personnel used the same list of factors. Table 2 shows the factors used in each

(DOCUMENT CONTINUED ON NEXT PAGE)

of the four studies, mean response, and their rank in terms of relative importance.

TABLE 2

Six Factors that May Contribute to Unethical Behavior
With Means and Rank of Importance

Factors	1986 Study Mean	1986 Study Rank	1984 Study Mean	1984 Study Rank	1961 Study Mean	1961 Study Rank
Behavior of Superiors	2.31	1	2.17	1	1.9	1
Behavior of One's Peers in the Organization	3.08	2	3.30	2	3.1	3
Personal Financial Need	3.18	3	4.09	6	4.1	5
The Ethical Practices of One's Industry	3.75	4	3.57	3	2.6	2
Formal Organizational Policy	4.32	5	3.84	5	3.3	4
Society's Moral Climate	4.38	6	3.79	4	N/A	

(DOCUMENT CONTINUED ON NEXT PAGE)

Place notes on separate page

NOTES

[1]Hong Kong Business Today reporting the New York Times/ CBS News Poll, (September 1985), p. 42.

[2]Martha Brannigan, "Auditor's Downfall Shows a Man Caught in Trap of His Own Making," The Wall Street Journal, (March 4, 1987), p. 31.

[3]Barry Z. Posner and Warren H. Schmidt, "Values and the American Manager: An Update," California Management Review, (Spring 1984), pp. 202-216.

[4]Raymond C. Baumhart, "How Ethical Are Businessmen?" Harvard Business Review, (July/August 1961), p. 163.

[5]Posner and Schmidt, p. 213.

S5-DOC7R

1. Revise S5-DOC7 as marked.
2. When you delete the column in Table 1, key the necessary commands to readjust the remaining columns between the margins. Make Column 1 wider and readjust text as marked.
3. Copy S4-DOC11 to page 3. Renumber the table to read Table 3. If the table was originally produced with lines, delete all except the double-ruled line above the column heads and the single-ruled line below the column head and at the end of the table. Delete the reference following the table.

TIPS TO OPERATOR

- Make all revisions to the document before moving text.
- When moving text from one page to another, use the command or key often labeled "Go to" to efficiently move the cursor to the desired page where text will be moved.
- Carefully check that all superscripts are numbered sequentially in the report and on the NOTES page after items are moved.
- S4-DOC11 may be copied into S5-DOC7r several different ways depending on your software. With WordPerfect, you could use the append command available with the move command. The file that will be appended to the end of the file then must be moved within the document to the desired location. You could also retrieve S4-DOC12 into S5-DOC7r. Some software such as DisplayWrite 4 offers a command called Notepad to copy text from one file to another. Check your software manual for steps.

An Excerpt from

ETHICAL PERCEPTIONS AND ATTITUDES OF BUSINESS PERSONNEL

Published in

American Business Review

January 1988

by

Maynard M. Dolecheck
James Caldwell
Carolyn C. Dolecheck

College of Business Administration
Northeast Louisiana University
Monroe, LA 71209

(DOCUMENT CONTINUED ON NEXT PAGE)

ETHICAL PERCEPTIONS AND ATTITUDES OF BUSINESS PERSONNEL

Recent events in financial communities have raised sharp questions about unethical conduct and moral leadership. A prominent financial entrepreneur was fined $100,000,000 for illegal insider trading in stocks involved in take-over actions. A leading defense contractor was found guilty of fraudulently overcharging the U.S. Government for military supplies. A producer of baby food admitted selling colored, flavored water as pure apple juice.

A New York Times/CBS News Poll conducted in June 1985, revealed that 55% of the American public believed that most corporate executives are dishonest; 59% thought white-collar crime occurs very often.[1] The implication is that fraud and lying are typical of American business policy.

Counsel for Ethical Situations

Because extreme value conflicts can be a result of today's rapidly changing environment, counseling with others about ethical situations in the workplace can provide perspective, understanding, and comfort. Recently, an accountant in an accounting firm knowingly approved another firm's false financial statements and is now facing a prison sentence. He stated in retrospect, "If I had sought counsel from someone that I had respect for, if I had even talked to my wife . . . ."[2]

To determine with whom or if respondents have discussed an ethical dilemma occurring at work, the respondents were asked to

(DOCUMENT CONTINUED ON NEXT PAGE)

mark one of seven choices they would make when confronted with an ethical dilemma. The list of choices selected for inclusion is one established by Posner and Schmidt and other researchers.[3] Percentage responses are shown in Table 1.

TABLE 1

Percent Responses to Statement: When You Are Confronted with an Ethical Dilemma in Performing Your Job, Whom Do You Usually Consult?

Source	Percent
Boss	41.7
Colleague or Friend at Work	21.7
No One	17.7
Spouse	10.2
Friend Outside Work	6.0
Legal Staff	1.7
Clergy	1.0
Total	100.0

Reasons for Engaging in Unethical Conduct

With the fact of unethical conduct clearly established as an occurrence, the question remains as to why persons engage in such activities. Various studies have attempted to determine the relative importance of various factors that could contribute to unethical conduct. In 1961, Raymond Baumhart surveyed Harvard Business Review readers asking them to rank a list of five factors.[4] Barry Posner and Warren Schmidt reported on their similar survey in the California Management Review in 1984.[5] The authors' study (labeled as the 1986 study in Table 2) of business personnel used the same list of factors. Table 2 shows the factors

(DOCUMENT CONTINUED ON NEXT PAGE)

used in each of the four studies, mean response, and their rank in terms of relative importance.

TABLE 2 1

Six Factors that May Contribute to Unethical Behavior with Means and Rank of Importance

Factors	1986 Study Mean	1986 Study Rank	1984 Study Mean	1984 Study Rank	1961 Study Mean	1961 Study Rank
Behavior of Superiors	2.31	1	2.17	1	1.9	1
Behavior of One's Peers in the Organization	3.08	2	3.30	2	3.1	3
Personal Financial Need	3.18	3	4.09	6	4.1	5
The Ethical Prac-tices of One's Industry	3.75	4	3.57	3	2.6	2
Formal Organiza-tional Policy	4.32	5	3.84	5	3.3	4
Society's Moral Climate	4.38	6	3.79	4	N/A	

¶ The most important finding of the 1986 study and the previous studies is the significance of one's organizational superiors as role models in the determination of one's ethical behavior. It was rated as the most important factor that contributed to unethical behavior in each study.

Insert A

General Attitudes Concerning Business Ethics

So that general attitudes toward business ethics could be analyzed, the questionnaire recipients were asked to respond to four statements shown in Table 3.

Operator: copy S4-DOC11 here. Change Table 1 to Table 3.

(DOCUMENT CONTINUED ON NEXT PAGE)

4

NOTES

[1]Hong Kong Business Today reporting the New York Times/CBS News Poll, (September 1985), p. 42.

[2]Martha Brannigan, "Auditor's Downfall Shows a Man Caught in Trap of His Own Making," The Wall Street Journal, (March 4, 1987), p. 31.

[3]Barry Z. Posner and Warren H. Schmidt, "Values and the American Manager: An Update," California Management Review, (Spring 1984), pp. 202-216.

[4]Raymond C. Baumhart, "How Ethical Are Businessmen?" Harvard Business Review, (July/August 1961), p. 163.

[5]Posner and Schmidt, p. 213.

SOFTWARE FUNCTION SUMMARY

SECTION 5

List the commands for the following:

Page break (hard) ______________________________

Widow\orphan protect ______________________________

Page numbering ______________________________

Header ______________________________

Footer ______________________________

Subscript ______________________________

Superscript ______________________________

SECTION 6

PREPARING FORM DOCUMENTS

Functions

- Merge
- Document Assembly

MERGE

Merge, also known as mail merge, is the process of combining information from two or more sources into a single form document. Merge is often used to create form documents (letters, memos, legal forms) when routine information is sent to several people. Form documents are produced by creating two separate documents: 1) a primary document that contains that portion of the form document that is the same for everyone, and 2) a secondary file that contains the information that will be different for each individual.

The **primary document** (also called the shell document, main document, or broilerplate) contains the text of the document and the merge commands at each variable position. The merge commands tell the software where to find the variable information. These commands vary with each software.

The **secondary document** (also called an address file, variable document, or data file) contains the variables necessary to individualize each document. Some software refers to all variables for one person as a *record* and each specific variable as a *field.* (Record and field are common terminology used in spreadsheet software.)

When preparing the primary document, each variable may be numbered or named. Use a descriptive name to identify each variable if your software allows. Fewer mistakes will be made when preparing the secondary document if you give the variable a name such as *date*, rather than *variable 1*.

When preparing the secondary document, it is extremely important to proofread the information carefully against the primary document. Because the variables appear out of context, proofreading must be done with extreme care.

List the steps for using merge.

FUNCTION	STEPS REQUIRED
Prepare Primary Document	____________________
	____________________
	____________________
Prepare Secondary Document	____________________
	____________________
	____________________
Merge/Print	____________________
	____________________
	____________________

S6-EX1

1. Key the primary document. At each variable position, insert the commands appropriate for your software.

```
Dear (variable 1 - salutation)

Thank you for your inquiry of (variable 2 - date).
This request has been referred to our (variable
3 - department name) Department for appropriate
handling.

Sincerely


Mr. Akeo Mitsui
```

2. Proofread the text carefully and correct any errors. Save the document as S6-EX1.PRI.

3. Prepare the secondary file containing the variables for both persons. Include the appropriate commands for your software.

```
Variable 1    Mrs. Simms
Variable 2    October 20
Variable 3    Accounting

Variable 1    Mr. Garcia
Variable 2    October 21
Variable 3    Human Resources
```

4. Proofread the variables carefully.
5. Save the variables as S6-EX1.SEC.
6. Merge the primary document S6-EX1.PRI with the secondary document S6-EX1.SEC. You should print two documents complete with the variables inserted.

S6-DOC1

1. Key the S6-DOC1 primary document in block letter format with mixed punctuation. Identify each variable according to your system's specifications by numbering or using a descriptive name. To assist you, each variable is numbered and identified with a name. Do not key the parenthesis. Select a file name that identifies the primary document. (For example, S6-DOC1.PRI.)
2. Check spelling, save, and print a copy. (Do not be concerned if the right margin appears very uneven; when the variable information is merged into the document, the margin will be the desired width.)
3. Key the secondary document containing the variable information for each addressee (see Variable Sheet). You will have four separate records. Be sure the names or numbers given each variable in the primary document match those in the secondary document. Select a file name that identifies the secondary document. (For example, S6-DOC1.SEC.)
4. Merge the primary and secondary documents, printing a copy for each addressee.

TIPS TO OPERATOR

- When keying the primary document, be sure to key it in correct format, including all punctuation and returns. Do not attempt to leave space for the variable information. Your system will automatically allow for space and adjust the margins appropriately.
- The address block for S6-DOC1 is set up with the complete name as one variable; however, some offices prefer to make each part of the name a separate variable in case they want to sort the file by last name.
- Because secondary files are often sorted by ZIP code or state, the city, state, and ZIP code for each record are keyed as separate variables.
- The variable name **company** appears three times in the primary document (Variables 3, 10, and 11); the same variable name can be used when the *same variable information* will appear at each point.

S6-DOC2

1. To prepare for merging, key the S6-DOC2 primary document in simplified block format. Identify each field according to your system's specifications by numbering or using a descriptive name. **Read Step 2 below before keying the "title" field.** To assist you, each field is numbered and identified with a name.

2. All addressees do not have a title; therefore, the "title" field will be empty for some records. To prevent a blank line in the address where the title would normally appear, you should key a command (conditional statement in WordPerfect) that instructs the system to skip this field if blank. Check with your instructor or your software manual to determine the command to key when the field is sometimes empty.

3. Check spelling, save the document, and print a copy.

4. Key the secondary document containing the variable information given on the variable sheet for each addressee.

5. Merge the primary and secondary documents, printing a copy for each addressee.

TIPS TO OPERATOR

- Check the printed copies for correct format of the address block.

current date

(variable 1 - name)
(variable 2 - title)
(variable 3 - company)
(variable 4 - address)
(variable 5 - city), (variable 6 - state) (variable 7 - zip)

PURCHASE ORDER NUMBER (variable 8 - number)

Your order for (variable 9 - amount1) diskettes will be processed as soon as we know the diskette density you need. Please check your system manual for diskette specifications, and then mark the enclosed card indicating whether you need 5 1/4-inch double-density or 5 1/4-inch high-density disks.

Also, if you want the diskettes preformatted for your system, please check the box labeled IBM or Macintosh.

Return the reply card by (variable 10 - date) and receive a (variable 11 - amount2) percent discount.

Ms. Virginia Hui
Shipping Agent

doc code

Enclosure

(DOCUMENT CONTINUED ON NEXT PAGE)

VARIABLE SHEET

Stored Document S6-Doc 2 Requested By Virginia Hui Date current

1.	Mr. Robert Moats	1.	Miss Ranesha St. Clair
2.	—	2.	—
3.	Woodland Hills	3.	Cloyd & Cloyd, Inc.
4.	510 Penn Avenue	4.	P.O. Box 669
5.	Pittsburgh	5.	Falls Church
6.	PA	6.	VA
7.	15222-1134	7.	22041-0669
8.	567-7888Y	8.	778-3344Z
9.	six dozen	9.	two dozen
10.	March 16	10.	April 14
11.	12	11.	10
12.		12.	
13.		13.	

1.	Ms. Meridith Arneson	1.	Mr. Fred VanGilder
2.	Office Manager	2.	Purchasing Officer
3.	Bechtel Production Company	3.	Strom Electrical Services
4.	150 Market Street	4.	3345 Prospect Street, Northwest
5.	Charleston	5.	Washington
6.	SC	6.	DC
7.	29401-2144	7.	20007-0123
8.	896-1111X	8.	1145-66770
9.	three dozen	9.	three dozen
10.	April 1	10.	May 1
11.	10	11.	12
12.		12.	
13.		13.	

1. To prepare for merging, key the S6-DOC3 primary document as a two-page letter in block format with mixed punctuation. Correct spelling errors. Identify each variable according to your system's specifications. If your software permits naming the variables, create an appropriate name for each. (The draft identifies each variable by number only.) See TIPS TO OPERATOR below for suggestions.

2. Set the following formats:
   1" margins
   block header at top of page 2 (See TIPS below.)

3. Check spelling, save, and print a copy.

4. Key the secondary document containing the variable information given on the Variable Sheet for each addressee.

5. Merge the primary and secondary documents. Print a copy for each addressee.

TIPS TO OPERATOR

- If your software permits naming variables, the variable names should be descriptive. For example, the variable names under the "Subject" heading might be: **claim no policy no insured**.

  Some software will allow a space in the variable name; if yours does not, key a hyphen (if your system permits) to separate words. Also, the number of keystrokes allowed in a variable name is limited; therefore, you may have to abbreviate some names such as **beneficiary**.

- The header for page 2 should include variable names (or variable numbers if your system does not permit naming) for addressee, page number, and current date. Refer to S5-DOC4 for header format, if necessary.

Document begins on following page.

(current date)

CERTIFIED MAIL-RECEIPT REQUESTED

(variable 1)
(variable 2)
(variable 3), (variable 4) (variable 5)

Operator: Help with spelling.

Dear (variable 6):

Subject: Claim No. (variable 7)
Policy No. (variable 8)
Insured: (variable 9)

Thank you for notifying us of a claim against the policy listed above. Since this claim occured during the contestable period, an investigation regarding the health history and cause of death will be made by our field representive in your area. The representive will reach the family to interview each member and secure an authorization, which is needed to complete the investigation. Please explain this matter to the family and request ~~their~~ cooperation. each member's

In addition to the investigation, each death claim require^s the following for complete consideration:

1. A claimant's statement form from each claimant. Note that this is a four/part form. Please have this statement and authorization completed by the primary beneficiary.

Our files indicate that the primary beneficiary is (variable 10).

2. A copy of the deeath certificate, for the insured. an uncertified copy is not acceptable. If you can not obtain a death certificate, a completed copy of the enclosed physicians statement will be considered.

3. A newspaper clipping, if available containing notice of the death.

Read the instructions on the back of the claimant's statement form carefully as well as the material about the handling of claims ~~that is to be~~ found in the Claims section of Agent's Service. If you have any quesitons about this statement or have any difficulty obtaining anyof the requested material itemized above, call me immediately at 601-555-3344.

Please send the requested items to:

(DOCUMENT CONTINUED ON NEXT PAGE)

add header { Name
Page 2
Date

Equality Life Insurance Company
Benefits Department
P. O. Box 6688
Tempe, AZ 85282-6688

} center each line

Sincerely,

Ms. Sookham Dhaliwal
Benefits Department

Enclosures: Claimant's Statement
Physician's Statement

(DOCUMENT CONTINUED ON NEXT PAGE)

VARIABLE SHEET

Stored Document S6-Doc 3 Requested By Sookham Dhaliwal Date current

1. Mr. Peter Hunger	1.
2. 5020 Wyoming Road	2.
3. Bethesda	3.
4. MD	4.
5. 20816-7712	5.
6. Mr. Hunger	6.
7. 602211	7.
8. X23-8811290	8.
9. Miss Jimmye Drapeau	9.
10. Mr. Zane Luse	10.
11.	11.
12.	12.
13.	13.
1. Ms. Keli Bobo	1.
2. P.O. Box 315	2.
3. Albuquerque	3.
4. NM	4.
5. 87103-3150	5.
6. Ms. Bobo	6.
7. 518980	7.
8. Y11-0011211	8.
9. Mr. Reynolds Kelley	9.
10. Mrs. Tammera Kelley	10.
11.	11.
12.	12.
13.	13.

S6-DOC4

1. Key the S6-DOC4 primary document in the appropriate legal format. Identify each variable according to your system's requirements. Turn hyphenation on. See the Reference Section for directions for formatting legal documents.

   If you name variables, carefully study the Variable Sheet - Legal Documents as well as the primary document to determine the information to be inserted so that you can compose descriptive variable names.

2. Check spelling, save, and print.

3. Prepare the secondary document containing the variable information for two clients.

4. Merge the two files. Print two copies of each completed Bill of Sale.

TIPS TO OPERATOR

- To key the heading for this document, key one space between each character and three spaces between each word. (A heading keyed in this manner is called a spread heading.)

- You must be very careful to key accurate information, particularly names, dates, and amounts, in legal documents. Check your work carefully.

- Key a format change for single spacing where the goods description is inserted, and key the indent command for the goods description. Change to double spacing for the following paragraph. Reset to single spacing before keying the signature blanks and the information printed under them.

- If following the merge command, one of the documents flows onto a second page, delete a line (return) between the signature lines to make one page.

B I L L   O F   S A L E

STATE OF (variable 1)

COUNTY OF (variable 2)

Before me, the undersigned authority, this the (variable 3) day of (variable 4), 19(variable 5), personally came and appeared (variable 6), who declared that for the sum of (variable 7) cash in hand paid, the receipt of which is hereby acknowledged; (variable 8) does by these presents Bargain, Grant, Sell, Convey and Deliver, without any warranty whatsoever, but, with full warranty of title and with complete transfer and subrogation of all rights and actions of warranty against all former proprietors of the property herein conveyed unto (variable 9) the following goods, to-wit:

(variable 10)

Who also declares and affirms that there is no mortgage, lien, or encumbrance of any nature whatsoever against the above described goods.

WITNESSES:

_______________________________ _______________________________
Vendor (Seller)

_______________________________ _______________________________
Vendee (Purchaser)

SWORN TO AND SUBSCRIBED TO before me this the (variable 11) day of (variable 12), 19(variable 13).

____
NOTARY PUBLIC

(DOCUMENT CONTINUED ON NEXT PAGE)

VARIABLE SHEET - LEGAL DOCUMENTS

Stored Document: S6-Doc 4 Requested By: Brown Date: 2-16

1. Michigan
2. Washtenaw
3. 17th
4. February
5. current year
6. Gary Giglio
7. Two Thousand Fifty Dollars ($2,050)
8. he
9. Stephanie Sistrunk
10. *see below
11. 17th
12. February
13. current year
14.
15.
16.
17.
18.
19.
20.

COMMENTS/NOTES: *Tandy 3000 personal computer HL, Serial no. 19157, Samsung EGA monitor

(DOCUMENT CONTINUED ON NEXT PAGE)

VARIABLE SHEET - LEGAL DOCUMENTS

Stored Document: S6-Doc 4 Requested By: Brown Date: 2-16

1. Michigan
2. Wayne
3. 16th
4. February
5. current year
6. Sonja K. Adams
7. Nineteen Hundred Dollars ($1,900)
8. she
9. Erik Fogger
10. *see below
11. 16th
12. February
13. current year
14.
15.
16.
17.
18.
19.
20.

COMMENTS/NOTES: *1989 Honda, Model ORV, VIN JR2TE1006ED145106, Title No. C6155215

DOCUMENT ASSEMBLY

Document assembly allows standard (form) sentences and paragraphs to be combined to create a document. This process may also be referred to as *append*. Document assembly is often used in legal offices, insurance offices, and medical offices to include specific paragraphs or sentences in all similar documents.

To use the document assembly feature, the standard paragraphs must first be created and stored. Depending upon the software, each paragraph may be saved as a separate file and then retrieved or appended into the final document.

Standard paragraphs may also be set up as macros (see page 278). Another procedure is to key special merge commands within the primary document to insert the desired standard document as the primary and secondary files are merged.

List the steps for using document assembly.

FUNCTION	**STEPS REQUIRED**
Document Assembly	________________________________
	________________________________
	________________________________
	________________________________
	________________________________

S6-DOC5

1. To prepare for document assembly, key the needed paragraphs following the suggestions below:

2. Depending on the method to be used with your software for inserting variable paragraphs into a merged document, key the three paragraphs labeled ARKANSAS, LOUISIANA and MISSISSIPPI so that each can be included in a merged document. Do not key the labels (ARKANSAS, LOUISIANA, MISSISSIPPI). For ease in locating the files, you may key file name extensions (AR, LA, MS) to identify the paragraphs by state as follows: S6-DOC5.AR, S6-DOC5.LA, and S6-DOC5.MS. Print each paragraph.

3. Key S6-DOC5 as a primary document, identifying each variable in the proper manner.

   At the point where one of the paragraphs is to be inserted, follow these steps: (a)double space, (b)key an indent command so that the paragraph is indented five spaces from the left margin, (c)key the appropriate merge command if you are merging paragraphs, and (d) double space. Do not key the explanatory statment at the point where the paragraph is to be inserted. (If you are using WordPerfect 5.1, you may key a Comment by selecting that capability from the Merge menu; it will not print in the document.) If you are going to append or retrieve a paragraph, omit step (c).

4. Check spelling, save, and print the primary document.

5. Prepare the secondary document containing the variable information for the two addressees.

6. Merge the primary and secondary files. If a merge command was not keyed to insert the needed paragraphs, retrieve or append the desired paragraph into each merged document.

7. Print.

TIPS TO OPERATOR

■ Once you have learned to use macros, you may want to save paragraphs such as the ones in this project as macros.

S6-DOC5 PARAGRAPHS

LOUISIANA (Key only the paragraphs, not the state names.)

Any employer whose liability for claims arising under the provisions of this Chapter is not covered by insurance, shall pay within 60 days after receipt of written notice. Failure to have such payment within 60 days after receipt of notice, when such failure is found to be arbitrary, capricious, or without probable cause, shall subject the employer to a penalty, in addition to the amount of the claim due, of 12 percent of the total amount payable to the claimant, together with all reasonable attorney's fees for the prosecution and collection of such claim. The provisions of R. S. 23:1141 limiting the amount of attorney's fees shall not apply in cases wherein the employer is found liable for penalties and attorney's fees under the provisions of this Section.

ARKANSAS

The first installment of compensation shall become due on the fifteenth day after the employer has notice of the injury or death, as provided in Section 17, on which date all compensation then accrued shall be paid. Thereafter compensation shall be paid every two weeks except where the Commission directs that installment payments be made at other periods. If any installment of compensation payable without an award is not paid within 15 days after it becomes due, there shall be added to such unpaid installment an amount equal to 6 percent.

MISSISSIPPI

If any installment of compensation payable without an award is not paid within 14 days after it becomes due, as provided in subdivision (b) of the section, there shall be added to such unpaid installment an amount equal to 10 percent thereof, which shall be paid at the same time as, but in addition to, such installment, unless notice is filed under subdivision (d) of this section, or unless such nonpayment is excused by the Commission after a showing by the employer that owing to conditions over which he had no control such installment could not be paid within the period prescribed for the payment.

current date

(variable 1)
(variable 2)
(variable 3)
(variable 4)
(variable 5), (variable 6) (variable 7)

Dear (variable 8):

Subject: Claim No. (variable 9)
Insured: (variable 10)
Claimant: (variable 11)
Date of Accident: (variable 12)

This claim recently reported to us was not reported in accordance with the requirements of the Worker's Compensation statutes. Such action may not only cause a financial hardship on the injured employee but also may result in a statutory penalty on your firm.

The statute is as follows:

Do not key {(optional paragraph goes here--append either paragraph ARKANSAS, LOUISIANA, or MISSISSIPPI)

In view of the above, please report all future Worker's Compensation claims promptly in accordance with the letter previously forwarded to you along with your policy.

Sincerely,

Charles Greer
Claims Department

doc code

(DOCUMENT CONTINUED ON NEXT PAGE)

VARIABLE SHEET

Stored Document S6-Doc5 Requested By Charles Greer Date current

1. Ms. Marla Goldstein	1.
2. Personnel Manager	2.
3. Highland + Highland Trucking	3.
4. P.O. Box 6611	4.
5. Little Rock	5.
6. AR	6.
7. 72201-6611	7.
8. Ms. Goldstein	8.
9. CY-77236Y	9.
10. Mr. John T. Adams	10.
11. Highland + Highland Trucking	11.
12. March 11, 19--	12.
13. Insert Arkansas paragraph	13.

1. Mr. Frank Miller	1.
2. Manager	2.
3. Mississippi Shipping, Inc.	3.
4. P.O. Box 1459	4.
5. Biloxi	5.
6. MS	6.
7. 39534-1459	7.
8. Mr. Miller	8.
9. CR-11876Y	9.
10. Mr. Harrison White	10.
11. Mississippi Shipping, Inc.	11.
12. March 15, 19--	12.
13. Insert Mississippi paragraph	13.

SECTION 6

SOFTWARE FUNCTION SUMMARY

List the commands for the following:

Merge ____________________

Prepare primary document ____________________

Prepare secondary document ____________________

Document assembly ____________________

SECTION 7

USING SPECIALIZED FEATURES

Functions

- Macros
- Overstrike, Redlining, Strikeout
- Thesaurus
- Changing Fonts
- Converting Files

MACROS

Macros, also called glossaries or stored keystrokes, allow you to save a series of keystrokes and retrieve them each time you need them. Macros are created for keystrokes that you know you will be repeating many times, such as the signature block of a letter, frequently used phrases, technical terms that are difficult to spell, and formats. Macros can also be created for a command that involves a series of keystrokes (such as printing on a network). Macros save keying and proofreading time.

Generally the following steps are required to create a macro. The series of keystrokes are created, assigned to a letter on the keyboard, saved, and then retrieved as they are needed.

Some software saves a macro with a file name rather than to a key on the keyboard. When a macro is saved with a file name, the name should be short and utilize the first characters of the major term. Examples of file names are *e* for the format for envelopes, *m* for memo, *l* for legal format, and *c* for complimentary closing.

List below the steps for using macros.

FUNCTION	STEPS REQUIRED
Create a Macro	____________________
	____________________
	____________________
	____________________
Use a Macro	____________________
	____________________
	____________________
	____________________

S7-EX1

1. Create a macro for the complimentary closing of a letter prepared in block format. Include your reference initials. Use the default margins.

   ```
   Sincerely



   LuAnn Mace
   Finance Director
   xx
   ```

2. Name the macro *c* for closing.

S7-EX2

1. Key the letter shown on the following page in block format, using the default margins of your software. Use the *c* macro to enter the closing.

```
January 3, 19


Mr. Ralph Watrous
Marketing Manager
Alpha Foods
5001 Madison Way
Phoenix, AZ  85001-1122

Dear Mr. Watrous

We received your request for the credit rating of
Mrs. Eleanor Brown of Los Angeles, California.
You will find the credit report enclosed.  Please
let me know if you need any additional informa-
tion.

(Insert the macro c.)
```

2. Save and print the document.

S7-DOC1

1. Before you key S7-DOC1, create a macro containing the standard memo headings and margin settings.

   Key the appropriate command to create a macro. The macro will contain the following format changes and headings in the order shown:

   begin on line 10 or leave a 1 1/2-inch top margin
   set a 1/2-inch left margin for headings
   key headings in ALL CAPS bold with with two spaces following the colon
   double-space between each heading (see illustration below)
   set 1 1/2-inch left and right margins after the **SUBJECT** heading

   TO: (line 10)
   DS
   FROM:
   1 1/2" left margin DS
   DATE:
   DS
   SUBJECT:
   DS

2. Save the macro using the name *M* for memo. Clear the screen (if prompted to "Save document?" key **N** for No).

3. On a clear screen, key the command to run the macro saved as *M*. The memo heading should appear on the screen and the margins should be set.

4. Key S7-DOC1 as a memo. To fill in the information for the **TO** heading, move the cursor to the position where the text is to begin and key the text. DO NOT RETURN. Position the cursor where the **FROM** text begins and key. Follow these steps for all four lines in the heading.

   Move the cursor to the point where the memo message begins. Be sure the cursor is at the new left margin (reveal formatting codes if you are not sure the cursor is positioned correctly). Text should align under the first character of the text in the heading. Key the memo.

5. Save, check spelling, and print. Check for correct formatting.

TO: Members of the Research Committee

FROM: Bill Gritzmacher

DATE: October 11, 19--

SUBJECT: Meeting on October 15

The Research Committee will meet at 1:30 p.m. on Thursday, October 15, in Room 3-49.

The agenda for the meeting is as follows:

1. The definition and role of the committee will be outlined.

2. Methods and procedures for accomplishing the committee functions will be discussed.

Please plan to attend.

doc code

S7-DOC2

1. In preparation for keying S7-DOC2 as a memo, run the macro saved as *M*.
2. When the memo headings appear on the screen, fill in the heading text and key the memo.
3. Save the memo as S7-DOC2, check spelling, and print.

TO: Mary Tilton

FROM: Marc White

DATE: December 2, 19--

SUBJECT: Lunch With Prospective Employee

Will you please plan to take Ms. Janet Schumacher, an applicant for the Training Supervisor's position, to lunch at noon on Monday, December 7. Juanita will be happy to make reservations for you; just tell her where you plan to go.

Please stop by my office before Monday to review Ms. Schumacher's vita.

S7-DOC3

1. Create a macro containing the letter address and salutation of a client whom you write often. Key the macro beginning on line 1.

```
Mr. Brett B. Dole
Systems Manager
Sicard Association
3600 Washington Blvd.
Ogden, UT  84403-0221

Dear Mr. Dole
```

2. Save the macro with the name **dole**.

3. Key S7-DOC3 in block format. Run the macro named **dole** for the letter address and salutation.

4. Check spelling, save, and print.

current date

(insert macro named dole)

Here is the information you requested about the VAX training program to be offered next month.

As you can see from the enclosed brochure, the five-day seminar covers basic internal controls essential to VAX managers. Please enroll early to assure that a place is reserved for each one on your staff who wishes to participate.

If you have questions about this seminar, please call me at 1-800-555-0022.

Sincerely

Ms. Jackie Hulbert
Training Coordinator

Enclosure

S7-DOC4

1. Create a macro containing the standard notary public statement to be included on legal documents. Set margins: 1 1/2" left, 1/2" right. Indent 10 spaces. Make signature line 3" long. Beginning on line 1, key the following statement:

```
STATE OF ____________________

COUNTY OF ___________________

          WITNESS my hand and seal as such
Notary Public on this ______ day of_________, 19—.

        My Commission expires: ___________________


                                ______________________
                                Notary Public
```

2. Save the macro with the name **NP**.

3. Refer to the Reference Section for legal document formatting instructions.

   Key S7-DOC4 as a two-page affidavit with the following format:

   1 1/2" left margin
   1/2" right margin
   2" top margin on each page
   double space*
   justify right margin
   precede and follow page number by a hyphen on page 2 and center at bottom of page
   8 1/2" x 11" paper
   indent paragraphs 10 spaces

4. For the notary public statement, run the macro saved as **NP**.

5. Save, check spelling, and print.

TIPS TO OPERATOR

- *Key the heading (all text through the ruled line before the body) with the single space setting. Return twice to make double spacing except **before** ruled lines. Set line spacing to double space at the first paragraph. Reset line spacing to single space before keying the line for the signature.

DISTRICT COURT, CITY AND COUNTY OF DENVER, STATE OF COLORADO

Civil Action No. 92CV20334, Courtroom 3

AFFIDAVIT OF BRANDON LEWIS SMITH

EDWARD J. EISENSTAT, Agent, et al.

Plaintiffs,

vs.

JOHNSON VALLEY MEDICAL FOUNDATION, et al.

Defendants

COMES NOW Brandon Lewis Smith, affiant, being first duly sworn upon his oath, and deposes and states as follows:

1. The affiant is over the age of twenty-one (21) years, is competent to testify in a court of law, and has personal knowledge of the matters contained herein.

2. In the fall of 1988, the affiant visited the Four-B Ranch property with Robert H. Cooper to view said property for the purpose of purchase. Affiant was interested in purchasing said property as co-investor with Mr. Cooper.

3. On the occasion that the affiant visited the Four-B Ranch property, affiant traveled across a dirt road that led to a hydroelectric plant close to the Four-B Ranch property. Said road that affiant traveled passed through the Lake Ouachita property. Affiant recalls seeing no signs or evidence of any

(DOCUMENT CONTINUED ON NEXT PAGE)

kind that would restrict access to the Four-B Ranch property through the Lake Ouachita property.

4. The owners, managers, and employees of Lake Ouachita property were advised and aware that affiant and Mr. Cooper were traveling through said property to the Four-B Ranch and made no objection to use of the road in question.

Further the affiant saith not.

Brandon Lewis Smith

(insert macro named **NP**)

2

OVERSTRIKE, REDLINING, AND STRIKEOUT

Overstrike superimposes one character over another to form special characters such as accent marks (résumé) and mathematical and scientific symbols (≠, ~). Overstrike characters may not be displayed on the screen because the overstrike occurs during the printing process. Some software such as DisplayWrite utilizes the overstrike feature to mark over existing text with another character. This procedure is described below as redlining or strikeout.

Redlining or **strikeout** is a method of marking text that has been edited, added to, or marked for deletion. When several people work together to produce a document, redlining or strikeout is a useful way to let everyone know of changes that are proposed. In WordPerfect, the redlining feature is recommended for marking text to be added; strikeout is recommended for marking text to be deleted. The combination of using redlining and strikeout is kown as *document compare* in WordPerfect.

Most software allows the user to select how the text is to be marked. For example, the diagonal (/) or hyphen (-) are often selected for superimposing over each character in the block of text to be revised.

This sentence is marked to show added text.

~~This sentence is marked to show text that is to be deleted.~~

List below the steps for overstrike, redlining, and strikeout.

FUNCTION	STEPS REQUIRED
Overstrike	______________________
	______________________
Redlining/Strikeout	______________________
	______________________

S7-EX3

1. Key the sentence below and save it as S7-EX3.

   Please send your résumé to the personnel director immediately.

S7-EX4

1. Key the sentence below and save it as S7-EX4.

   City Charter prohibits the use of firearms and alcohol within the immediate vicinity of educational institutions.

S7-EX5

1. Retrieve S7-EX4.
2. Add the following text as the second sentence. Use the redlining or overstrike feature of your software to mark the added text. If you can choose a character for marking, use the diagonal (/).

   ```
   Religious institutions cannot be located within
   500  feet of an establishment selling alcohol.
   ```

3. Using the strikeout (or overstrike) feature of your software, mark the first sentence for deletion. If you can choose a character for marking, select the hyphen (-). Save and print the exercise.
4. Remove the redlining and strikeout (overstrike) commands from the file. Save and reprint the document. The print should appear normal.

S7-DOC5

1. Key S7-DOC5 as a letter in block format with mixed punctuation. Set 1-inch side margins.
2. When keying the name in the signature block, use the overstrike feature to make each accent mark (apostrophe) so that it will print over the character.

current date

Dear East Central Graduate:

Have you looked at East Central University's accomplishments recently? The decade of the 80's has been one of growth in land and facilities as well as in quality of faculty, academic programs, athletics, and students.

9 new buildings since 1986
22 nationally accredited programs
900 students on scholarship

ESU represents the efforts of many people--people who were committed to building a quality program of higher education.

The 90's will, however, be a period of inflation and rising costs. It will be challenging to maintain the present rate of growth and development. Although most of the ESU budget comes from student fees and state appropriations, these funds alone do not allow us to achieve excellence in every area. Private gifts often provide funds for an extra margin of quality.

As individuals, we can do little, but together we can accomplish a great deal. Since ESU is a young school, we need participation from all alumni.

Why should you give to the ESU Alumni Fund? Your dollars will insure continuing growth at ESU in the 90's. Won't you send your check in the enclosed envelope today and help make ESU an even greater university.

Sincerely,

René Courégé
Secretary, Alumni Fund

Enclosure

S7-DOC5R

1. Revise S7-DOC5 by making the changes requested.
2. To mark the text that is recommended for deletion, use the strikeout feature of your software. If strikeout is not available with your software, you may select the overstrike feature and select a character such as the hyphen (-) for striking over each character in the block of text.
3. To mark the text that is inserted, use the redline feature of your software. If redline is not available with your software, you may select the overstrike feature and select another character such as the slash (/) for striking over each character in the block of inserted text.

TIPS TO OPERATOR

- If your software offers strikeout and redline, the characters that strikeover the text are printer dependent; you cannot select the characters that the printer will print over the text.

current date

University

Dear East Central Graduate:

Have you looked at East Central University's accomplishments recently? The decade of the 80's ~~has been~~ was one of growth in land and facilities as well as in quality of faculty, academic programs, athletics, and students.

Bold

9 new buildings since 1986
22 nationally accredited programs
900 students on scholarship

ESU represents the efforts of many people--people who were committed to building a quality program of higher education.

The 90's will, however, be a period of inflation and rising costs. It will be challenging to maintain the present rate of growth and development. Although most of the ESU budget comes from student fees and state appropriations, these funds alone do not allow us to achieve excellence in every area. Private gifts often provide funds for an extra margin of quality.

Leave in but mark for possible deletion.

As individuals, we can do little, but together we can accomplish a great deal. Since ESU is a young school, we need participation from all alumni.

Why should you give to the ESU Alumni Fund? Your dollars will insure continuing growth at ESU in the 90's. Won't you send your check in the enclosed envelope today and help make ESU an even greater university.

with fewer graduates than some other universities in the state,

Sincerely,

insert and mark to show new material

René Courégé
Secretary, Alumni Fund

Enclosure

no ¶ Insert and mark to show new material

People make the university grow. ESU is prospering, and as an alumnus, you should know that ESU needs your help to maintain that prosperity.

S7-DOC5RR

Revise S7-DOC5r by deleting the paragraph marked for strikeout and removing the commands that mark the inserted text.

current date

Dear East Central University Graduate:

Have you looked at East Central University's accomplishments recently? The decade of the '80s was one of growth in land and facilities as well as in quality of faculty, academic programs, athletics, and students.

9 new buildings since 1986
22 nationally accredited programs
900 students on scholarship

ESU represents the efforts of many people--people who were committed to building a quality program of higher education. People make the university grow. ESU is prospering, and as an alumnus, you should know that ESU needs your help to maintain that prosperity. *Remove red line markings.*

~~The '90s will, however, be a period of inflation and rising costs. It will be challenging to maintain the present rate of growth and development. Although most of the ESU budget comes from student fees and state appropriations, these funds alone do not allow us to achieve excellence in every area. Private gifts often provide funds for an extra margin of quality.~~ *Delete ¶*

As individuals, we can do little, but together we can accomplish a great deal. Since ESU is a young school, with fewer graduates than some other universities in the state, we need participation from all alumni. *Remove red line markings.*

Why should you give to the ESU Alumni Fund? Your dollars will insure continuing growth at ESU in the '90s. Won't you send your check in the enclosed envelope today and help make ESU an even greater university.

Sincerely,

René Courègé
Secretary, Alumni Fund

doc code

Enclosure

1. Key S7-DOC6 as a two-page legal document following the format directions for legal documents in the Reference Section. Turn on hyphenation.
2. The inserted paragraph is to be marked to show new material using the redline or overstrike feature.
3. Run the macro saved as *NP* (Notary Public statement) when directed.

WARRANTY DEED

with relinquishment of dower

DAVID T. GUTEK and BARBARA HAZEN GUTEK, Husband and Wife; and Francis D. Huybregts and Ying Yee Huybregts, husband and wife, hereinafter called Grantors, for and in consideration of the sume of FIVE HUNDRED AND NO/100 Dollars($500.00) AND OTHER VALUABLE CONSIDERATION in hand paid by JAMES MCQUILLIN and VALLERIE WHITE MCQUILLIN, husband ans wife the receipt of which is here by acknowledged, do here by grant, baargin, and convey un-to JAMES MCQUILLIN and VALLERIE WHITE MCQUILLIN, husband and wife, here in called Grantees, and unto thier hiers and assigns forever, the following lands laying in Union County, Iowa, to-wit:

Lot 8, Block 10, Platt River Subdivision per recorded plat or plats, and subject to the notes and other indicated restrictions, if any, on siad plat or plats and subject to the conditions, covenants, reservations easement, charges and liens reflected in the Declaraditons and Supplemental Declarations filled in connection therewith in the office of the Circuit court clern and ex officio recorded of Union County Iowa.

TO HAVE AND TO HOLD the same unto the said GRANTEES, and unto their heirs and assigns forever, together with all improvements thereon and all rights, priviledges, and appurtenances thereunto belong.

AND GRANTORS HEREBY COVENANT with said GRANTEES that they will forever warrant and defend the title to the siad lands against all lawful claims whatever.

AND WE, THE UNDERSIGNED, for and in consideratoin of the sum of money do here by convey and relinquish unto the said GRANTEES and their heirs and assign all our rights of dower and homestead in and to said lands.

WITNESS our hands on this third day of April, 19--.

David T. Gutek	Francis D. Huybregts
Barbara Hazen Gutek	Ying Yee Huybregts

(insert Notary Public statement saved in macro named NP)

The Grantees are authorized at any time and from time to time to appropriate and apply any or all of the net cash receipts from any of said property and/or any balance account.

Operator: Insert as new ¶ with Redline to show new material.

-2-

PRINTING DIRECTORY

1. Display the directory of your data disk revealing the names of files you produced using this text.

2. Use the Print Screen command on your keyboard (Shift+PrtSc) and print a copy of the directory. If your directory is longer than one screen, display the next screen and print the screen again.

3. Fold and place the printed directory in the paper jacket with your diskette.

THESAURUS

Thesaurus helps you find the right word when you are composing or editing a document. The thesaurus will display a list of synonyms (words with similar meanings) for a word that you identify. Some software will also display a list of antonyms (words with opposite meanings).

After displaying the list of synonyms, you can either select an alternate word or leave the original word intact. When using the thesaurus feature, be careful to select a word with the meaning you intend. Using the thesaurus improves your writing because it provides you with a list of words that can be used as possible substitutes for a word that you have selected.

List the steps below for using the thesaurus.

FUNCTION	STEPS REQUIRED
Thesaurus	____________________
	____________________

S7-EX6

1. Key the following words.

   revenue
   prospect
   accommodate

2. Use the thesaurus feature and select a synonym for each word.

S7-DOC7

1. Key S7-DOC7 as a one-page report with the following format settings:
   1 1/2" left margin
   1" right margin
   justify right margin
   double space

2. After the document is keyed, access the thesaurus feature of your software and replace each circled word with an appropriate synonym.

3. Check spelling, save, and print. Proofread to determine that the synonyms selected are appropriate, that they are in the proper tense, and that any preceding article adjective is correct.

TIPS TO OPERATOR

- When you check some words, a suitable synonym may not be available for selection; some software offers the capability for you to search for a synonym of the words in the list on the screen. You may find a better synonym if you check other words.

- When selecting the best synonym, you may have to edit the selected word for tense. For example, when you search for a synonym of *identified*, your software may show synonyms for *identify*; therefore, you may have to key the past tense of the word selected. Also, sometimes an adjective preceding the synonym must be changed (i.e., *a* and *an*).

SELECTING A JOURNAL FOR PUBLICATION

After you have chosen your topic, written a draft, and identified your audience, you must decide which journal is best for your article. Although you may have a particular journal in mind and are sure your paper is appropriate, look for other journals which might also be appropriate for your writing.

Articles in professional journals may be categorized into three groups: essay, secondary researched material, and primary researched material. A current study of over 40 journals which accept articles related to business revealed that 76 percent of the articles did not utilize statistical material. Some journals do not even accept manuscripts with statistical data. Therefore, if your material includes statistical data, you should select a journal which includes articles with statistical analysis.

Examine the Directory of Publishing Opportunities in Business Administration or a similar directory to begin your search for a journal. These directories provide information about many journals which publish articles by people other than their editorial staff.

1. Retrieve the file S3-DOC13. (If you cannot locate S3-DOC13 on your disk, look for S3-DOC6 that was to be renamed S3-DOC13 as a renaming activity in Section 3.)
2. Access the thesaurus feature and replace each word circled on the copy with an appropriate synonym. (Refer to Step 3 in the S7-DOC7 DIRECTIONS.)
3. Save this file as S7-DOC8.* Check spelling and print. Proofread to determine that the synonyms selected are appropriate, that they are in the proper tense, and that any preceding article adjective is correct.

TIPS TO OPERATOR

- *If your software does not permit saving an original file with a different name, save it with its old name and then rename the file S7-DOC8.

OFFICE LIGHTING: ILLUMINATING THE BOTTOM LINE

Excerpt from Modern Office Technology, March 1990

If you're involved in office management and make or influence decisions about lighting, ask yourself this question: Why did we install lighting in here in the first place? The answer is basic: **So people can get their work done.**

It can affect productivity and/or error rates, either one of which can have a substantial impact on the bottom line . . . not to mention ripple effects: e.g., better productivity can shorten turnaround time, which can enhance customer satisfaction and create a superior competitive position. It can also result in more output per unit of input, increasing profitability, and the like.

The National Lighting Bureau recently published a guide titled **OFFICE LIGHTING AND PRODUCTIVITY.** Its listing of benefits--primary and those derived secondarily--is impressive. The listing includes, in addition to productivity and error rate reduction, quality control, reduced absenteeism, inexpensive space differentiation, accommodation of frequent spatial changes, enhanced business image, effective mood setting, lower utility costs, and improved profitability.

doc code

CHANGING FONTS

Font describes all the characters for one typeface in one size. Common typefaces (styles) include Times Roman, Helvetica, and Universe. The height of a character is measured in *points*. In one inch, there are 72 points. Characters printed in 18 point are approximately one-fourth inch tall. On the other hand, typewriter pitch (pica or elite) refers to the width of typewriter type.

Varying the fonts on the page adds variety and emphasis to text. Headings, for example, are often formatted in larger fonts. Some software will not allow you to select a specific point size such as 10 or 12 point. Instead the software may give you the option of selecting fine, small, or large. To print in various fonts, your printer must be able to print the font you select.

Following are examples of different fonts:

This is 10 point Helvetica.

This is 18 point Helvetica.

This is 12 point Times Roman.

List below the steps for changing fonts.

FUNCTIONS	STEPS REQUIRED
Selecting a Font	______________________
	______________________
	______________________

S7-EX7

1. Format the following sentences in the font listed. If you are unable to select a specific typesize, then format the sentences in three different sizes.

   This sentence appears in 10 point Helvetica type.

   This sentence appears in 18 point Times Roman type.

   This sentence appears in 8 point Times Roman type.

2. Print the exercise.

S7-DOC9

1. Key S7-DOC9 as a one-page announcement with the following formats:
   1 1/2" top margin
   1" side margins
   single space
   left align tab, 25 spaces from left margin
2. Key the appropriate command to print in a size larger than normal for the lines marked "large." For the text to be printed smaller than normal, key the command to print in a size smaller than normal.

TIPS TO OPERATOR

■ Some software offers a selection of font sizes in small, large, very large, and extra large. Other software offers a a selection of pitch sizes; therefore, if your software permits changing pitch, print the large lines in the largest pitch available and the small lines in the smallest pitch available.

If you are using a laser printer with soft fonts, font cartridges, or PostScript fonts, you may select a typestyle and change the point size to a size larger than normal for "large" and a point size smaller than normal for "small." For example, you may select a point size of 14 for large, 12 for normal, and 8 or 10 for small.

The University of Southern Texas) Large

Faculty Position Available) Large

Position Available:	Assistant Professor Office Information Systems Tenure track, 9-months
Salary:	Dependent upon experience and degree
Position Availability:	August 20, 19--
Qualifications:	Doctorate preferred. Competence in WordPerfect, Lotus 123, Quattro, dBase III Plus, DOS, and local area networks. Evidence of research and publications. Minimum of three years' teaching experience.
Responsibilities:	Duties include teaching undergraduate courses in information systems (word processing, spreadsheet, database, PC operations using DOS), engaging in research and publication, student advising, and service to the university, profession, and community.
Applications:	Send resume, three letters of recommendation, and transcripts to: Dr. Maria Z. Hatcher, Head University of Southern Texas Department of Office Information Systems El Paso, TX 79996-0210 Telephone: 915-555-1000
Closing Date:	Application deadline: February 1, 19--, or until position is filled.

center each line (The University of Southern Texas is an
Affirmative Action/Equal Opportunity Employer.
Women and minorities are encouraged to apply.) Small

S7-DOC10

1. Retrieve the file saved as S3-DOC7.
2. Key the commands to print the lines marked "large" in a size larger than normal. Insert the text at the bottom in a size smaller than normal.
3. Save as S7-DOC10. If necessary, rename the file.

TIPS TO OPERATOR

- If your system has a View feature for examining the format of a document before printing, use it to determine if the document is attractively formatted.

THE STUDENT ORGANIZATIONS OF THE
COLLEGE OF BUSINESS ADMINISTRATION) Print in large font

Cordially Invite You to a

Faculty and Staff Reception

on Thursday, November 30, 19--

From 2 p.m. - 4 p.m.

at the Alumni Center

ENTERTAINED BY:) large

Miss Heather Henann, Miss University
Mr. Karl Rubrecht, Pianist

SPONSORED BY:) large

Collegiate Secretaries International*
Pi Omega Pi
Pi Sigma Epsilon

Come and enjoy the food and entertainment!

small (*Directed by the Institute for Educating Secretaries, a department of Professional Secretaries International.

CONVERTING FILES

Because there are many different word processing programs available today, it is often necessary to convert (change) a document created using one program to a different word processing program. For example, a document created in WordPerfect may need to be converted to MultiMate so that another user can edit and print the document.

Conversion may be completed in more than one way with some software.

a. You may save a document in the American Standard Code for Information Interchange format (ASCII pronounced as kee) using a menu or a special key such as Textin/Out. The menu for saving a file in ASCII may list the selection as DOS Text.
b. With a file on disk (not on the screen), you may enter the Conversion Menu (for example, Convert in WordPerfect) and select ASCII Text File.
c. Some software provides a Utilities Menu for file conversion.

A file saved in ASCII format can be used with any software. Therefore, when you cannot convert to the desired application software or do not know which application software will be used, you may convert to ASCII. Conversely, an ASCII file can then be converted to the desired word processing software format.

During conversion, all formatting codes (tabs, centering, etc.) are stripped from the document and replaced with spaces and hard returns. Also, soft returns inserted by word wrap become hard returns. Therefore, ASCII files converted to another software must be reformatted with the new software. To confirm this fact, you may convert the ASCII file to your software format. When you retrieve the converted file to the screen, reveal formatting codes and check formatting codes and the return at the end of each line.

List below the steps for converting files.

FUNCTION	STEPS REQUIRED
Convert a File to ASCII	______________________________
	______________________________
	______________________________
Convert a File to Another Word Processing Software	______________________________
	______________________________
	______________________________

S7-DOC11

1. Using the conversion capabilities of your software, convert the file saved as S5-DOC2 to a standard text file (ASCII) so that it can be used with any software.

2. Name the converted file S5-DOC2.ASC. ASC is the standard extension for ASCII files. Any time you convert a file, always keep the original file name changing only the extension.

3. Do not print the ASCII file.

4. Check your directory to confirm that both S5-DOC2 and S5-DOC2.ASC are saved on your disk. Conversion does not affect the original file.

S7-DOC12

1. Using the conversion feature of your software or a special conversion software, convert the file saved as S5-DOC3 to another word processing format or an older version of the software you are using.*

   For example, if you are using WordPerfect you may convert the file to Revisable-Form-Text (DCA format) or Final-Form-Text for use with DisplayWrite, or convert it to WordStar 3.3, Multimate, Microsoft Word, or a few others.

   If you are using DisplayWrite, convert to Revisable-Form-Text for conversion to other DOS-based software.

2. Name the converted file S5-DOC3.RFT if you convert to Revisable-Form-Text. If you convert to other software format such as WordStar, select a suitable extension (different from one that your software may append) so that you can distinguish between files.

3. If you have access to other word processing software, see if you can retrieve the converted file with that software. If the file is not compatible, you will see a message on the screen that the file is not a supported file type or that it is incompatible. If you can retrieve the converted file using another software, check the formatting commands to see if they were converted.

TIPS TO OPERATOR

- New versions of software often are not compatible with older versions of the same software; therefore, if a file is to be revised using the old version of software, it must be converted. For example, if a WordPerfect 5.1 file is to be used with WordPerfect 4.2 software, the WordPerfect 5.1 file must be converted to WordPerfect 4.2. Typically, if a file created with an old version of software is to be used with a new version of the same software, it will be converted automatically when the file is retrieved with the new version.

SECTION 7

SOFTWARE FUNCTION SUMMARY

List the commands for the following:

Macro ______________________________

Create a macro ______________________________

____

Use a macro ______________________________

Overstrike ______________________________

Redlining/Strikeout ______________________________

Thesaurus ______________________________

Select font

Convert file to ASCII ______________________________

____

Convert file to another word processing software ______________________________

____

REFERENCE SECTION

DOCUMENT CODES

A document code is helpful for retrieving a file saved on disk. The document code identifies who keyed the document and the document file name. If a number of disks are used for storing files, the document code may include the disk label or number.

The document coding recommended for documents in this text will help you in document retrieval and will aid your instructor in recording the progress of your work. For each document you process in this text, key a document code at the point where the **doc code** notation appears. Although the doc code notation may not be shown on some documents, you should key the code in the appropriate position as recommended below:

- Memos and letters: a double space below the originator's name or title.
- Reports, tables, and legal documents: a double space below the last line of text.

The document code should include your initials, a space or a separator symbol such as the : or /, and the document file name. Example: **xxx/s3-doc1.**

For each document revision, cursor to the end of the document code and key an **r** to indicate revised copy. Example: **xxx/s3-doc1r**.

PROOFREADING PROCEDURES

1. Proofread using the spelling checker feature of your software.
2. Before printing the first draft, proofread from the screen by scrolling line by line through the document. Compare the copy on the screen with the original copy to be sure that no copy has been added or deleted. Be sure that all edits have been made on the screen.
3. Check the accuracy of all figures and calculations.
4. Check punctuation and capitalization.
5. Check the format of the document—margins, line spacing, page numbers, and headers and footers. Check that numbered items are in the correct order.
6. Print the document. Proofread the printed document again. Check format.
7. If you locate any errors, correct them, save the document, and print.

PROOFREADERS' MARKS

Mark	Meaning	Example	Result
^	insert	Please send me the ^ copy. [hard]	Please send me the hard copy.
^,	insert comma	Las Vegas ^, Nevada	Las Vegas, Nevada
' (insert)	insert apostrophe	The meeting begins at 8 oclock.	The meeting begins at 8 o'clock.
=/	insert hyphen	The 10 day trip begins Monday.	The 10-day trip begins Monday.
⊙	insert period	Please come by 7:30 a m.	Please come by 7:30 a.m.
⁀ (close up)	close up space	per cent	percent
#	add space	hardcopy	hard copy
(transpose)	transpose	Read only the last chapter.	Read the last chapter only.
lc	lowercase	John has studied Word Processing.	John has studied word processing.
(delete)	delete	Key the documents by tomorrow.	Key the document by tomorrow.
(delete and close up)	delete and close up space	She is committted to her work.	She is committed to her work.
/	replace	of the sisteenth floor [x]	on the sixteenth floor
___	underline	The Balance Sheet	The Balance Sheet
≡	capitalize	office information systems 210	Office Information Systems 210
sp	spell out	(5) days	five days
¶	new paragraph	A hard copy is printed. ¶ Clear the screen.	A hard copy is printed. Clear the screen.
stet	do not change; ignore the correction	~~Nevertheless,~~ she went to the play. [stet]	Nevertheless, she went to the play.
(straighten line)	straighten line	students.[1] Many others came	students.[1] Many others came
(move right)	move right	You will key S5-Doc6.	You will key S5-Doc6.
(move left)	move left	You will be able	You will be able
(move copy)	move copy as indicated	You can revise copy easily.	You can easily revise copy.
SS	single-space	501 Lake Shore Drive SS Chicago, IL 60611-1199	501 Lake Shore Drive Chicago, IL 60611-1199
DS	double-space	DS Dear Ms. Sabo	Dear Ms. Sabo
QS	quadruple-space	PROOFREADERS' MARKS QS A quadruple-space follows titles, which leaves three blank lines.	PROOFREADERS' MARKS A quadruple-space follows titles, which leaves three blank lines.
~~	print bold	Qualifications:	**Qualifications:**

WORD DIVISION RULES

To keep an attractive even right margin on text documents, most word processing users hyphenate words following word hyphenation rules by inserting a syllable hyphen at the appropriate point. Follow these rules consistently as you key documents in Part 2 of this book.

Begin using the hyphenation feature of your word processing system after you learn the hyphenation function. Your system, however, may sometimes hyphenate words at inappropriate points (for example, it may hyphenate a proper noun or leave only two characters for the next line). If the system inserts or suggests hyphenation at a point that is incorrect, cancel the system's hyphen and insert one at the proper point or omit the hyphen altogether. The following hyphenation rules should be followed as you produce the following documents.

1. Divide words between syllables only. Check a dictionary when in doubt about syllabication:

   knowl- edge   length- wise   pre- ferred

2. Do not divide words containing five or less syllables. These words should not be hyphenated:

   ideal   begin   apple

3. Divide words only between syllables. One syllable words cannot be divided.

   passed   wrapped   eighth   drowned

4. Do not divide after a one-letter syllable at the beginning of a word; do not divide before a two-letter syllable at the end of a word.

   enough   reader

5. Do not hyphenate proper nouns, dates, or addresses. If necessary, separate proper nouns at a logical point that will provide the best readability.

   New/ Orleans   Dr. Timothy/ Vines
   November 18,/ 1990   Shreveport,/ LA 71161-1100

6. Divide compound-hyphenated words only at the hyphen.

   self- contained   mid- 1980s

7. A line may end at the right margin with a dash; do not add a hyphen:

   Some attorneys prefer titles keyed as spread headings— one space between characters and three spaces between words.

8. Do not divide numbers, abbreviations, or words containing apostrophes:

   C.O.D. $7,155.99   didn't

9. Be careful of suffixes such as -able, ible, icle, or ity; hyphenate before the single-vowel syllable:

   secur- ity   crit- ical   perish- able

   (However, applica-ble and surgi-cal are divided after the vowel since the vowel is a part of the preceding syllable.)

10. When 2 one-letter syllables occur together, divide between the one-letter syllables:

    mime- ograph   continu- ation

11. General hyphenation rules for a document follow:
    a. Do not hyphenate words on more than two consecutive lines.
    b. Do not hyphenate a word at the end of a page.
    c. Avoid hyphenating words at the end of the first and last lines of a paragraph.

INTEROFFICE MEMORANDUM: SIMPLIFIED FORMAT

Correspondence between offices in an organization is usually in memo format. The simplified memo format includes the date, addressee's name, subject line, message, and sender's name; the headings TO, FROM, DATE, and SUBJECT are omitted. Position memo parts as shown in the example.

- Set side margins of 1" or use the defaults margins.
- Begin each line at the left margin.
- Begin the date 1 1/2" (line 10) from the top.
- Key the name of the addressee. Titles are usually omitted on interoffice memos.
- Key the subject line in ALL CAPS.
- Key the sender's name followed by the document code. (See the section on Document Codes in this Reference Section.)
- If enclosures or photocopies are noted, key that notation.

January 15, 19-- Line 10 or 1½"

QS

Department Personnel

DS

ELECTRONIC MAIL SYSTEM FOR DEPARTMENT

DS

The departmental electronic mail system is now in operation. I will use the electronic mail system entirely for departmental communication. Unless we find a very serious deficiency in this mail system, this will be the last paper memo you will receive from me! In fact, you have an electronic message waiting for you now. By the way, the certification feature lets the sender know when the recipient has read the message.

DS

When you log into the network at your computer each day, be sure to look for your mail messages. When you are logged in during the day, your system will beep and a note will appear on your computer screen indicating that you have a mail message. Please use our electronic mail system for all department correspondence.

QS

John Mayer

DS

doc code

LEGAL DOCUMENTS

Although formats for legal documents vary somewhat from state to state as well as from court to court, most legal documents follow certain standard formats for margins, line spacing, paragraph indention, and page-numbering procedures.

Side Margins: The left margin is 1 1/2". The right margin is 1/2" and may be justified.

Top and Bottom Margins. The top margin is 2" on all pages. The bottom margin is about 1".

Spacing: All copy is double spaced except land descriptions and quoted material, which are single spaced and indented 10 spaces from both margins. Notary public acknowledgments are single spaced. Paragraphs are indented 10 spaces.

Document Titles: Titles are usually centered in ALL CAPS. If a caption identifying the court, case number, and other pertinent information precedes the title, horizontal lines are keyed to set off the title. (See the illustration following.)

Names: The names of principals within a legal document, along with certain phrases at the beginning of a paragraph, are keyed in ALL CAPS.

Page Numbers: Page numbers are preceded and followed by a hyphen (e.g., -2-) centered 1/2" from the bottom of the page. While the first page of a will must always be numbered, other legal documents are usually numbered beginning with the second page.

Signature Lines: Lines for signatures should be about 3". Leave two or three blank lines between signature lines to leave space for the handwritten signature. At least two lines of the document should appear on the page containing the signature of the maker and any witnesses.

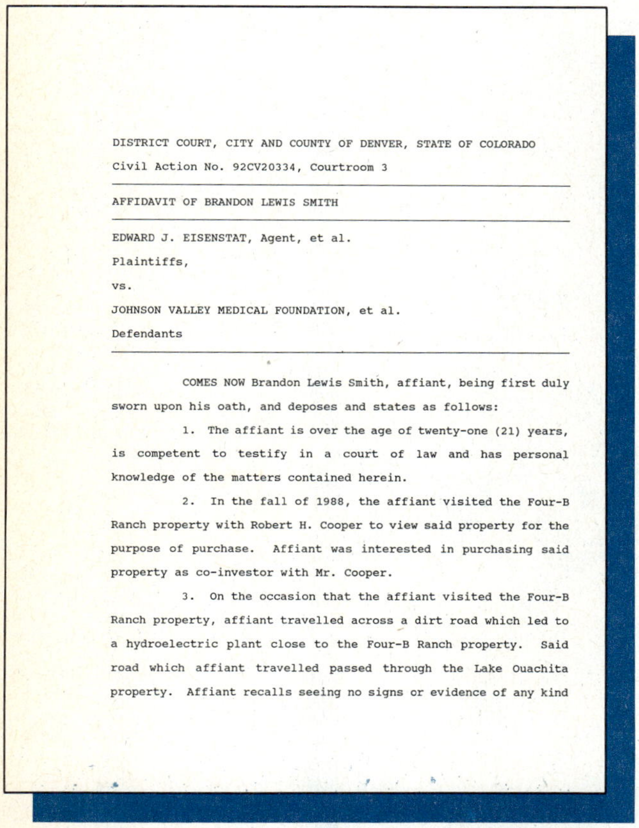

DISTRICT COURT, CITY AND COUNTY OF DENVER, STATE OF COLORADO

Civil Action No. 92CV20334, Courtroom 3

AFFIDAVIT OF BRANDON LEWIS SMITH

EDWARD J. EISENSTAT, Agent, et al.

Plaintiffs,

vs.

JOHNSON VALLEY MEDICAL FOUNDATION, et al.

Defendants

COMES NOW Brandon Lewis Smith, affiant, being first duly sworn upon his oath, and deposes and states as follows:

1. The affiant is over the age of twenty-one (21) years, is competent to testify in a court of law and has personal knowledge of the matters contained herein.

2. In the fall of 1988, the affiant visited the Four-B Ranch property with Robert H. Cooper to view said property for the purpose of purchase. Affiant was interested in purchasing said property as co-investor with Mr. Cooper.

3. On the occasion that the affiant visited the Four-B Ranch property, affiant travelled across a dirt road which led to a hydroelectric plant close to the Four-B Ranch property. Said road which affiant travelled passed through the Lake Ouachita property. Affiant recalls seeing no signs or evidence of any kind

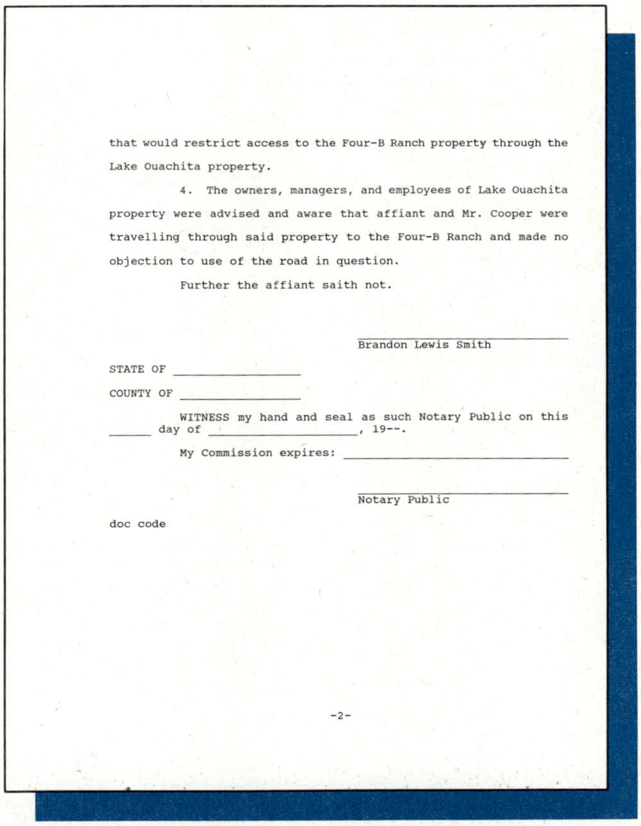

that would restrict access to the Four-B Ranch property through the Lake Ouachita property.

4. The owners, managers, and employees of Lake Ouachita property were advised and aware that affiant and Mr. Cooper were travelling through said property to the Four-B Ranch and made no objection to use of the road in question.

Further the affiant saith not.

Brandon Lewis Smith

STATE OF ________________

COUNTY OF ________________

WITNESS my hand and seal as such Notary Public on this _____ day of ____________________, 19--.

My Commission expires: ______________________________

Notary Public

doc code

-2-

LETTERS: BLOCK FORMAT

The block letter format has become popular in many organizations. Because all lines begin at the left margin, this style is easy to use. Business letters keyed on company stationery have the following parts: date, name and address of recipient, salutation, message, complimentary closing, and sender's name and title. Special lines such as a mailing notation, attention line, subject line, enclosure, and copy notation may also be included. Position letter parts as shown in the illustration. Special lines used in letters in this text will be positioned for you.

The following guides are to be followed for all block letters unless special directions are presented with a document:

- Set 1" side margins or use the defaults of your system.
- Begin the date about 2" from the top (lines 12-14).
- Most letters in this text are shown with open punctuation—no punctuation follows the salutation or closing.
- Key the document code a double space below the writer's title. (Refer to Document Codes in this Reference Section for directions.)
- If the letter requires more than one page, add a header to the second and subsequent pages, beginning on line 6. Double-space below the header to continue the body of the letter. The header includes the first line of the letter address, page number, and date.

Mr. Mark Stidham Page 2 Current Date

CBi

Connors & Brennan, Inc.

8044 Montgomery Street San Francisco, CA 94104-6713 (415) 555-4078

Current Date

QS

Mr. Mark Stidham
Route 2, Box 36
Council Bluffs, IA 51501-1136

DS

Dear Mr. Stidham

DS

A stop transfer has been entered against your Certificate No. C07555586-2 for 13 shares of Jaguar common stock issued May 15, 1987.

Enclosed are forms of affidavit of loss and indemnity agreement to be completed in order to secure issuance of a replacement certificate.

A check for $45.50 representing payment of the premium due the insurance company, made payable to The Henry Piatt Company should accompany the three copies of the affidavits. The above premium includes a $10 nonrefundable processing fee.

The instruments should be executed and acknowledged before a notary public. All questions must be answered by completing the blank areas of items 1, 2, 3, and 7. All notarized copies must then be forwarded to The Henry Piatt Company, 1605 Bond Court, Cleveland, Ohio 44114-1105, for assumption of liability under lost security blanket bond No. 8847011.

If you have any questions in regards to the above matter, please contact one of our shareholder representatives at (216) 555-7747 between the hours of 9 a.m. and 4:30 p.m. (EST).

Very truly yours

DS

QS

Ms. Ginette Evgenidi
Shareholder Communications

jp/s2-doc8

Enclosure

LETTERS: SIMPLIFIED BLOCK FORMAT

The simplified block letter format is the same as the block letter format except the salutation and closing are omitted and a subject line is always used. If a window envelope is to be used, the address may be keyed in ALL CAPS with no punctuation except the hyphen in the ZIP code. If the address is keyed with all capital letters, the signature line should also be in capital letters. The simplified block format is illustrated below in two formats: with the address keyed in the traditional format and with the address and signature block keyed in all caps.

SIMPLIFIED BLOCK LETTER

CBi
Connors & Brennan, Inc.
8044 Montgomery Street San Francisco, CA 94104-6713 (415) 555-4078

June 15, 19--

QS

Ms. Jane Bittle
Office Manager
Office Products, Inc.
770 North Titan
Fullerton, CA 92631-6111

DS

DESCRIPTION OF SIMPLIFIED BLOCK LETTER FORMAT

DS

The simplified block letter style differs from traditional business letter styles for several reasons. It was devised to improve efficiency of keying, to aid readability, and to remove outdated salutations and complimentary closings. The simplified block letter style has these characteristics:

All lines begin at the left.

The letter address may be keyed in the traditional style of lower case with initial caps with punctuation as shown in this illustration. The address, however, may be keyed in ALL CAPS with no punctuation so that it can show through a window envelope. The signature block may be keyed in all caps, also.

The salutation and complimentary closing are omitted.

The subject line is keyed in ALL CAPS without the word <u>subject</u>, with a double space before and after it. The subject line, however, may be keyed in lower case with initial caps.

The signature block (name and title) is keyed a quad space (four returns) below the message.

Let me know how well this style is accepted by your organization's originators.

QS

Ruth McGraw
Training Supervisor

DS

ccd/f:\dole\s-block.w51

SIMPLIFIED BLOCK LETTER WITH ADDRESS AND SIGNATURE IN ALL CAPS

CBi
Connors & Brennan, Inc.
8044 Montgomery Street San Francisco, CA 94104-6713 (415) 555-4078

June 15, 19--

MS JANE BITTLE
OFFICE MANAGER
OFFICE PRODUCTS INC
770 NORTH TITAN
FULLERTON CA 92631-6111

DESCRIPTION OF SIMPLIFIED BLOCK LETTER FORMAT

The simplified block letter style differs from traditional business letter styles for several reasons. It was devised to improve efficiency of keying, to aid readability, and to remove outdated salutations and complimentary closings. The simplified block letter style has these characteristics:

All lines begin at the left.

The letter address may be keyed in the traditional style of lower case with initial caps with punctuation as shown in this illustration. The address, however, may be keyed in ALL CAPS with no punctuation so that it can show through a window envelope. The signature block may be keyed in all caps, also.

The salutation and complimentary closing are omitted.

The subject line is keyed in ALL CAPS without the word <u>subject</u>, with a double space before and after it. The subject line, however, may be keyed in lower case with initial caps.

The signature block (name and title) is keyed a quad space (four returns) below the message.

Let me know how well this style is accepted by your organization's originators.

RUTH MCGRAW
TRAINING SUPERVISOR

ccd/f:\dole\s-block.w51

PERSONAL BUSINESS LETTERS

Personal business letters may be formatted in block style with all lines beginning at the left margin. Since personal business letters are printed on plain paper rather than letterhead stationery, a return address must be included. Begin the return address immediately above the date. The return address should include the following: street or post office box; the city, state, and ZIP code.

P. O. Box 1132 Line 14
Silver Spring, MD 20910-4162
January 12, 19--

QS

World Travel Club
Attention Membership Director
3110 Forbes Blvd., Suite 110
Lanham, MD 10706-3698

Ladies and Gentlemen

World Travel Club Membership No. T516X

Please cancel my membership in World Travel Club. I am returning the World Travel Club Savings Card and related materials, which you sent to me. I do not wish to continue my membership which expires in February 19--.

Please credit my Express charge card for $50.

Sincerely yours

David T. Hotvedt

doc code

Enclosure

REPORTS

Unless otherwise directed, follow these directions for formatting reports in this text.

Side margins: The side margins for an unbound report are 1"; for a leftbound report use a 1 1/2" left margin and a 1" right.

Top and bottom margins: The top margin of the first page is 1 1/2" (line 10). Most operators strike the return key, to move to the desired line. If the line spacing has been set to double space, one can begin on odd-numbered lines only—1, 3, 5, 7, 9. If you want to begin on an even-numbered line, strike the return to the desired line and then set the format to double spacing.

The top margin for the second and subsequent page is 1" (line 6). The bottom margin should be about 1" on all pages.

Spacing: Double-space reports and use a 5-space paragraph indention. Double-space above and below side headings.

Headings: Center the main heading in ALL CAPS. Quadruple-space below the main heading. If a secondary heading follows the main heading, double-space below the main heading and quadruple-space below the secondary heading. Key side headings even with left margin and underline.

Page Numbers: The first page is not numbered. The second and following pages are numbered at the top right margin 1" from the top (line 6), unless specific directions are given otherwise. Double-space below the page number to the body of the report—the default on most software.

If a header is to be keyed on the second and following pages, position it at the left margin 1" from the top (line 6).

A text footer and page number appearing at the bottom of the page should print 1/2" from the bottom of the page.

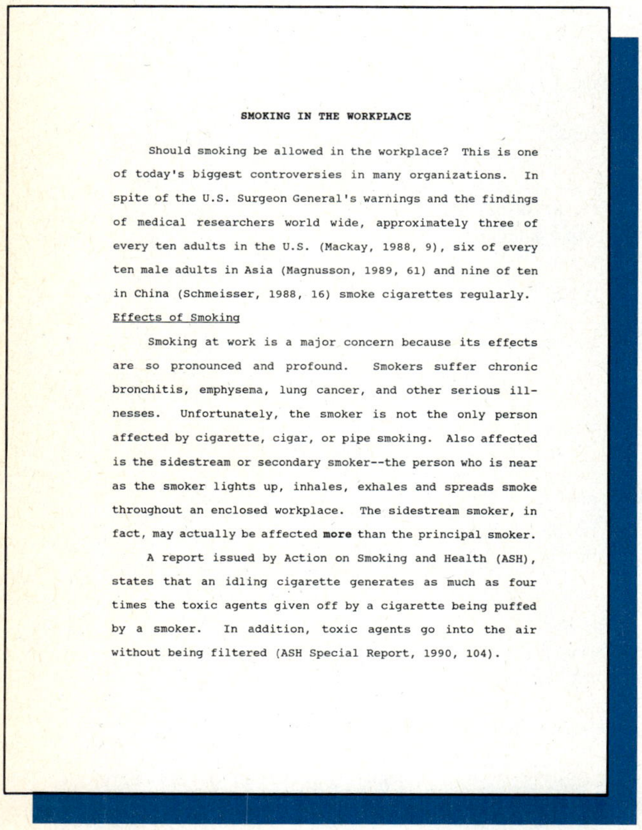

SMOKING IN THE WORKPLACE

Should smoking be allowed in the workplace? This is one of today's biggest controversies in many organizations. In spite of the U.S. Surgeon General's warnings and the findings of medical researchers world wide, approximately three of every ten adults in the U.S. (Mackay, 1988, 9), six of every ten male adults in Asia (Magnusson, 1989, 61) and nine of ten in China (Schmeisser, 1988, 16) smoke cigarettes regularly.

Effects of Smoking

Smoking at work is a major concern because its effects are so pronounced and profound. Smokers suffer chronic bronchitis, emphysema, lung cancer, and other serious illnesses. Unfortunately, the smoker is not the only person affected by cigarette, cigar, or pipe smoking. Also affected is the sidestream or secondary smoker--the person who is near as the smoker lights up, inhales, exhales and spreads smoke throughout an enclosed workplace. The sidestream smoker, in fact, may actually be affected **more** than the principal smoker.

A report issued by Action on Smoking and Health (ASH), states that an idling cigarette generates as much as four times the toxic agents given off by a cigarette being puffed by a smoker. In addition, toxic agents go into the air without being filtered (ASH Special Report, 1990, 104).

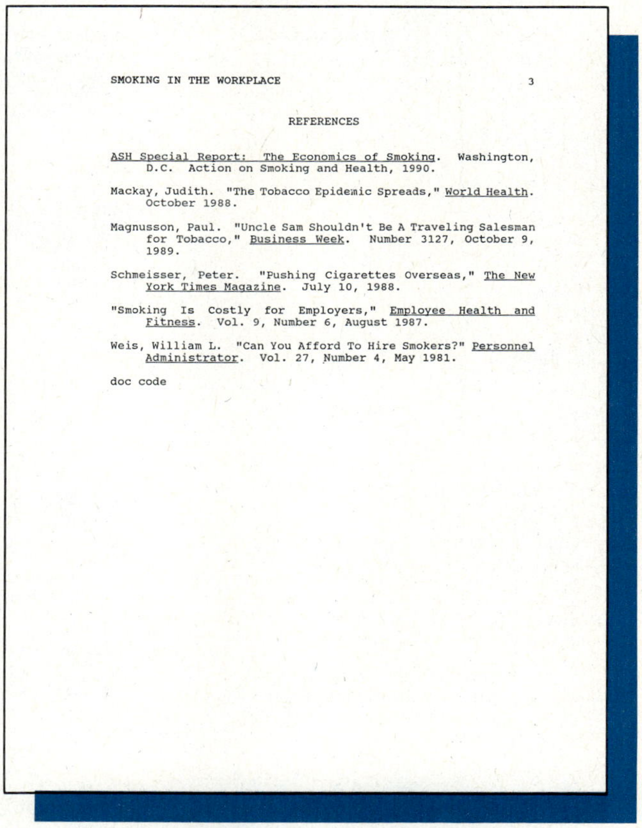

SMOKING IN THE WORKPLACE 3

REFERENCES

ASH Special Report: The Economics of Smoking. Washington, D.C. Action on Smoking and Health, 1990.

Mackay, Judith. "The Tobacco Epidemic Spreads," World Health. October 1988.

Magnusson, Paul. "Uncle Sam Shouldn't Be A Traveling Salesman for Tobacco," Business Week. Number 3127, October 9, 1989.

Schmeisser, Peter. "Pushing Cigarettes Overseas," The New York Times Magazine. July 10, 1988.

"Smoking Is Costly for Employers," Employee Health and Fitness. Vol. 9, Number 6, August 1987.

Weis, William L. "Can You Afford To Hire Smokers?" Personnel Administrator. Vol. 27, Number 4, May 1981.

doc code

INDEX